Manifesto to the Mexican Republic

Manifesto to the Mexican Republic

which *Brigadier General José Figueroa,*
Commandant and
Political Chief of Upper California,
presents on his conduct and on that of
José María de Hijar and *José María Padrés*
as Directors of Colonization in 1834 and 1835

TRANSLATED, WITH AN INTRODUCTION AND NOTES BY

C. Alan Hutchinson

University of California Press

Berkeley   Los Angeles   London

University of California Press
Berkeley and Los Angeles, California

University of California Press, Ltd.
London, England

Copyright © 1978 by
The Regents of the University of California

ISBN 0-520-03347-7
Library of Congress Catalog Card Number: 76-47992
Printed in the United States of America

1 2 3 4 5 6 7 8 9

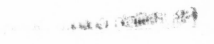

For Jean, Robert, and Mary

Contents

Preface

MY INTEREST in José Figueroa's *Manifesto to the Mexican Republic* was first aroused while I was engaged in a study of Mexican California. Because it was one of the most valuable sources available, I decided to prepare an introduction and explanatory notes for the original English translation made in 1855. I discovered, however, that this translation, although presented in smooth-running English prose, contained numerous errors and omissions which made it unacceptable for scholarly purposes. The original Spanish book of 1835 also contained misprints. I then enlarged my project to include a fresh translation of the text, which has been carefully revised by Professor Hernán Vidal of the Department of Spanish and Portuguese at the University of Minnesota and Señora Silvia Cubillos de Vidal, to whom I am greatly indebted for their expert assistance. My thanks also go to Marjorie Hughes of the University of California Press for her careful editing of the manuscript. The explanatory notes for the text of the *Manifesto* are designed to clarify obscurities and offer other biographical and historical information essential for an understanding of the work.

I wish to thank the Committee on Faculty Fellowships for Summer Research in the Humanities at the University of Virginia for assistance which enabled me to complete this volume; and I am indebted to the late John Cook Wyllie, former Director of Libraries at the University of Virginia, for his interest and helpful suggestions. I would also like to acknowledge the aid of William H. Runge, Curator of the McGregor Collection at the Alderman Library of the University of Virginia. I take particular pleasure in recording my continuing gratitude to the staff of the Alderman Library, who cheerfully gave me their wholehearted assistance, and I appreciate the services of Mary Topping and Suzanne Sweet, who typed the manuscript. I am grateful to the Bancroft Library of the University of California for permission to reproduce a facsimile of the original *Manifiesto a la República Mejicana*.

C. Alan Hutchinson

Charlottesville, Va.

INTRODUCTION

JOSE FIGUEROA AND HIS *MANIFESTO*

Some day the whole of this affair will come to light:
all men will be acquainted with the motives of each party,
they will make a judgment between the two
and render their verdict.

JOSÉ MARÍA DE HÍJAR

A GREAT DEAL of attention has been paid to Governor José Figueroa's *Manifesto to the Mexican Republic,* the first book-length imprint published in California,[1]* as a valuable rare item of Californiana, but little thought seems to have been given to its significance in the history of Mexican California or to the light that it sheds on the Mexico of its day. Printed at the press of Agustín Vicente Zamorano in Monterey in 1835, it put forward persuasively Governor Figueroa's point of view in his recent dispute with José María Híjar and José María Padrés over the settling of a colony on the northern frontier of the Territory. Contemporaries of Governor Figueroa used it to exalt his name,

*Notes to introduction follow on page 15.

and historians have accepted it with virtual unanimity (the major exception being Hubert Howe Bancroft) as an impartial document proving the rascality of Híjar and Padrés.[2]

The new Anglo-American residents of California became interested in the *Manifesto* in 1855, following discussion in the press of the validity in United States courts of titles to lands formerly held by Indians under Mexican law. An English translation of the *Manifesto* by an unknown hand appeared on June 18, 1855, and it was advertised in the *San Francisco Daily Herald* regularly almost every day for the rest of the year until increasing Christmas advertisements finally drove it out about the middle of December. The notice called attention to the *Manifesto*'s "incalculable interest and value to real estate owners and dealers, and particularly to those interested in the mission lands of the state."[3] Despite the inaccuracies and omissions in the translation, it probably did encourage would-be purchasers of mission lands, since Governor Figueroa seized every opportunity to state that they belonged to the mission Indians.[4]

Figueroa's main concern in writing his *Manifesto*, however, was not merely to argue that the mission Indians owned the lands of the missions on which they lived; he wanted to justify his measures hindering the colony headed by Híjar and Padrés from being established on the northern frontier of California, adjacent to the Russian settlements of Bodega and Ross, and his arresting the leaders of the expedition and sending them back to Mexico. Mexican newspapers during 1833 and 1834 had carried numerous reports of the attempts being made to colonize California, which had long been considered threatened by the Russians and was now beginning to be reached by Americans traveling overland. Governor Figueroa felt it necessary to put his case before the public in the normal way employed at the time by prominent persons in Mexico: a ringing manifesto pointing out the errors of his opponents and the righteousness of his own actions.

Figueroa probably wrote his *Manifesto* during July and August of 1835. While he admits that he is no literary man and that his work is devoid of frills, he prides himself on presenting his facts clearly and accurately.[5] He does, in fact, include in the work a great many letters he wrote to Híjar and to the Minister of Internal and Foreign Relations in Mexico, as well as replies by Híjar, so that it is a valuable compilation of documents in the case. Furthermore, comparison of these documents with some of the originals shows that he has not attempted to alter or omit passages in order to better his arguments. If Figueroa's charges against Híjar, Padrés, and some of the other leaders of the colony are accepted at their face value, it appears that he dispersed the colony for excellent reasons: its members were not only unfit for the task they had undertaken, they were conspirators, aiming to remove him from power and make off with the wealth of the missions. Closer investigation reveals, however, that this simple explanation does not do justice to the colonists and their leaders or to the Farías administration, which organized and sent out the colonizing expedition.

Valentín Gómez Farías was a medical man from Guadalajara who had practiced his profession in Aguascalientes and then represented the states of Jalisco and Zacatecas in the Mexican Chamber of Deputies and the Senate. He was a reformer whose roots went deep down into the fertile soil of the eighteenth-century Enlightenment. He had been interested in protecting California from foreign threats by colonization since the early days of independence, and when he came to power as Vice-President in 1833 one of his first concerns was California, which he felt needed populating and economic development.[6] There was nothing new in this, for Lucas Alamán, the conservative-minded Minister of Internal and Foreign Relations under President Guadalupe Victoria and also under Vice-President Anastasio Bustamante, felt the same way.[7] The difference was that Farías was ready to take more immediate and radical action. His administration submitted to the Mexican Congress an act to secularize the Franciscan missions of California, making them into parishes, which was passed into law on August 17, 1833.[8]

The reasoning behind this law was that the Franciscan missionaries were slow and ineffective in civilizing the Indians who, under Mexican law, were held to be citizens equal in every way with the whites. Another reason for taking this step was the desire to remove all Spaniards from Mexico, following a long period of suspicion and hatred which culminated in the abortive Spanish invasion of Mexico in 1829; the Franciscan missionaries in California were mostly Spaniards. The secularization law said nothing about distribution of the vast estates of the missions in California or of their large herds of cattle and horses. Previous legislation had stopped short of colonizing mission lands until it could be decided who was to get them. It had been suggested that mission property might be divided among the mission Indians and the Mexicans resident in California.[9]

In a bill which has hitherto escaped the attention of historians, the Farías administration presented its views on these important matters to the Chamber of Deputies on April 16, 1833.[10] In this bill, mission lands were to be divided according to the following priority: Indian families living in California; the military in the garrisons of California, to whom pay was owing; Mexican residents of California who owned less than the minimum acreages to be distributed under the law; Mexican families who emigrated to California; foreign families who went at their own expense to California; entrepreneurs who brought families to the Territory; and convicts who completed their terms of imprisonment there and wished to stay. It should be noted that the bill gave top priority to California Indians, without distinguishing between mission Indians and non-Christian Indians living in the interior. It was clearly designed to win the approval of the military in California, who had been unable to draw their pay for many years because of the Government's perennial shortage of funds. Mexican residents of California were not to obtain land under this bill if they already possessed more than the minimum amounts stipulated in the law, which were 52 acres (21 hectares) of irrigable land, 826 acres (335 hectares) of arid land dependent on rainfall, or 1860 acres (753 hectares) of land suitable only for grazing. Presumably these conditions would have made it difficult for the leading Mexican residents of California to obtain mission land, which was admitted to be the best in the Territory.

The bill also provided that mission stock was to be divided among the Indians, each family getting a certain number of oxen, steers, cows, sheep, horses, and mules. The remaining stock was to be distributed among the other groups, with the exception of the foreigners, but the whites were only to receive half the number of animals given to the Indians. Not only did the bill give preference and priority to the Indians, it gave them special protection by prohibiting them from selling their newly granted land until they had possessed it five years, and even then permitting them to sell only those parts of it which they had farmed and which they would presumably be least interested in selling.

The debates in the Chamber of Deputies reveal that this last method of protecting the Indians was a controversial one, for an amendment was proposed by which non-Indian colonists were to be given the same protection, but it was narrowly defeated.[11] There were, in fact, two schools of thought in Mexico at the time on how to deal with the Indian problem. José María Luis Mora, one of the leading intellectuals of the day and a highly trusted advisor of the Farías administration, believed that the Indians should not be protected but should be treated as equals of the white man. Those who wanted to protect the Indians, Mora reasoned, really believed that the whites were superior to them.[12] Opponents of this argument, like Juan Rodríguez Puebla, a distinguished Indian who was Rector of the College of San Gregorio in Mexico City, claimed that the Indians should get special assistance or protection because they were what would today be called culturally deprived, and needed it.[13] It can be seen from this bill that the Farías administration tended to side in this case with those who sought special protection for the Indians, although they preferred not to use the word Indian at all and thought of them rather as the poor or lower classes of the population.

Painstakingly prepared, as it clearly was, this bill was approved by the Chamber of Deputies on May 9, 1833,[14] and immediately went to the Senate. For reasons unknown, but possibly connected with the devastating cholera epidemic which hit Mexico that summer and disorganized all Government action, the bill never emerged from the Senate and did not become law. Knowledge of it nonetheless reached California, where, as will be seen, the recently arrived Governor Figueroa read its provisions with disapproval.[15]

The reasons behind the appointment of General Figueroa as Political Chief and Military Commandant of Upper California are not entirely clear. He was in 1833 a short, dark-skinned man of 40 from Jonacatepec, near Cuautla in the present state of Morelos. Having established a fine record in the Mexican War for Independence,

fighting from the first with the revolutionary forces, he emerged as a trusted aide of the distinguished General Vicente Guerrero. President Victoria sent him to the state of Occidente (Sonora and Sinaloa) as Commanding General in 1825. There, after playing a part in reopening the overland route to California through the Yuma country, which had been closed since 1781, he became engaged in putting down the Yaqui and Mayo Indian insurrection led by Juan de la Bandera. When Spanish forces attacked Tampico in 1829, General Figueroa hastened overland to defend his country, but the enemy was defeated before he arrived.

General Guerrero had by now become President of the Republic, but his Vice-President, Anastasio Bustamante, revolted against him in December 1829 and took over on Guerrero's departure from Mexico City in 1830. At first General Figueroa proclaimed his loyalty to his old chief, President Guerrero, but Guerrero's star began to fade and Figueroa was arrested and jailed on March 25, 1830, for reasons which were not announced but presumably because of his known friendship for Guerrero. Although other persons accused of conspiring against Vice-President Bustamante were tried and exiled from the country, Figueroa apparently made his peace with the new regime. In fact, sometime later in 1830, perhaps shortly after the death of one of the generals on the Supreme Military Tribunal early in October, Figueroa was made a substitute judge of that court, a position he kept until he was appointed to replace the unpopular Colonel Manuel Victoria as Governor of California on April 17, 1832. Whether Vice-President Bustamente was thinking of keeping Figueroa in a kind of exile in California or whether he was appointing him to the position on his merits is not clear. Perhaps there was a mixture of these motives behind his decision. At all events, Lucas Alamán, the distinguished former Minister of Relations who was once more in office, thought highly of Figueroa.[16]

It was one of Alamán's responsibilities, as Minister of Relations, to take charge of the affairs of the Territory of Upper California, and he accordingly briefed Figueroa on the unsettled situation there, basing his views on those of former Governor Victoria. On the all-important matter of the missions, Alamán instructed Figueroa to distribute suitable-sized lots of mission lands to competent mission Indians, while keeping intact mission lands whose revenues were used for supporting the church, schools, and other general needs. By this method, Alamán considered, the mission system would in the course of time be slowly replaced by one in which the Indians owned their own land, and the work of the missionaries would eventually be reduced to their religious duties only. Finally, the missions would be secularized, with the whole process having been so gradual that it would not arouse the feared dissatisfaction among the missionary Fathers. Alamán also ordered Figueroa to continue to encourage colonists to come to California and, in particular, to endeavor to found new towns at sites that he thought the Russians or the Americans were planning to seize.[17] Alamán's instructions were virtually the same as those given to Figueroa's two predecessors in the position, José María Echeandía and Manuel Victoria.

Figueroa was undoubtedly the best-prepared and most experienced Mexican officer until then to become Governor of California. Furthermore, he was evidently intelligent and public-spirited. Yet he had his weaknesses: He had deserted his wife shortly after marrying her, and the government had been forced to subtract a modest amount from his salary so that she and his son should not starve.[18] He lived openly with a mistress. He was inordinately fond of gambling and had run up considerable gambling debts while he was in Sonora, which he still owed when he left it.[19]

Figueroa arrived at Monterey about the middle of January 1833 and quickly began to restore order to the Territory. This was accomplished within little more than two months although, complaining of illness, he asked to be relieved of his job. The administration of Vice-President Bustamante had now been toppled, however, and the new regime of President Santa Anna and Vice-President Gómez Farías was just embarking on its extraordinarily difficult task. So Governor Figueroa went on with his work, and his health began to improve. He sent Ensign Mariano Guadalupe Vallejo north to find a good location for a settlement to offset possible Russian advances and to spy on the Russians at Bodega and Ross. Following some Indian disturbances on the missions in southern California, Figueroa went to San Diego, where he decided that the turbulence was due to secularization attempts made by former Governor Echeandía who, in Figueroa's view, had promised the Indians more than he had given them.

Nevertheless, Figueroa decided to put Alamán's instructions on the missions into effect, and on July 15 issued his "Provisional Steps for the Emancipation of Mission Indians." Under this scheme, which was similar to an earlier one tried by Echeandía in 1826, married mission Indians who had been Christians for twelve years, and who were willing and able to earn their own living, could leave their missions. If enough of them did so, they were to receive lots in new towns to be founded for them, in which they would run their own affairs under city councils made up of men selected from their number.

Figueroa was not sanguine about the success of this program, and wrote frankly to the authorities in Mexico that the Indians were still children, while the white settlers who pretended to be interested in freeing the Indians from the missions were in reality scheming to seize both mission lands and Indian labor. He pointed out that California depended entirely on the missions, which were valuable haciendas whose products supported both the Territorial Government and the military garrison, since the Federal Government was unable to pay their salaries. Many California families obtained loans and other assistance from the missions, while the common whites, who did no work, occupied their time by swindling the mission Indians: They gambled with them at cards, provided liquor for them, and in return took their clothing and their food; they even persuaded the Indians to become robbers and then took what they had stolen. The missions were also hostels where travelers and the poor found food, lodging, and horses, or whatever they needed, free of charge. It could be seen, he concluded, that the missions were the sole source of the prosperity of the Territory, and that all of the inhabitants depended in some way on their preservation. In view of this situation, Figueroa did not think it wise to give wholesale grants of land to mission Indians, for they would be likely to lose it and such a course would ruin the missions whose products kept California going.[20]

It was evident to Figueroa, and to others, that if the missions supported California society, the burden fell directly on the mission Indians, for they did the manual labor in the fields and looked after the mission herds of cattle. Everyone in California pitied the mission Indians, but while the military and some Californians blamed the Franciscans for their unfortunate condition, the Franciscans pointed out that the hard labor that the Indians had to perform on the missions was caused by the demands of the garrison and the Territorial government, which depended on them. Secularization and distribution of mission lands to the Indians would break the vicious circle, but then who would pay the garrison or perform the other services long left to the missions? And who, asked the Franciscans, would protect the Indians from the greed of the scheming whites?[21]

While Governor Figueroa was attempting to put his provisional emancipation program into effect (it ran into numerous difficulties), he read the accounts of the debates in the Chamber of Deputies about the bill to secularize all the missions. He also read the bill to colonize mission lands which was proposed by the Farías administration. He at once wrote to Mexico City expressing his disapproval of both bills. It was premature to secularize all the missions, he said, and he pointed out that it had long been held in California that the mission Indians owned mission lands.[22] This may have stemmed from the provisions of the Spanish law of September 13, 1813, still considered valid in the Republic, which ordered secularization of the missions and provided that mission lands be divided up among the Indians living on them. It was evident, however, that this was no longer the view of the Federal Government, and indeed, one of the articles of the mission colonization bill specifically declared the law of September 13, 1813, to be null and void.[23] When this colonization bill failed to emerge from the Senate, the government put forward a bill drawn up by Juan Bandini, the representative from Upper California in the Chamber of Deputies, which was hurriedly approved on November 26, 1833. It provided that the government was "empowered to take all necessary steps to assure colonization, and bring about secularization of the missions of Upper and Lower California. . . ."

Governor Figueroa's reaction to this new mission legislation in Mexico was to suspend his own emancipation program and consult the Territorial Deputation (or Legislature) as to whether he had the power to put the secularization law into effect at once. He did not think he had the power to do so, because there were no regulations provided in the law for distributing mission lands and stock. The Deputation agreed with Figueroa that he could not implement the law until he had received the necessary additional instructions. By the middle of June 1834, Figueroa knew that another Political Chief, who would presumably bring these instructions with him, was to come out, and he therefore opposed any further secularization steps.

Within a month, for reasons that are not entirely clear, Figueroa had given his consent to the provisional secularization program drawn up by the Deputation. In hazarding a guess as to how this came about, it should be borne in mind that Figueroa, and probably the Deputation, thought that the instructions dividing up mission property would be based on the mission colonization bill, which they must have assumed was still being debated by the Senate. Because of the restrictions this bill placed on the acquisition of mission lands by the white Californians, it would be surprising if they had not opposed it, and in fact the Deputation proceeded to put pressure on Figueroa to take some action. They suggested that mission boundaries, which were not exactly known, should be surveyed. Unless this was done, they pointed out, mission lands could not be distributed; surveying the boundaries of the missions would permit Figueroa to make grants of land adjacent to them. Figueroa once more demurred, saying that he had suspended these grants until the new instructions arrived.

A Committee of the Deputation then suggested that Governor Figueroa assign each mission the amount of land he considered it needed, in accordance with the number of cattle it possessed. It would appear from this move that the Committee believed that the missions claimed more land than they needed, and that if Governor Figueroa assigned them the amount of land he calculated they actually required to pasture their herds, vacant land, which could then be granted to white Californians before the mission land itself was divided up, would become available. Again Figueroa refused to act. It was pointed out to him that the missions were slaughtering an unusually large number of cattle and that, as a result, the value of the missions was being rapidly reduced. Figueroa agreed with this, and apparently did not oppose the Deputation's view that the missionaries were deliberately reducing their herds to cash because of the coming secularization. Actually, what extra slaughtering was being done at the time was probably due to the need to settle mission accounts before the closing down of what in effect were profitable ranches. In addition, it is known that the Indians were slaughtering cattle without permission.

Sometime between the middle of June 1834 and the middle of July, Governor Figueroa changed his mind and agreed to go along with a new proposal put forward by the Deputation. They had been debating putting administrators in the missions, presumably to curb what they considered to be the excessive slaughtering and to take over the business management of the institutions. Then, following Figueroa's opposition, they presented a full provisional set of regulations for secularizing the missions which were probably worked out with Figueroa himself. These were approved virtually without debate by the Legislature and officially announced by Governor Figueroa on August 9, 1834.[24] A fact which may have helped persuade Figueroa to go along with the Deputation was that he had just acquired, for the remarkably small sum of 500 pesos, a 26,000-acre (10,530-hectare) ranch near Los Angeles.[25] The evidence is not sufficient to state categorically that this was a bribe, but the possession of such a ranch would, in any case, be likely to make Figueroa see eye-to-eye with the landowning members of the Deputation.

The regulations provided that ten missions were to be partially converted into towns at once and the remainder were to follow suit in due course. The Territorial Government was to take charge of the business management of the missions, or the "temporalities," as they were called, the mission Fathers being relegated to their religious duties. Under an important section devoted to distribution of mission property, the regulations granted heads of former mission Indian families not more than 33 acres (13 hectares) of land from the mission. In addition, each Indian town was to have common land for pasturing stock and for obtaining town revenue. Half of the mission stock, implements, and seed was to be divided up among those who received grants of mission land. All former mission land that remained undivided, following this distribution to mission Indians, was to be put in charge of an official appointed by the Governor. This official's salary, the stipends of the missionaries, the expenses of schools, and other needs of "good government" were to be met from the revenues of these undivided lands.

An important article made it obligatory for Indians freed from the mission to cultivate these undivided tracts of land—so that, in fact, they would still be subjected to forced unpaid labor. The new commissioners who took over the former missions were warned, perhaps wisely, to use "sweetness and patience" in explaining these regulations to the emancipated Indians. The regulations also prohibited the Indians from selling or otherwise disposing of their newly granted property, and anyone who attempted to buy it would lose his money. These paternalistic measures to protect the Indians would undoubtedly have won the support of men like Juan Rodríguez Puebla, with whose ideas on protection for the Indians Figueroa agreed. Another important provision in this section of the regulations was that mission property recovered from someone who tried to buy it from a mission Indian would be considered as "belonging to the nation." And if an Indian owner of former mission land died without heir, the land was to "return to the power of the nation." In other words, mission lands belonged to the nation, which was granting them to the former mission Indians and could get them back, under certain conditions.[26]

In the meantime, while Governor Figueroa had been busying himself with mission problems, some 239 colonists bound for California had slowly been making their way in covered wagons from Mexico City to Guadalajara and then on to Tepic and San Blas. Vice-President Gómez Farías had appointed José María Híjar, a man of 40 from a well-known Guadalajara family who was prominent in political circles in the state of Jalisco, to be Director of the new colony and to succeed General Figueroa as Political Chief, or Governor. Híjar had met Gómez Farías, who was then Minister of the Treasury, in Mexico in 1832, although he may have known him previously, since Farías was also from Guadalajara. Second in command of the colony was Adjutant Inspector José María Padrés, an officer of engineers, who was to take Figueroa's position as Commandant of the California garrison if Figueroa "continued to be ill and wished to retire."

Padrés had previously come out with Echeandía, who took office as Governor of California in 1825. Padrés did not get beyond Lower California at that time, however, and in 1827 he was back in Mexico City representing Lower California in the Chamber of Deputies. Here he made a name for himself as a strong opponent of Spaniards in Mexico, and in 1828 he was ordered to return to Upper California as Commandant of the garrison. He did not reach San Diego, however, until July 1, 1830, where his reputation as an opponent of the missionaries and a proponent of exile for Spaniards had undoubtedly pre-

ceded him. Colonel Manuel Victoria, who had by this time succeeded Echeandía as Governor, became convinced that Padrés was more of a troublemaker than the Spanish missionaries, and sent him back to Mexico at the end of 1831.

After a period of inactivity due to ill health, Padrés worked in the office of the Military College of the Corps of Engineers. While he was there, the Government ordered him to prepare plans for the defense of the northernmost region of California against the Russians at Bodega and Ross, and it was probably in the course of this work that he came into touch with Vice-President Farías, who was deeply interested in preserving California from foreign encroachments. At all events, Farías asked him to return to California to put his plans into effect. Padrés at first refused, but finally consented and was made Assistant Director of the colonizing expedition led by Híjar.[27]

The most complete source for what happened to the colony in California is Figueroa's *Manifesto to the Mexican Republic*, but before proceeding to discuss the limitations of this work it may be helpful to provide a brief synopsis of its argument and conclusions:

After passage of the act of August 17, 1833, secularizing the California missions, Governor Figueroa learned unofficially that Híjar was preparing to bring a colony to California to settle the northern frontier, which was threatened by the Russians. Figueroa selected a suitable site in the north for the colony and awaited further regulations from the Federal Government in Mexico on how to proceed with secularization, in particular what to do about the vast mission properties in land and cattle which the secularization act had not mentioned. After having waited for a year, Governor Figueroa reluctantly consented to put into effect a provisional regulation for secularization, drawn up by the Territorial Deputation, on August 9, 1834.

While engaged in this, Figueroa learned of the arrival of Híjar with part of the colony at San Diego, closely followed by the arrival of the second portion of the colony under Padrés at San Francisco. Figueroa had already received an unfavorable account of Padrés' previous activities in favor of secularization in California in 1830–31, and his suspicions were aroused when Padrés refused to perform his military duties, preferring to act as Assistant Director of the colony.

At the same time that Figueroa learned of Híjar's arrival, he was informed by a special messenger, who had come overland from Mexico City at record-breaking speed, that he was not to permit Híjar to become the Political Chief, or civilian head, of the Territory, as he had previously been informed. When they met at Monterey, on October 14, Figueroa told Híjar this surprising news and Híjar, in turn, surprised Figueroa by showing him the instructions he had received as Political Chief and Director of Colonization, authorizing him to take over all mission property and use it to finance the settlement of his colony. After consultation with the Deputation, Figueroa refused to hand over mission land and cattle to Híjar, and the Deputation backed him— suggesting, however, that Híjar might continue in California as Director of Colonization, despite serious doubts as to whether he could hold that position after being deprived of the post of Political Chief, which appeared to go with it.

Híjar at first refused to submit to measures drawn up by the Territorial Deputation for his colony, on the ground that

only the Federal Government had the right to enact these regulations. Figueroa and his advisers countered this argument by citing numerous Spanish laws and the Spanish Constitution of 1812, which Figueroa claimed was in effect in California, to show that the Legislature and Political Chief did have this power. Figueroa proceeded further to assert that mission land and property belonged only to the mission Indians, and that Mexican law prohibited colonization of such land. Híjar replied to this by citing the law of November 26, 1833, which ran as follows: "The Government is empowered to take all necessary steps to assure colonization, and bring about secularization of the missions of Upper and Lower California. . . ." Híjar interpreted this law as giving him full powers to assure the colonization of all available public land in California, including mission lands. Governor Figueroa and the Deputation interpreted the law as simply giving the Territorial Government the right to secularize the missions. It was, in any case, unconstitutional for the Government to seize mission lands, according to Figueroa, for the mission Indians knew that these lands were theirs. When Híjar called Figueroa's attention to the very small plots of land his own provisional secularization program gave the mission Indians, Figueroa became angry and retorted that all that Híjar was going to do for the Indians was to keep them working on the missions for wages, making them submit to a new form of serfdom. Híjar categorically denied this.

After conferences on October 25 and 26, 1834, in between which Figueroa accused Híjar of attempting to bribe him (labeling the alleged transaction, however, an accommodation), Híjar and Padrés agreed to act as the Directors of

Colonization under Governor Figueroa who, in his turn, promised to provide the implements and food pledged by the Federal Government to the colony during its first year. Figueroa then assisted Híjar in endeavoring to reunite the colonists, who were strung out along the line of missions between San Diego and Monterey. He also helped him make preparations to send the colonists to San Francisco Solano (Sonoma), close to the site that it was planned they should occupy.

But no sooner did a measure of harmony finally prevail between Governor Figueroa and Híjar than news of non-Christian Indian depredations in the south reached the Governor, along with complaints that they had been instigated by the colonists. Further disquieting rumors reached Figueroa that some of the colonists were plotting against him. Public opinion in California, in the meantime, had become exercised over what appeared to be an attempt by the Federal Government in Mexico to prevent the division of civil and military authority between two men, a Political Chief and a Military Commandant, which was a long-desired objective of the native sons. Governor Figueroa's refusal to allow Híjar to take over as Political Chief, keeping in his own hands both civil and military control, seemed to those who held this view a retrograde step. Rumors also began to spread that President Santa Anna was aiming at doing away with the federal form of government in order to set up a centralized state—an eventuality which also displeased the Californians. Confronted with what looked to him like a threatening situation, which he blamed on the leaders of the colony, Figueroa acted energetically against the non-Christian Indians and kept close watch on Híjar. In the meantime Padrés had moved some of the colonists to their

northern rendezvous at San Francisco Solano, to which Híjar was planning to go in a few weeks' time.

Governor Figueroa was now becoming increasingly suspicious of the leaders of the colony. He suggested to Híjar that his colonists, who were mostly from the city, were not suited for heavy manual labor in the fields and that, as many of them were people with a trade, they would do better for themselves if they were allowed to settle where they wanted instead of having to congregate on the northern frontier. Híjar rejected this, but said that if the Governor could not provide the necessary support for the colony, it would be better if he would openly say so at once rather than lead the colonists on further with false hopes. Figueroa then gave orders that the colonists should be allowed to settle where they wanted, and stated that he did not have sufficient funds to provide all that the Federal Government had promised. Híjar set out himself for San Francisco Solano early in March 1835, closely shadowed by Governor Figueroa. At a conference with Híjar at San Francisco de Asís (San Francisco), Figueroa told him that some of his colonists were conspiring against the Territorial Government and that he would have to take action against them unless Híjar curbed them himself. Híjar professed ignorance of the whole affair.

Finally, on March 7, a revolt broke out at Los Angeles in which one of the colonists, Francisco Torres, was involved. Governor Figueroa was at once convinced that Torres was responsible for the outbreak and quickly marched south to take charge of the affair himself. He also sent instructions to Ensign Mariano Vallejo, his commander at San Francisco Solano, to arrest Híjar, Padrés, and some of the other leading colonists and have them put on board the Sardinian frigate *Rosa*, then at San Francisco. Governor Figueroa thought that the revolt at Los Angeles was designed to coincide with another revolt at San Francisco Solano, and he enjoined Vallejo to seize at once all the arms and munitions which he knew Padrés had. Híjar wrote Figueroa an indignant letter denying any knowledge of a conspiracy and doubting whether Torres had involved himself in one.

The *Rosa*, with its cargo of dispirited colonists, stopped at Santa Barbara, where its passengers were transferred to the brigantine *Loriot* which took them on to San Pedro. Here Torres joined them for the voyage to San Blas. The rest of the colonists scattered to the various towns of California. At this point the *Manifesto* ends.

It may be argued on behalf of Governor Figueroa that he could hardly help being suspicious of Híjar and Padrés from the beginning. He had already been warned against Padrés by Alamán, and it must have seemed incredible to him that Padrés should be sent out to California by the new administration in Mexico. Híjar he does not appear to have known previously, but President Santa Anna's special message, with its laconic order not to allow Híjar to be Political Chief, must surely have made Híjar suspect in Figueroa's eyes. The brief instructions which Híjar presented to him, ordering Figueroa to hand over all mission property to the leaders of the colony, would be likely to convince him that some devious scheme was afoot which he must at all odds prevent until he received further instructions from the Federal Government. The fact that the people of Upper California were unhappy over the continued failure of the Territory to achieve a separation of civilian from military rule,

and were apparently concerned about Santa Anna's moves in the direction of centralism, could only add to Governor Figueroa's worries. Had not Governor Manuel Victoria been removed by revolutionary action? In addition to all this, there was the constant danger that both the mission Indians and the non-Christian Indians in the Territory would go on the warpath and endanger the very existence of Mexican California.

Perhaps even weightier than these fears, plausible as they appeared, were some concrete objections to the colony shared by Governor Figueroa and the Territorial Legislature, of which the most important was the order presented by Híjar requiring Figueroa to hand over to him all mission lands and cattle, the most valuable prize in the Territory. Figueroa inferred that the mission Indians were not to get anything, and that all other Californians were equally excluded.[28] However objectionable it had seemed, the Farías bill to colonize mission land, which had not become law, did grant the garrison and the white Californians their share of this wealth. Now these Mexican colonists were to get it all! And in Figueroa's view these people were not capable of farming, indeed had hardly ever gone into the country from the towns in which they had plied their trades.

In vain Híjar pointed out that "colonists" meant Californians, whites as well as Indians.[29] Híjar seems, in fact, to have been orally instructed to divide the mission lands in a way similar to that set forth in the colonization bill. But Figueroa would have none of it—the Indians, he said repeatedly, were not to be done out of their birthright. The Government, he vigorously affirmed, could not touch mission lands. It was unconstitutional to do so. He had never heard of eminent domain.[30] Yet he had previously approved the secularization regulations drawn up by the Legislature, in which mission lands were said to belong originally to the nation. Surely if the nation owned them, it could distribute them as it wished?

There can be little doubt that Figueroa's attitude on this crucial matter coincided with that of many of the leading Californians, who felt that they had more right to mission lands than immigrant Mexicans, for whom they had little use. There was also the important question of what was to happen when the mission estates were broken up and no longer produced the revenue that kept California going. Híjar's plan included elaborate provisions whereby a monopoly corporation known as the Cosmopolitan Company was to run them, paying the former mission Indians a daily wage for their work. But this Company was to have a virtual monopoly of all shipping as well as control of the former mission farms. It was true that it was supposed to provide fast transportation overland in California and stimulate exports of the hides and other crops that California produced, but how would it affect California ranchers and foreign ship-owners who then had the lion's share of the business?[31]

Governor Figueroa, it has been seen, opposed the colony's objective of taking over mission property and distrusted its leaders. His *Manifesto* reveals that he became convinced that Híjar and Padrés were aiming at making their fortunes by seizing mission property from its rightful owners. Actually, there is no evidence that this was the case. But Figueroa also criticized the rank and file of the colony. They were tradespeople, he claimed, quite unsuited to the hard manual labor of a farmer. He felt that he was doing these

"young girls, ladies, and delicate young men," as he called them, a favor by persuading them not to settle the northern frontier.[32] In reality some 20 percent of the colonists were farmworkers, or men engaged in food processing; 20 percent were garment workers; 14 percent were in the building trades; and 6 percent in the medical arts. All of these skills were badly needed in California. The remainder included silversmiths (presumably to make or repair mission silver ornaments), saddlers, teachers, tinsmiths, printers, lawyers, distillers, a miner, smelter, surveyor, bookbinder, secretary, and several others.[33]

Figueroa became convinced, however, that the colony was conspiring against him. He began to oppose uniting them in one place because it might lead to trouble. The Government had supplied them with guns, he remembered, and in a moment the "delicate young men" became dangerous revolutionaries.[34] If he had not previously made such a point of emphasizing the weakness and incapacity of the colonists, over half of whom were women and children, Figueroa's new argument that they were potentially dangerous would have been more convincing. As one of the colonists succinctly remarked: "If the intentions and plans [of the Directors] were hostile, they would have been able to carry out their plans at less cost, and with greater security, if they had brought along a force of military men instead of good family men of intelligence with some knowledge of the sciences and arts."[35]

It was perhaps with almost a sigh of relief that Governor Figueroa finally seized upon tangible evidence that a conspiracy had been going on in Los Angeles. It was reported that one of the colonists, Francisco Torres, a young physician from Guadalajara, was involved in it, and

Figueroa quickly came to the conclusion that he was the leading figure in the attempted revolt.[36] The available evidence does not offer sufficient corroboration for this view. But Figueroa went further still; admitting that he had no evidence to incriminate Híjar and Padrés in the revolt, he nonetheless had them arrested and deported on suspicion of being involved.[37]

In Figueroa's view, then, there was little good that could be said for Híjar, Padrés, and their colony: they were scheming to feather their nests with booty from the missions that by right belonged to the Indians, they were not capable of being settlers on the frontier, and they were revolutionaries who were plotting to get rid of Governor Figueroa. On the other hand, from Híjar and Padrés' point of view, Governor Figueroa was thwarting the colony for some mysterious ulterior purpose of his own.

It must be admitted that the Farías administration was itself responsible for some of the difficulties between Figueroa and Híjar. Figueroa had not been directly informed by the Government, it would appear, of the makeup of the colony, nor had he previously been told how much the Territorial Government should provide for it. Híjar's instructions were too brief to give a clear idea of how the new system was to be set up. Behind these inadequacies lay the growing mutual distrust between President Santa Anna and Vice-President Gómez Farías: the need for hasty action on the part of Farías to get the colony sent off before Santa Anna tried to prevent it from going. There was also general confusion in Mexico caused by a series of military revolts, and panic at the approach of Asiatic cholera which, when it did appear in Mexico City, wrought fearful havoc amongst the poor.[38]

The imprecise wording of Juan Bandini's act of November 26, 1833, may be ascribed to the haste with which it was passed. The Government's special powers, which had been granted to deal with emergencies, were due to expire on November 30, and the Government asked for passage of the bill without sending it through all the usual committee channels. This was done, and it was signed into law by President Santa Anna. "The Government," it stated, "is empowered to take all necessary steps to assure colonization, and bring about secularization of the missions of Upper and Lower California. . . ." Híjar took this to mean that it gave the Government the power to take *all* necessary steps to assure the colonization of the missions of the Californias, as well as their secularization. Such an interpretation is clearly in line with the aims of the Farías colonization bill which had not passed. But, as has been noted, Figueroa interpreted it as simply giving the Government the power to colonize non-mission land in California.

Perhaps if the colony had had energetic and effective help from the Federal Government after it had started on its way, it might have been successful. But unfortunately, Gómez Farías, who had organized and sponsored the colony from the first, was removed from power shortly after it left Mexico City. In September 1834, the same month that Híjar and Padrés reached California, Farías set out with his family for exile in the United States.[39]

To sum up, it is evident that Figueroa's *Manifesto to the Mexican Republic* was an unusually effective piece of personal propaganda which, ever since it was written, has cast the spell of a black legend over the colonizing project of Híjar and

Padrés. It also convinced many contemporary Californians that the Mexican Government was ready to give away their richest lands to penniless Mexican tradespeople, and thereby weakened Mexico's hold on their loyalties.

That Figueroa and Híjar differed profoundly in their views is clear: Figueroa insisted on paternalism and protection for the California mission Indians, whereas Híjar, following the Farías administration, wanted a more egalitarian attitude toward them; Figueroa repeatedly claimed that mission property belonged to the mission Indians, whereas Híjar, following the ideas of José María Luis Mora, considered the missions to be "moral bodies" which could merely administer the prop-

erty in their charge. Such property, according to Mora, belonged to the public or the nation as a whole.[40]

But Figueroa did not limit himself to combating what he considered to be the erroneous views of Híjar; he set out to prove that Híjar and Padrés were traitors and conspirators who were undermining Mexico's hold on California. It is here that Figueroa is at his weakest; indeed, his paranoid style has the unfortunate effect of casting suspicion on his own motives. Perhaps the controversy may be set to rest by reflecting that there were honest differences of opinion separating Figueroa and Híjar, which were sufficient in themselves to explain their mutual animosity.

FOOTNOTES

1. Robert Ernest Cowan, in his *A Bibliography of the History of California and the Pacific West, 1510–1906* (San Francisco, 1914), pp. 86 and 187, says that Figueroa's *Manifiesto* is "the second and most important of the early books printed on the Spanish press of California." Cowan regards the *Reglamento provicional para el gobierno interior de la Ecma. Diputación territorial de la Alta California* (Monterey, 1834) as the first book printed in California. The *Reglamento*, however, was only 16 pages long, whereas the *Manifiesto* had 184 pages, a fact which has made others differ with Cowan on this point. Edward Eberstadt, for example, says in his Americana catalogue no. 128 (1951) that the *Manifiesto* is "the most precious and famous of California books. Not only is it the first book printed in California (four single-sheet hand bills and a 16-page pamphlet being all that are known to have preceded it) but it is likewise by far the most important, and indeed the most pretentious volume printed in California during the twelve years in which the Spanish press was in operation." More recently (1961), Robert Greenwood, in *California Imprints, 1833–1862* (p. 40), describes the *Manifiesto* as "the most extensive volume printed in California during the period of the Mexican press." Perhaps the last word on this matter should go to the printer of the work, presumably Agustín Zamorano, who in an anonymous note at the beginning of the volume begged the

indulgence of his readers for his lack of sufficient accents and for any other typographical errors they found in the book, "taking into consideration that it is the first of its kind to appear from the only printing press in this Alta California."

Whether the *Manifiesto* is regarded as the first book printed in California or not, there is no question that it is extraordinarily rare. George Harding, in his "A Census of California Imprints, 1833–1845," lists (in 1933) five institutions and five individuals possessing copies of the *Manifiesto*, the Bancroft Library of the University of California at Berkeley having three copies. A single copy sold for $7500 at an auction in 1964. One of the printers at the Zamorano press was José de la Rosa, who was born in Puebla, Mexico, on January 5, 1790. Possibly he was a relative of Pedro de la Rosa, who had a printing press in Puebla in 1830. (John E. Baur, "José de la Rosa, Early Ventura's Centenarian Printer," pp. 14 and 16.) See also article by Alex[ander] S. Taylor dated Monterey, Jan. 31, 1855, in the *San Francisco Daily Herald*, May 8, 1855.

2. Spanish-speaking residents of California who reveal in their memoirs that they accept the conclusions of the *Manifiesto* include Juan B. Alvarado, Mariano G. Vallejo, José Fernández, Antonio María Osío, José de Jesús Vallejo, Vicente P. Gómez, and Manuel Castro. These memoirs may be consulted in the Bancroft Library,

University of California, Berkeley, hereinafter cited as BL. Among the large body of historians who appear to have accepted Figueroa's *Manifiesto* uncritically are: Charles Edward Chapman, Zoeth Skinner Eldredge, Zephyrin Engelhardt, Theodore H. Hittell, Irving Berdine Richman, and Franklin Tuthill.

3. *San Francisco Daily Herald*, June 18 and 19, 1855. Perhaps the translator was the indefatigable Alexander S. Taylor. For an interesting sketch of Taylor, see Robert Ernest Cowan, "Alexander S. Taylor, 1817–1876, First Bibliographer of California." The 1855 translation is also a rare item; see Greenwood, *California Imprints*, p. 194. This translation is not listed in Edith Margaret Coulter's 1943 article on "California Copyrights, 1851–1856," nor in the enlarged version of this article in *California Imprints*, pp. 480–504.

4. The original English version was reprinted in 1952 by Biobooks, Oakland, Calif., with a brief introduction by Joseph A. Sullivan. The 1952 edition reproduces the 1855 translation verbatim except for two changes: a running title on each page, and one word on almost every page in italics.

5. Figueroa, *Manifesto*, p. 95. (References in these notes to this work, hereinafter cited as *Manifesto*, are to the translation presented here.)

6. *El Telégrafo* (Mexico City), April 22, 1833.

7. *Memoria que el secretario de estado presenta*, p. 33.

8. Manuel Dublán and José María Lozano, eds., *Legislación mexicana*, II, pp. 548–549.

9. "Plan de colonización de nacionales," p. 7 in *Colección de los principales trabajos en que se ha ocupado la junta . . .*

10. *El Telégrafo*, April 22, 1833. For a discussion of the bill, see my article, "The Mexican Government and the Mission Indians of Upper California, 1821–1835," p. 352.

11. *El Telégrafo*, May 17, 1833. The voting on the amendment was given in this issue of *El Telégrafo* as 24 to 22 in favor, but this was corrected to 24 to 22 against in the May 22 issue.

12. *El Indicador de la Federación Mexicana* (Mexico City), Dec. 4, 1833.

13. José María Luis Mora, *Obras sueltas*, I, p. cclxiii.

14. *El Telégrafo*, May 21, 1833.

15. José Figueroa to Minister of Relations, Oct. 5, 1833, State Papers, BL, vol. 2, p. 70. (Minister of Relations is used herein as an abbreviated term for Minister of Internal and Foreign Relations.)

16. See my article, "General José Figueroa's Career in Mexico, 1792–1832," pp. 277–294 passim; and also my *Frontier Settlement in Mexican California*, p. 156.

17. Hutchinson, *Frontier Settlement*, pp. 156–157.

18. Hutchinson, "Figueroa's Career," pp. 286–287.

19. José María Mendoza, "Reclamación contra el Gral. Figueroa," Departmental State Papers, Benicia Military, BL, vol. 77, p. 455.

20. Hutchinson, *Frontier Settlement*, pp. 216–220, 222–227.

21. Zephyrin Engelhardt, *The Missions and Missionaries of California*, III, pp. 492–493.

22. Hutchinson, *Frontier Settlement*, pp. 236–239.

23. Article 39. (*El Telégrafo*, May 21, 1833.)

24. Hutchinson, *Frontier Settlement*, pp. 189–191, 240–241, 246–256.

25. Robert Glass Cleland, *The Cattle on a Thousand Hills: Southern California, 1850–1870*, pp. 252–256.

26. See Articles 18 and 19. Engelhardt, *Missions*, III, pp. 523–530, has a translation of the regulations.

27. Hutchinson, *Frontier Settlement*, pp. 182–185.

28. *Manifesto*, pp. 39–42.

29. *Ibid.*, p. 35.

30. *Ibid.*, pp. 52–53, 54.

31. *Reglamento para la Compañía Cosmopolitana*, passim. There is a translation of the *Reglamento* by Keld J. Reynolds in the *Historical Society of Southern California Quarterly* of December 1946.

32. *Manifesto*, pp. 68–69.

33. *El Telégrafo*, Sept. 14, 1834. See also my article, "An Official List of the Members of the Híjar–Padrés Colony for Mexican California, 1834," pp. 407–409.

34. *Manifesto*, p. 70.

35. Antonio Franco Coronel, "Cosas de California," BL, pp. 17–18.

36. *Manifesto*, p. 75.

37. *Ibid.*, pp. 86–87.

38. *Ibid.*, p. 60. For an account of this epidemic, see my article, "The Asiatic Cholera Epidemic of 1833 in Mexico."

39. *La Lima de Vulcano* (Mexico City), Sept. 9, 1834, cited in Vicente Riva Palacio, ed., *México a través de los siglos*, IV, p. 347.

40. Mora, *Obras*, I, pp. 223–224.

Manifesto to
the Mexican Republic

TRANSLATION

Manifesto to
the Mexican Republic

THE WIDESPREAD publicity which the attempt to colonize the Territories of the Californias has received all over the Republic, and the events which followed the expedition undertaken by José María Híjar and José María Padrés[1] for that purpose, force me to lay before the public a brief but accurate account of the matter. Since the undertaking did not turn out as the Directors proposed, an attempt is being made to blame me for its errors, when these are entirely due to the Directors' lack of preparation, poor management, and underhanded scheming. Confronted with the facts, the public will pass judgment on the persons involved.

In April 1832 the Federal Government appointed me Political Chief and Military Commandant of Upper California, and I arrived in January 1833[2] to take up my duties. In March of that year I became gravely ill, for which reason I asked to be relieved.[3] Since at that point the Territory had just emerged from a dangerous crisis, and I did not yet consider the causes of the revolution which had divided its inhabitants to be entirely extinguished, I did not think that it was the proper time to separate the civil and military commands in the hands of two different individuals, as had been urged, but that one single individual should hold both positions. I officially presented this view to the Federal Government when I asked to be relieved; it seemed to me appropriate under the circumstances, as I was not even remotely thinking of staying in command, because my health was badly broken and I was anxious only to return to the bosom of my family.

In 1830, Adjutant Inspector José María Padrés, pretending to have a great interest in improving the lot of the natives—although not with very good intentions, as has been revealed—devised a scheme to

1. For a discussion of the careers of Híjar and Padrés, see the Introduction, p. 9. I have given a detailed account of the Híjar and Padrés expedition in *Frontier Settlement in Mexican California*.

2. The administration of Vice-President Anastasio Bustamante appointed General Figueroa Inspector and Military Commandant of Upper California on April 17, 1832. On May 9 it made him Political Chief, or Civil Governor, as well, thus continuing the joint civil–military command which many Californians opposed. Figueroa arrived at Monterey on January 14 or 15, 1833.

3. Figueroa wrote to the Minister of War on March 25, 1833, asking to be relieved of his duties. For an account of General Figueroa's career in Mexico before coming to Alta California, see my article, "General José Figueroa's Career in Mexico, 1792–1832."

secularize the missions of this Territory in accordance with the law of September 13, 1813.[4] At that time the Governor of the Territory was Lieutenant Colonel José María de Echeandía,[5] whose aid Padrés easily enlisted by presenting him with a plan, which Echeandía forthwith ordered proclaimed and put into effect, at a time when Lieutenant Colonel Manuel Victoria had just arrived to relieve him.[6] Both for this reason and because the Federal Government had not been consulted, Governor Victoria ordered that the project be halted. Since Padrés had surreptitiously enlisted several patriots who in good faith wanted secularization, he had many collaborators who, both because of the exaggerated ideas that had been inculcated in them and because of the severity with which Victoria attempted to govern them, later joined the ranks of Victoria's opponents in the revolution against him led by Echeandía.[7]

4. This law provided that all missions in overseas provinces which had been in existence ten years were to be turned over to parish priests immediately. The missionaries were also immediately to cease their administration of the Indians' lands, and mission lands were to be distributed as private property. The law is reprinted in Francisco de la Maza, ed., *Código de colonización y terrenos baldíos*, pp. 152–153.

5. Governor of California 1825–1831.

6. Governor Victoria arrived at Santa Barbara on December 31, 1830, and took his oath of office on January 31, 1831. The secularization plan to which Figueroa refers was issued by Echeandía on January 6, 1831. Since this plan was similar to Echeandía's 1828 secularization proposal, which was modified in 1830, it is inaccurate to say, as Figueroa does here, that José María Padrés "presented" Echeandía with the plan. It is possible, however, that Padrés may have had some influence on the wording of the preamble to the plan.

7. Governor Victoria, convinced that he was defending mission property from greedy Californians, refused to call together the Territorial Deputation and ran the Government in dictatorial fashion.

Whatever the causes of this revolution, it threw the Territory into disorder, both because the government was destroyed, and the consequences of this were felt, and because it divided the citizens in general and made them enemies. So it was that when I arrived to take command, the Territory was in a state of complete anarchy, from which it has not yet completely recovered. The Federal Government highly disapproved of the conduct of Echeandía and Padrés, and gave orders that if I found the secularization decree in effect I was to suspend it and restore the missions to their former state, but nonetheless to report whether or not they were in a condition to be secularized, so as to undertake it with due circumspection, and also to slowly go ahead dividing up mission lands among the neophytes, to imperceptibly convert them to private property. Padrés was thrown out of this country[8] by Victoria, but he had sown the seeds of the revolution which later flared up and which owes its origin to the scheme to secularize the missions.

Since the distance from here to Mexico City is so great, I had recovered my health before I knew the Government's decision [on my request to be relieved], and I informed them that I was able to continue to discharge my duties. The Government then ordered me to continue in both my positions, as I was doing, despite the fact that when they had received my first communication they had ordered Adjutant Inspector José María Padrés to proceed to California and take over the military command "in case" I continued to be ill and wanted to return to Mexico.[9]

8. Padrés sailed for San Blas on November 8, 1831.

9. Figueroa wrote to Mexico on March 25, 1833, asking for permission to resign because of his

When this dispatch was sent, the Government was in the hands of Gómez Farías, who reposed great confidence in Adjutant Inspector José María Padrés, as Padrés himself has made known.[10] Padrés availed himself of this opportunity to use his influence effectively to obtain passage of the law of August 17, 1833, which was designed to secularize the missions of the Californias and to undertake colonization of both Territories, and to have José María Híjar appointed Political Chief of Upper California and Director of Colonization. One could be readily persuaded of the utility and propriety of these projects if they did not involve other aims which time has revealed;[11] but the Government, motivated by the best wishes for the hap-

piness and progress of this country, gave its protection to these grandiose schemes. Padrés was delighted at seeing the plans he had been preparing since 1830 being realized, and he himself was rewarded with the position of Assistant Director of Colonization.

Preparations were made for the journey and people were recruited in the name of the Government to be colonists. I do not know what help they received, but it is well known that up to the time when the expedition embarked at the port of San Blas, the Government spent a great deal of money.[12]

In February 1834 I received the following Government order:

Mexico City
July 15, 1833

General José Figueroa
Political Chief of Upper California

His Excellency the Vice-President, exercising the Federal Executive Power,[13] has been pleased to grant you relief from your position of Political Chief of the Territory and appoint to that post José María Híjar, to whom you will at once turn over the command.

At the same time His Excellency orders me to thank you, as I do, for the zeal with which

---

health. After April 1, 1833, however, a new liberal administration under President Santa Anna and Vice-President Valentín Gómez Farías took over, following the defeat of Anastasio Bustamante and the interim presidency of Gómez Pedraza. Owing to the alleged indisposition of Santa Anna, Gómez Farías became Acting Chief Executive on April 1. On July 12, 1833, José Joaquín de Herrera, Minister of War in the Farías administration, informed Padrés that he was to go to California as Military Commandant if Figueroa "continued to be ill and wished to retire." At this same time the Farías government appointed José María Híjar to the post of Political Chief, the civil arm of the California government which the Californians wanted separated from the military. During one of the periods in which Santa Anna took over the presidency himself, the Minister of War wrote Figueroa (in a letter dated December 7, 1833) that he was to remain Commandant. It was not until July 25, 1834, that Santa Anna sent out a special courier instructing Figueroa not to turn over the office of Political Chief to Híjar, but to keep this position himself. Figueroa's statement here, that "the Government then ordered me to continue in both my positions," is misleading, since it does not mention the passage of time between these orders.

10. For a discussion of Padrés' activities in Mexico, see the Introduction, p. 9.

11. The "other aims" mentioned by Figueroa probably refers to the Cosmopolitan Company plans discussed in the Introduction, p. 13.

12. It is difficult to estimate the amount spent by the Mexican Government on the colony. Híjar estimated his expenses for the colony in November 1833 at 6,985 pesos (Departmental State Papers, C-A40, BL, vol. 1, p. 165). This included surveying instruments, horses, saddles, forage, etc. It is likely, however, that expenses were considerably higher than this. In Mexico City each family was to receive 10 pesos for the purchase of necessary equipment for the trip to California. The expenses of the journey by land and sea were to be paid by the Government, and the colonists were to be given the saddles bought for the expedition. From the day that they reached their place of settlement in California, all colonists over four years old were to be given 4 reales a day; those under, 2 reales a day.

13. Vice-President Gómez Farías, acting as President.

you have performed your duties, and hopes that you will continue your services in support of order.

I communicate this to you for your information and compliance.

God and Liberty.
García[14]

My answer was as follows:

Monterey
May 18, 1834

Esteemed Sir:

As soon as Señor José María Híjar presents himself in this Territory I shall hand over to him the civil government which has been in my charge, as His Excellency the Vice-President disposes and Your Excellency informs me in your official letter of July 15, 1833, which I have received after much delay.

I am exceedingly grateful to His Excellency the Vice-President for having relieved me of this position, which is so far above my limited attainments, and for his distinguished expressions of satisfaction with my conduct in the performance of my duties. Indeed, although I cannot pride myself on having fulfilled the wishes of the Government, I at least have the satisfaction of having reestablished tranquility and constitutional order, which, on entering this Territory, I found slackened in all branches of the administration. Fortunately peace and unity are enjoyed today, and I have spared no pains nor efforts to attain them. I declare that I shall continue to do so until the moment my successor arrives, hoping that the results will testify to my good or bad conduct.

Meanwhile, please convey my sentiments to His Excellency the Vice-President, to whom I respectfully tender my gratitude and acknowledgment.

God and Liberty.
José Figueroa

Unofficially the news reached me that along with José María Híjar a multitude of families were coming as colonists, supported by the Government, and although neither the Government nor Señor Híjar depended on the local authorities for this undertaking,[15] it seemed to me prudent to make some preparations for settling them. With this in mind, I went on an expedition to the frontier up to Fort Ross, which is the Russian settlement closest to us; I reconnoitered the land there and selected what seemed to me the best site to establish the colony.[16] I left a detachment there for the protection of the colony and returned to Monterey to await it.

On September 11, the day before I reached Monterey, I received a special courier from the Federal Government who had come overland from Mexico City with the following order:[17]

Mexico City
July 25, 1834

José Figueroa
Political Chief of Upper California

His Excellency the President, having been informed by your dispatch of May 18, in which

---

14. Carlos García, Minister of Relations. (See the Introduction, n. 15.)

15. In actual fact the colony did depend on the California authorities, but possibly when Figueroa first learned about the coming of the colony he thought it might not have to rely on local funds.

16. Figueroa left Monterey shortly after August 21, 1834, on this expedition. With him were Captain Agustín Zamorano, the engineer and printer, who was to do the surveying, and Ensign Mariano Guadalupe Vallejo. A site for the new town, to be called Santa Anna and Farías, was located on what is now known as Mark West Creek, a few miles north of Santa Rosa. The main square and some of the blocks surrounding it were laid out from August 29 to August 31. On September 1 the expedition marched to San Francisco Solano (Sonoma). It may have been at this point that Figueroa visited Ross, for he did not return to Monterey until September 12. Figueroa had previously sent Vallejo up to investigate Ross in the spring of 1833 (April 21–May 5). (Figueroa to Vallejo, May 15, 1833, Cowan Collection, BL.)

17. The courier was Rafael Amador, a native of Lower California. He completed the arduous trip

you reply to the order relieving you from the post of Political Chief of Upper California, saying that you will hand over the command as soon as Señor Híjar arrives, has ordered in reply that you are not to hand over the command and that you are to continue to fulfill the office of Political Chief.

God and Liberty.
Lombardo[18]

By the same courier I received the first communications sent to me by Señor Híjar from San Diego, where he disembarked on September 1 with part of the colony. On September 25 the naval corvette *Morelos* arrived here in Monterey with José María Padrés, several employees, and the rest of the colony.[19]

From that day my difficulties began, and it was easy to foresee the consequences. Señor Padrés officially asked me for help for the colonists who had come with him, and that was the first news that he gave me of his assignment. The Federal Government had given me no previous notice regarding the colonization project,[20] nor had it given any orders to Treasury officials to disburse funds for the colony. Nor had the Government even informed me that José María Padrés, a military offi-

cer who was to serve under my orders, had been selected as Assistant Director of the colony. For all of these reasons, therefore, Padrés' conduct seemed strange to me, and although he tried to satisfy me by showing me a document that the Minister of Relations[21] had directed to him, by which he was appointed Assistant Director of Colonization, that is not the way it should have been done, nor should an order from the Government have been communicated to me through Padrés. And the Minister of Relations should not have made use of the services of a military officer without a prior order from the Secretary of War. In spite of this, I thought it prudent to say nothing and to give him to understand that my responsibility had not been discharged.

No payment should be made in Government offices unless it is preceded by an order transmitted through established channels, based on some law, and approved by the Houses of Congress of the Union in the general budget for the fiscal year. Although it was contrary to these express precautions and despite the great needs of our civil and military employees, I ordered that the colony should be supported to prevent it from perishing while the Government was being asked for orders about it. This is irrefutable evidence of the lack of skill and foresight and the faulty planning of the Directors, who should have prepared everything necessary for the people they brought with them to avoid exposing them to suffering. The Directors should have known that the salaries of the few military and civilian employees of the Territory have not been paid in full for more than twenty years, for lack of money, and that besides adding to the distress of these people, they

---

overland in the record time of 48 days and is said to have died as a result of his exertions.

18. Francisco María Lombardo took over the Ministry of Relations from Carlos García on December 16, 1833.

19. Híjar arrived on the *Natalia*, belonging to the Cosmopolitan Company, with 127 members of the colony. Padrés arrived in Monterey on the corvette *Morelos* on the night of September 24, 1834, with 112 colonists. The names, ages, and occupations of the colonists, including spouses and children, are given in my article, "An Official List of the Members of the Híjar–Padrés Colony for Mexican California, 1834."

20. Information about the forthcoming colony had been appearing in the official Government paper *El Telégrafo*, however, and it is from this source that Figueroa apparently picked up his advance information.

21. Francisco María Lombardo.

would compromise the responsibility of the officials of the Treasury who had no orders to make payments to the colony.

Since it is 468 miles from San Diego to Monterey,[22] Señor Híjar did not arrive here until October 14.

I received him with public demonstrations of friendship and respect. I treated him with the greatest distinction and courtesy, and I put him up in my home. After the first compliments were over, I showed him the order from the Federal Government and told him that I was bound to obey it, although I regretted having to do so because of its reflection on his honor and interests. In all sincerity and good faith I placed my limited influence at his disposal and said that I would urge the Territorial Deputation[23] to ask the Government to return to him the post of Political Chief; in the meantime, he should carry out his special assignment as Director of the Colony. Finally, I told him that if I found a legal means to hand the command over to him, without compromising my own responsibility, I would gladly do so, for I had no desire to retain it.[24]

Persuaded of my good will and perhaps convinced that he could not aspire to the command, Señor Híjar resigned himself to his special assignment as Director of the Colony, which the Government had not expressly mentioned. Although I was in doubt whether he should be considered as having this position after he had been deprived of the civil government, I could see no danger in his being Director of the Colony, and I at once agreed that he should undertake this assignment, subject to my notifying the Government. Then he demanded that I hand over to him the property of the missions, as if it were something intrinsic in the aforesaid assignment. I answered that I was unaware of the basis for such a presumption, and forthwith he handed me a document containing the following instructions:

Mexico City
April 23, 1834

Instructions in accordance with which José María Híjar, Political Chief of Upper California and Director of Colonization of Upper and Lower California, is to regulate his conduct:

Article 1. He will begin by occupying all the property belonging to the missions of both Californias, and the Military Commandant, under his responsibility, will, whenever he is called upon, provide the necessary assistance for doing so.

Article 2. For the period of one year, counted from the day that the colonists reach the place where they are to settle, each colonist over four years old is to be supplied with four reales a day, and two reales a day for those under four.

Article 3. The expenses of the trip by sea and land will be met by the Federal Government. The colonists will be given full possession of the mounts that have been purchased or will be purchased for their transportation.

Article 4. Towns will be formed by bringing together a sufficient number of families to live in safety, selecting suitable sites according to the quality of the soil, the abundance and healthfulness of the water, and the good quality of the air.

Article 5. It will be attempted as far as

22. The distance from San Diego to Monterey by road today is about 464 miles (747 km).

23. The term Territorial Deputation is an adaptation of Provincial Deputation, an institution provided in the Spanish Constitution of 1812. Since California was a Territory in the new Republic of Mexico, the name was modified, but the institution remained the same. It continued in existence because the Mexican Congress, although it was constantly urged to pass new legislation for the Territory of California, did not do so. For a detailed discussion of the Provincial Deputation, see Nettie Lee Benson, *La Diputación provincial y el federalismo mexicano*.

24. The command which Figueroa says he is not interested in keeping is the civil government only (Political Chief), not the military command.

possible to settle frontier regions with the greatest speed.

Article 6. Topographical plans will be drawn in which the blocks constituting the town will be named and marked out. The length of each side of the blocks will be 100 yards, and every side will be equal. The width of the streets will be 20 yards, and no alleys will be permitted. There will be a square at least every ten streets, in addition to the main square, which will be situated in the center of the town.

Article 7. Very special care will be taken to include Indians in the towns, mixing them with the other inhabitants, and towns composed solely of Indians will not be permitted.

Article 8. In each block of the towns, lots will be distributed to families so that they may build their houses; but they will not be permitted to do so beyond the lines marking the street.

Article 9. Outside of the towns, each family of colonists will be given full and exclusive ownership of 423 acres of land if it is irrigable, 846 acres if it is nonirrigable crop land, and 1692 acres if it is only suitable for raising cattle. Each family will also be given four cows, two yoke of oxen or two bulls, two tame horses, four colts, four fillies, four head of sheep—two female and two male—and also two plows ready for use.

Article 10. Between individual lots of land, one parcel of land equivalent to two lots will be kept unoccupied. The Government will be able to sell the land in this parcel when it wishes to do so, and the Director of the Colonies will give preference in this case, other circumstances being equal, to the neighboring colonists.

Article 11. When the movable property belonging to the missions of California has been distributed, up to half of the remainder will be sold in the most advantageous manner.

Article 12. Not more than 200 head of cattle of one kind may be sold to a single family.

Article 13. The remaining half of the movable property or cattle will be held in the account of the Government and applied to the costs of religious worship, stipends for the missionaries, salaries for the elementary school teachers and supplies for the children of both sexes in the schools, and for the purchase of farm equipment which is to be given free to the colonists.

Article 14. The Political Chief and Director of Colonization will prepare at this time, and annually thereafter, a detailed account of the yield of mission property, of the way in which it is invested, and of the property that remains after the distribution of movable property and cattle among the colonists.

Article 15. He will also report at least once each year on the state of the colonists, the reasons for their backwardness, if any, and the ways by which they may be made to progress.

Lombardo

I replied that as far as I was concerned these orders would be obeyed, although, in my opinion, it was unjust to deprive the neophytes of the wealth of the missions, which they considered their property.[25] Our private meeting on the night of October 15 ended at this point, and at daybreak on the 16th I received the following message:

Monterey
October 16, 1834

Commanding General José Figueroa

Among the orders and instructions of the Federal Government which I, as Director of Colonization, have shown you is the following article: "Article 1. He will begin by occupying all the property belonging to the missions of both Californias, and the Military Commandant, under his responsibility, will, whenever he is called upon, provide the necessary assistance for doing so."

Since it is therefore of the utmost importance that my assignment be begun, both to avoid the losses that the missions are suffering[26] and

25. For a discussion of the basic question of ownership of mission lands, see the Introduction, pp. 5–9.

26. The missions were losing many of their cattle. The missionaries were later accused of killing off large numbers of cattle in order to turn

to improve the lot of the natives and settle the families of colonists accompanying me, I beg you to give orders to the commissioners for secularization that they are to act under my direction, and to the military commanders in all parts of the Territory to provide me or my respective agents with whatever assistance may be needed for this end.

I repeat to you my declarations of esteem and great respect.

God and Liberty.
José María de Híjar
Director of Colonization
of the Californias

I replied with the following:

Monterey
October 16, 1834

José María de Híjar
Director of Colonization

As you requested, I shall direct the commissioners of the missions to act in accordance with the orders you send them, and the military commanders to render assistance, whenever necessary, in accordance with the resolutions of the Federal Government in Article 1 of the instructions which you were good enough to copy for me in your note of today's date, which I hereby have the honor of answering.

But you will permit me to first consult the Territorial Deputation, so as to obtain their acquiescence and better expedite your duties in this assignment.

God and Liberty.
José Figueroa

Back again came Señor Híjar with this:

Monterey
October 17, 1834

By your note of yesterday's date I was pleased to learn of your willingness to support the resolutions of the Federal Government, after prior consultation with the Territorial Deputation, concerning my colonization assignment.

I beg you that, if possible, this matter be brought to a conclusion this very day. The ruinous disorder of many of the missions through which I passed; the proximity of the time for planting wheat,[27] which the missionaries seem to have neglected, assuredly because they fear they will lose control of the temporalities; the outcries of the natives, who up until now have endured infinite suffering; the colony, which I am unable to settle until this matter is resolved; and the painfully short time remaining for the planting necessary to provide its subsistence for the entire year—everything, everything, General, indicates that not a moment must be lost.

In conclusion, I turn to you as a military authority to entreat that the assistance mentioned in Article 1 of my instructions, which I transcribed for you in my previous communication, be provided, and I should exceedingly regret your bearing the responsibility for the disorders and irreparable losses that delay may bring.

God and Liberty.
José María de Híjar

The clear and persistent desire to seize property owned by an abject and defenseless people; the reports, spread abroad by the colonists themselves and their Directors, about the grandiose speculations of the vaunted Cosmopolitan Trading Company, which owned the *Natalia*, that the missions were to pay for it with 89 short tons of tallow; and, above all, the Federal

---

their assets into cash before secularization. What evidence there is, however, reveals that restless mission Indians, working with non-Christian Indians, did much of the destruction, although on some missions the Franciscans were killing cattle in order to pay off mission indebtedness. More evidence is needed before the matter can be fully explained. Cases against the missionaries are presented by Hubert Howe Bancroft, *History of California*, III, pp. 348–349, and Theodore H. Hittell, *History of California*, II, pp. 207–208. The missionaries are defended by Zephyrin Engelhardt, *The Missions and Missionaries of California*, III, pp. 556–559, 654–663.

27. Contemporaries regarded November as the planting time in California for corn and other grains.

Government's having sent a special courier with the sole object of ordering me not to hand over the command, caused me to distrust their claims for property, and I consulted the Territorial Deputation, as is shown by the following communications:

Monterey
October 17, 1834
Territorial Deputation of Upper California

The law of June 23, 1813, in Article 15, Chapter 3, provides "that in certain serious matters" I should hear the advice of the Deputation, and avail myself of their knowledge.[28] The internal regulations of that body in Article 2, Title 1, authorize me to convene it for special sessions.[29] Making use of this power, I decided to summon you to this session which today I have the pleasure of seeing take place. The reason for this meeting has been explained; I am now going to indicate the objectives which must occupy your attention.

On July 15, 1833, the Federal Government was pleased to relieve me of my charge as Political Chief of this Territory and appoint José María Híjar in my place. On May 13 of this year I replied that I was ready to hand over the command as soon as he should arrive, and on July 25 the Federal Government ordered me by special express courier not to hand over my post to Señor Híjar and to continue filling the office of Political Chief. Everything is recorded in the documents which I hereby have the honor of submitting, and I request that they be read for your further enlightenment. Señor Híjar was also appointed Director of the Colony which has just arrived, as is shown by the Government order which I also submit for your information.

When the Federal Government advised me that I was not to hand over the command to Señor Híjar, it did not mention the other position or positions that it had entrusted to him. And since the position of Director of the Colony has a link, so to speak, with the post of Political Chief, I am in doubt as to whether he can undertake the former assignment, now that he has been removed from the latter, or, if he can, how this should be done; for although these positions are not incompatible with one another, I lack precedents, for the Government has not given me any information regarding colonization. His Excellency the President, by virtue of the law of April 6, 1830, may appoint commissioners to establish colonies,[30] and in my opinion Señor Híjar should carry out the task which he has been given. But since I wish to carry out my responsibility properly and not compromise it in any way, I thought it necessary to hear the Deputation's advice, believing that your integrity and knowledge would suggest a conciliatory and decorous solution.

On the 16th of this month Señor Híjar sent me a note, which I also send herewith. It contains within it an article of the instructions which he received from the Federal Government, and in accordance with this he asks that the commissioners appointed under Article 20 of the provisional secularization regulations operate under his orders.[31] Here is a question for Your Excellencies' attention: Is Señor Híjar Director of Colonization and Secularization, or only of the former? His appointment says that he is Director of the Colonies; are colonization and secularization the same thing? No. But the Federal Government orders him to occupy all the property belonging to the missions. In what role or position should he

28. The Law of June 23, 1813, is given in Manuel Dublán and José María Lozano, eds., *Legislación mexicana*, I, pp. 413–425.

29. These internal regulations are in the *Reglamento provicional para el gobierno interior de la Ecma. Diputación territorial de la Alta California*, or house rules for that body, which were published at Monterey in 1834. This 16-page pamphlet is sometimes regarded as the first book printed in California (see the Introduction, n. 1).

30. The text of the Law of April 6, 1830, is reprinted in Maza, *Código de colonización*, pp. 241–244.

31. These provisional regulations, entitled *Reglamento provisional para la secularización de las misiones de la Alta California*, were published on August 9, 1834. For locations of an original copy, a translation, and a synopsis, see n. 134 below.

be given jurisdiction over this wealth? I do not know. Let Your Excellencies ponder this matter and advise me what is most just.

God and Liberty.
José Figueroa

Monterey
October 17, 1834
Territorial Deputation of Upper California

Since I took over the reins of government of this Territory, I have been regarding with pleasure the constitutional progress being made by these peaceful inhabitants without any obstacle or disturbance. Since public trust has been placed in me, I have held in veneration the laws containing the social guarantees. But one of those misfortunes by which the genius of evil extends its malign influence seeks to take away from us the enviable tranquility which only Californians are permitted to enjoy. Events which produce differences of opinion in the public have unexpectedly become linked together, and Your Excellencies will not be unaware of the means which are being employed to wound us with the exaggerated notions which are unfortunately consuming our brothers in the interior of the Republic.[32]

The ostensible reason for discontent lies in the Government order, which I have shown you, referring to my not handing over the civil command to Señor José María Híjar, who had been appointed to that post. Your Excellencies are informed of the communications on this matter and know that I have had no part in this change, for I neither seek this position nor desire to continue in it. I have undertaken it and I shall continue to do so while the Federal Government and the residents of this land honor me with their confidence. But if my remaining in command is going to produce discord and discontent in the family of Californians, whose feelings I share, I am determined to give it up.

As a proof of my disinterestedness, I have proposed to Your Excellencies that if my duty

to obey can be reconciled with public demands, tell me what steps I must take, and no other consideration will deter me from handing over the command. In accordance with this declaration, I propose to you that I shall resign of my own accord, if at this price the tranquility of the Californians, whose fate is of such concern to me, can be preserved. My determination is supported by the public opinion actively expressed in favor of separation of the civil from the military command, and by the knowledge that the Federal Government, as interested as I in the progress of this fortunate country, will approve of my conduct and will appreciate it as emanating from true patriotism and current circumstances. No sacrifice, sirs, no sacrifice is too high for me to preserve the liberty and tranquility of the Territory. I should like to be the only victim immolated on the sacred altars of harmony.

May the Californians continue to live in peace, and let the results and the responsibility be mine. The wishes of this young society are my guide. The Deputation is the organ through which they must be expressed. May my prayers be granted and the desires of my compatriots be satisfied.

God and Liberty.
José Figueroa

I knew very well that the position of Director of Colonization did not give Híjar the power either to dispose of or to administer the property of the missions, but I wanted to humor his desires and only sought to establish guarantees to assure the security of this property, for which I as Political Chief was responsible. But the tricks with which he surprised me forced me to change my mind and put the matter in its true light.

Señor Híjar's followers tried to lead public opinion astray and alarm the inhabitants of this Territory in order to throw me out ignominiously and furtively seize the government. Subversive rumors were spread, under the pretext of dividing the command between two separate per-

---

32. For comments on the situation in Mexico at this time, see the Introduction, pp. 4–5.

sons, in order to become independent of the Republic of Mexico.[33] The abject natives were approached; ignoble interests and passion were called into play and, in brief, they tried to intimidate me with threats of revolution under diverse and specious pretexts, such as that His Excellency the President of the Republic had changed the federal system and destroyed by armed force the institution representing National Sovereignty. My conduct under such circumstances is shown in the declaration that I made to the Deputation: I would obey the Government and not oppose the general will. This was my decision: I had been ordered not to turn over the command to Señor Híjar, but I was ready to deposit it in the hands of the leading member of the Deputation, who is the person named by the law of May 6, 1822,[34] to govern when there is no Political Chief. Nonetheless, I wanted to have my resolution backed by the vote of the people's representatives.

In order to arrive at its opinion, the Deputation referred the matter to one of its committees, and it was during this time that there was most recourse to politics, friendship, and intrigue to take that body by surprise. In spite of this, the Deputation acted with a dignity in accord with its position and agreed to the following:

Monterey
October 21, 1834

The Committee on Government [of the Territorial Deputation] reports as follows: That

33. Figueroa's suspicions that the Californians wanted to separate the civil and military authorities in the Territorial Government so that they might obtain independence from Mexico are not supported by other available evidence.

34. The law of May 6, 1822, may be found in *Colección de los decretos y órdenes del soberano congreso mexicano desde su instalación en 24 de febrero de 1822 hasta 30 de octubre de 1823*, pp. 44–45.

the unforeseen events that have so justly attracted public attention were presented [by you] from a true point of view; and after prolonged examination, it appears that the Federal Government, resolved to separate the civil command from the military, appointed José María Híjar, who arrived at San Diego on September 1, 1833, bringing with him, as its Director, a colony of persons of both sexes. The same Federal Government, for reasons which it does not state, making use of its authority orders that the command is not to be handed over to Señor Híjar and that General José Figueroa is to continue to exercise it. This incident has been imperfectly transmitted to the public. The sense of the Government order has been altered, and it has been attributed to an attempt by the President of the Republic to change the system of government. Such ideas and other bitter statements have been voiced in public to mislead popular opinion, which has long been in favor of separating the commands. An event of such great importance was clearly alarming: it concerned the liberties of the land and the destiny of this Territory, and nobody can remain indifferent when the exercise of his rights is being discussed. But reason and truth make the darkness disappear, and so Your Excellency must rectify public opinion by presenting the events to the world just as they occurred.

We shall not attempt to discuss whether the commands should be separated or not, because the Federal Government has not refused to separate them, and the inhabitants of this Territory are not deprived of the right of petition; nor will the Deputation, as the immediate representative of the people, cease in its efforts to have its views heard by the Executive of the Union, and even in the very sanctuary of the laws, to demand the exercise of the political rights of its constituents. Is it simply a matter of knowing who is to exercise the powers of Political Chief? The Government order of July 25 leaves no room for interpretations. It states explicitly that the command is not to be handed over to Señor Híjar and that General Figueroa is to continue to exercise it. In that case, what cause could induce us to contravene this mandate? Would it not be said that it was rebellion or usurpation of the powers of the Executive against the provisions of the Constitution? Shall it be said that because the Republic is in a state of convulsion, and our brothers are divided by fatal discords, we should cease to proceed along constitutional paths? No, esteemed sir. Liberty endures while laws are respected, and unhappy is the people which attacks them for frivolous pretexts. The result is anarchy, and the consequences are the annihilation of the fortunes and the existence of the citizens. Let us keep free from the contagious poison of discord which is devouring our brothers, since nature has spared us by means of an impregnable wall. If enemies of liberty and order are provoking strife among them, we are not in that position; and if we should unfortunately become involved at some time, we know how to make use of our rights. Comply with the order in question, therefore, for the present, and we shall have fulfilled our duty by giving public testimony to our love of order and justice. At the same time, let us make a petition to the Federal Government that it be good enough to resolve the separation of the civil command, this Deputation to propose one or more persons from those that it considers qualified to undertake this task, and we venture to predict the best results.

Señor Figueroa, moved by his patriotism, offers to resign as Political Chief if this would serve the tranquility of the Territory, and to submit to whatever results and responsibility may fall on him; but public tranquility is assured under the command of this gentleman, and there is no merit in making such a change. The Deputation, which has been observing his conduct from close quarters, and which keeps a watch on the public welfare, knows that he has not become unworthy of public confidence, and thus it must continue to recognize him, although if he should go astray it must bring him to order.

Señor Híjar has been invested with the double position of Political Chief and Director of the Colony which he has brought with him, and we see that the Government has taken away from him the power of the first position and made no mention of the second. This Committee might consider the second position inherent in the first and consider him to be deprived of both positions at the same time, by virtue of the abovementioned order. But keeping to the literal meaning, we are of the opinion that he can continue with his special assignment as Director of the Colony that he has brought with him, as his appointment states, for which purpose he will be provided from the missions with whatever assistance the Political Chief can extend to him, without detriment to the natives and the other needs connected with these foundations; for the expenses of colonies must be borne either by the Pious Fund of the Californias, according to the decree of November 26, 1833,[35] which gave the government this authority, or by the Federal Government, according to the decree of April 6, 1830, which we suggest should be read. But under no circumstances should these expenses come from mission property, which is the exclusive fruit of the arduous work of the mission neophytes and the sole inheritance waiting for them in reward for a century[36] of slavery. By what right, then, can these unfortunates be stripped of the fruits of their labor and privations? Will they not say, and with justice, that they belong to a predatory society?

This, sir, is the time to rise above fine theories and preconceptions, the time to make the imperious voice of justice heard before the highest authorities so that, in vindication

35. The text of this decree may be found in Dublán and Lozano, *Legislación mexicana*, II, p. 641, no. 1309. It runs as follows: "The Government is empowered to take all necessary steps to assure colonization, and bring about secularization of the missions of Upper and Lower California, and for this purpose to make use, in the most suitable manner, of the estates belonging to the Pious Fund of those territories, in order to provide resources for the Commission and for those families going to them who are now here in Mexico City."

36. The Franciscan missions in Upper California date from 1769, when Spanish settlement commenced. By "a century of slavery," the Committee no doubt simply meant a long time.

of humanity, they may enforce respect for the properties of our unfortunate compatriots. It is not the Federal Government, sir, which is disposing of this wealth, but courtiers decked out in the mantle of patriotism who, by invoking sacred liberty and the public welfare, take the good faith of the first Magistrate of the Republic by surprise and inveigle him into taking steps which he thinks will make men happy but in fact cause their ruination and plunge them into misery. Let the veil be drawn aside, therefore, and let us show His Excellency the President, with due respect for his high position, that if he believes that he is helping our natives, the instructions conferred on Señor Híjar permit the destruction of their wealth in order to apply it to objects which, if worthy of attention in other respects, should be taken care of without injuring that unfortunate group of our brethren[37] who still groan in the darkness of ignorance. And since Your Excellency is charged with guarding and promoting their happiness, it falls to you to protect their rights, not with theories or sophistry, but on the basis of the eternal principles of justice. Men have joined together in society to assure their lives and property, and they may not be deprived of the smallest part of their possessions without violating the compact and the common law of nations.

Having established these incontestable principles, the Committee is of the opinion that the execution of that part of Señor Híjar's instructions which orders the property of the missions to be taken over, distributed, and converted into cash should be suspended, and that a petition should be made to the Federal Government, in which this report is included, asking that it revoke this decision. Let the property of the missions be distributed to the Indians and for purposes beneficial to them, since they are the sole owners. In the mean-

time, let a part of this property be used to assist the colonists, on condition that the owners be repaid from the Pious Fund of California or from the Federal Treasury.

From the foregoing it may be deduced that the property of the missions should not be placed at the disposition of Señor Híjar, for since he is not to assume the position of Political Chief, he should not play any part in putting the law of secularization into effect. The instructions which he presented are expressly entitled: "Instructions in accordance with which José María Híjar, Political Chief of Upper California and Director of Colonization of Upper and Lower California, is to regulate his conduct." The literal sense of these provisions leaves no room for doubt that they gave him authority as Political Chief and in no way as Director of Colonization, an appointment which does not give him political jurisdiction. He has no powers set forth in any law,[38] and the Federal Government, under the existing laws of colonization, has only delegated to him the power of conducting the colony, establishing it, and distributing lands to it. This is clear from the order of July 16, 1833,[39] and from the instructions which we have mentioned. But it must be repeated that these instructions were given to him as Political Chief, and it is in this respect that he was given the right to choose the place where the colony was to be established. But having been deprived of this post, he must subordinate himself to the actual Chief and defer to him with regard to where the families are to be located. To sum

37. The original Spanish version of the *Manifiesto* has the word *progenitores*, or ancestors, in place of "brethren." (See facsimile of *Manifiesto a la República Mejicana*, p. 28.) But in the printer's list of errata at the beginning of the book, *hermanos* or brethren is substituted for it, and is therefore used here.

38. While it is true that the powers of the Director of Colonization are not provided in a law, they were set forth in detail in the bill of April 16, 1833, which failed to become law and which has escaped the attention of scholars. This bill appeared in several issues of *El Telégrafo*, and was seen by Figueroa. There is a discussion of the bill in my article, "The Mexican Government and the Mission Indians of Upper California, 1821–1835."

39. The "order of July 16, 1833," probably refers to a letter Minister of Relations Carlos García wrote to Híjar on that date, outlining the duties of the Director of Colonization. The letter is in State Papers, Missions and Colonization, BL, vol. 2, pp. 207–209.

up, his special assignment is that of Director of the Colony and this he can certainly be, working in harmony with the Political Chief, from whom he must receive instructions and the necessary assistance, in accordance with Government orders on this matter.

The colonists deserve our consideration, and they have come out under the protection of the Federal Government. They will be given attention and special recognition in complete conformity with the promises of the Government, for a change in the person who exercises political authority must not have an adverse effect on the fortunes of these families, who, with the support of public good faith, have come to live with us. We shall hold them in high esteem, and the brotherly society of kinsmen, in peace and security, will ease the pains of their solitude. Californians, sir, are hospitable, and will gladly share their good fortunes with all people who come to their homes.

The public awaits the end of this drama which has attracted so much attention, and in order to guard against its being misled, with regrettable consequences, the Committee is of the opinion that the public should be informed of what has happened by having this report and the decision of the Deputation published, in order to avoid sinister interpretations, as they record conclusively the grounds on which the Deputation bases its decision. For this reason, we submit for your consideration the following proposals:

1. That the Government order of July 25, 1834, that the command not be handed over to José María Híjar and that José Figueroa continue in the position of Political Chief, be obeyed.

2. That José María Híjar, if he desires, shall undertake the special assignment of Director of Colonization, under the control of the office of the Civil Government of the Territory and subject to the bases agreed upon by the Deputation.

3. That José María Híjar will have no part in the secularization of the missions, nor will their property be handed over to him as he requests.

4. That while the Federal Government is determining what it deems suitable, the provisional Regulation agreed upon by the Deputation for the secularization of the missions shall be carried out, and the Indians be put in possession of their property and lands.

5. The Political Chief will order that the colonists be given, from mission stocks, the implements and other assistance that the instructions provide for, as soon as they reach the site where they are to settle, the contributions to be divided up proportionately so as not to hurt any one mission. In accordance with the amount allotted to each person, he will provide seed, meat, and whatever is most necessary for subsistence. The Director of the Colony will be subject to the Political Chief, and will give him a detailed list of the number of persons who are going out as colonists, and a budget of the payments to be made to them every month, so that the contributions for this purpose may be arranged proportionately. Mission lands belong to the Indians, and no colony will be established on them.

6. The Political Chief will retain the instructions given by the Federal Government to Señor Híjar, who will be given an authorized copy if he needs it, returning to him the order of April 23 of this year,[40] which he sent in with them.

7. That the Federal Government be informed with this report and notification of what has been decided upon, for its higher approval. That a statement also be sent asking for annulment of the instructions in that part that deprives the Indians of their property, and for approval of the provisional Regulation issued by the Deputation. And that a respectful petition be sent asking separation of the civil and military commands, and nominating three persons selected from those considered competent.

8. That this report and what has been decided upon by the Deputation be published

40. The order of April 23, 1834, is the order containing Híjar's instructions. These instructions are discussed in the Introduction on p. 12, and translated on pp. 24–25 as they appear in the *Manifiesto*.

and circulated as soon as possible for the information of the public.

José Antonio Carrillo
Pío Pico
José J. Ortega[41]

The foregoing questions impressed the public, and everyone discussed them. Several individuals who felt that their interests were being harmed and who were unable to conceal their feelings threw discretion to the winds and publicly revealed matters about which they should have kept quiet for their own honor. It was then that they disclosed the greed that was agitating their souls and the excessive ambition that was devouring their hearts. It was then that the commitments with which they had burdened the wealth of the missions were revealed. It was then that the commercial undertakings of the Cosmopolitan Company, which could not count on any other funds for its business ventures except mission capital, were made public. It was then, finally, that it was boasted that the Government itself— that is Señor Gómez Farías—had permitted one of the estates of the Pious Fund of the Californias to be put under an obligation, mortgaging it for 14,000 pesos, the sum agreed upon for the brig *Natalia*, which was to be paid with tallow

from the California missions.[42] In truth such an arrangement was unjust, for these communities were to get no benefit from it.

It was also publicly stated that the Cosmopolitan Company was to have exclusive control over the domestic and foreign trade of the Territory, placing an agency in each mission or town and having the necessary ships on the coast for the import of national and foreign goods and the export of local products. Here is the real object of the colonizing expedition which has been made at such cost to the nation. This was the aim of Señor Padrés' efforts, which he lauded to the point of weariness as being inspired by the highest patriotism. The people realized that an attack was being prepared against landed property, saw that bankruptcy threatened the only capital that provides public wealth, and recognized the ruinous monopoly that was being aimed at.[43] Thus the pretensions of Híjar and Padrés openly clashed with public opinion, and this is the origin of the ill will shown against them later on.

Blindly following their own false desires, they tried other, less decorous

41. The brothers José Antonio and Carlos Antonio Carrillo of Santa Barbara played a prominent part in the Territory under Mexico. José Antonio continued his political career after Upper California became part of the United States; for a brief but detailed outline, see Bancroft, *California*, II, pp. 745–746, and Leonard Pitt, *The Decline of the Californios*, pp. 3, 43, 45, 46, 138, and 205. Pío Pico and his brother Andrés Pico, from Los Angeles, were also well-known men; see Bancroft, *California*, IV, pp. 778–779; Pitt, *Decline*, passim; and Martin Cole and Henry Welcome, eds., *Don Pío Pico's Historical Narrative*. José Joaquín Ortega was likewise a member of a leading California family; see Bancroft, *California*, IV, p. 760.

42. The 185-ton brig *Natalia*, formerly Peruvian, belonged to a certain Miguel Palacios, who sold it to the Cosmopolitan Company for 14,400 pesos, which was to be paid by giving him 182,592 pounds of tallow in California. Palacios arranged for a wealthy capitalist, Pascual Villar, to guarantee the transaction, so that if Palacios was not paid he would not suffer a loss. Villar in his turn wanted security, and Gómez Farías ordered the hacienda called Ciénaga del Pastor, near Guadalajara, belonging to the Pious Fund of the Californias, to be turned over to a representative of Villar until Palacios was paid. The whole transaction was typical of the financial dickering the Government was forced into because of lack of funds. (Minister of Relations to Parres, April 1, 1834, and Junta de Californias to anon., January 17, 1837, "Californias," vol. 20, in Archivo General de la Nación, Mexico City.)

43. See the Introduction, p. 13.

means of getting the results they wanted. Señor Híjar, highly insulted by the Deputation's decision, sent me in reply a statement full of gratuitous insinuations. Along with them he added some scornful remarks that I attributed to a stirring up of the bile or lack of reflection, and without mentioning them I approached him to offer him my friendship and entreat him to take part in a conference to discuss the matters occupying our attention, to avoid odious disputes. I offered to show him the laws, orders, and regulations on which the Deputation based its resolution, and told him that if he proved to me that these provisions had been annulled, the resolution would be changed. This was agreed to, and on October 25 and 26 José María Híjar, José María Padrés, José Antonio Carrillo, Pío Pico, José Castro, District Judge Luis del Castillo Negrete, attorney Rafael Gómez,[44] and I met together. The discussion was opened by reading Señor Híjar's statement, and since it takes up diverse matters I shall divide it up into sections which I shall refute in turn, since this was the fundamental and primordial objective of the conference:

October 23, 1834

I have examined with care Your Honor's note of yesterday's date. It contains an order from the Federal Government that I am not to be given the civil government of the Territory which had been entrusted to me; a statement that Your Honor made to the Territorial Deputation on the harm that putting this order into effect could cause, after referring to the trend in the country for the separation of civil and military governments; and finally, eight proposals approved by the Deputation, with which it appears that Your Honor is in agreement. I would have preferred to have these matters treated with due separation from one another, but since it has not been found fitting to do so, I will answer them in the same sequence in which they appear.

With regard to the order that I am not to be given civil command of the Territory, I have no objection to make, since it emanates from the same Government that appointed me. I am a respectful servant of the Government, and I shall never disregard its orders if they are limited by the orbits of its powers. I am only surprised that no communication was sent to me so that I might know whether my authority is completely ended or whether Your Honor is to continue only because of some particular circumstance. But that is not a matter for us to decide, and consequently it would be useless to take it up at this point.

[Figueroa]: The order of July 25 that I should not hand over the civil government to Señor Híjar is very conclusive. Colonies, according to the Regulation of February 4, 1834, Article 9, will be transported under the direction of persons designated by the Government, and according to Article 10 "they will remain subject to the Chief or Political Chiefs that the Government designates."[45]

44. José Castro was one of the more prominent Californians of the time whose career is succinctly outlined in Bancroft, *California*, II, pp. 751–752; see also Pitt, *Decline of the Californios*, passim. Luis del Castillo Negrete was the brother of Francisco Javier del Castillo Negrete. Both of them came out with the colony under Híjar and Padrés, although they were not colonists; for a brief mention of their careers, see Bancroft, *California*, II, p. 749. Rafael Gómez was a Mexican lawyer who was legal adviser to the Territorial Government; for a brief outline of his career, see Bancroft, *California*, III, p. 759.

45. The text of the Regulation of February 4, 1834, is in Maza, *Código*, pp. 263–264. It refers to colonization in the Mexican States, and Article 10 decreed that colonies were to remain under the Chief or Political Chief whom the Federal Government designated. Figueroa interpreted this law to mean that since Híjar was no longer the Federal Government's appointed Political Chief, the colony must necessarily be subject to himself. But the law was actually designed for state governments, and there was a printer's error in Article 10 when it first appeared. A corrected version of Article

Therefore there can be no doubt that Señor Híjar's authority has completely ended. In spite of this, the Deputation says that although it might consider him removed from both positions—that is, both as Political Chief and as Director of Colonization—it is of the opinion that he may continue in the special position of Director of the Colony, subject to the Territorial Government. It appears that this is very much in conformity with the desires of Señor Híjar, in spite of the fact that the title of Director of Colonization is not a position determined by any law.[46]

[Híjar]: I have nothing to say about the statement that Your Honor made to the Deputation, for you must know what the situation of the Territory is and the opinion of its inhabitants. Nor will I add anything to the first proposal which the Deputation approved, since it is in agreement with principles that I have previously mentioned.

The second proposition may be summarized as saying that if I desire, I may continue to direct the colony, subject to the Territorial Government and the bases agreed upon by the Deputation. The two conditions with which this proposition concludes are certainly remarkable: the first because it is useless, since every man who does not have special privileges[47] must be subject to the local authorities; the second because it is a crime against the Federal Government, against me, and against the colony. Who empowered the Dep-

utation to issue bases for colonization? How can the Deputation attempt to abrogate powers that belong only to the Congress of the Union or to the Federal Executive if, as in this case, it is authorized by the legislative branch? So many errors, General, and causing such regrettable results! If I should continue to direct the colony on any other bases than those the Federal Government gave me, I should betray the very Government which appointed me; I should be unfaithful to the confidence with which I was honored, and to the duties of a good citizen, if I recognized orders from an illegitimate power, such as that of Your Honor and the Deputation in the present case.

If I do not[48] submit to the bases agreed upon by the Deputation, it must then be inferred that I shall not be Director of Colonization. And who has given Your Honor or the Deputation the power to remove me from a special assignment that the Federal Government has entrusted to me? Likewise, the colony that I have conducted cannot and must not be directed by bases other than those given me by the Federal Government. When the Government uprooted the 300 persons who accompany me from their homes,[49] it offered them certain conditions which must be kept if preserving the honor of the Government is of concern. On the other hand, what guarantees would the bases of the Deputation offer if, as I said before, they sprang from an illegitimate power? Your Honor must bear in mind that I am a Director of Colonization, not merely of the colony which has arrived. Consequently, natives of the country and foreigners who desire to do so have a right to be colonists.[50]

10 was issued which stated that colonies were to remain under the Chief or Political Chiefs whom the Government *of the State* designated (my italics). It is apparent that this law was not applicable to a *Territory* such as California. The corrected version of Article 10 is in Maza, *Código*, p. 266.

46. See n. 38 above.

47. The "special privileges" mentioned by Híjar refer to the legal rights of army men and ecclesiastics, under the Constitution of 1824 (Title V, Section VII, Article 154), to be tried, under certain conditions, in military or church courts rather than in the ordinary courts for citizens not so privileged.

48. The original Spanish has it "If I submit" instead of "If I do *not* submit," but the writer believes, since this is directly contrary to the sense of the passage, that "no" has been omitted from the original. The original text contains a number of printer's errors not mentioned in the list of errata.

49. Híjar's statement that 300 people accompanied him should probably be taken as an approximate figure. Some 239 colonists embarked on the *Natalia* and the *Morelos* at San Blas.

50. By "natives of the country," Híjar meant white Californians and mission and non-mission Indians. There had been no mention of white

But if the bases change, they will all withdraw for lack of security, and the misfortune will be the Territory's which so greatly needs useful hands.

[Figueroa]: The Deputation never vainly presumed to attribute to its decisions the character of laws, and for the very reason that it does recognize the limits of its authority, it wanted the Director of Colonization to have the necessary dependence on the Government. The Deputation and I have not tried to dictate general bases for colonization, but we did think that we should provide some rules for the colonization that was to be undertaken in this Territory, for the law has conferred sufficient power on us to do so. If there is any doubt about it, examine the Spanish Constitution, which is the one in effect in this Territory,[51] and the law of June 23, 1813, Chapters 2 and 3.[52] I shall not stop to copy out its articles, so as not to be too long-winded, because Señor Híjar is convinced that "every man who does not have special privileges must be subject to the local authorities," and because the Deputation, which never intended to oppose the laws and orders of the Government, explained its point of view, drawing up its proposal in the following terms: "That José María Híjar, if he desires, shall undertake the special assignment of Director of Colonization, subject to the Civil Government of the Territory and to the laws and regulations passed on the matter."[53]

Señor Híjar will now see that the proposal that he has fought is not, as he says, a crime against the Federal Government, against his person, and against the colony, and that although we could legally provide bases for the establishment of the colony, we refrained from doing so to avoid a purely nominal dispute, since Señor Híjar submits to the Territorial Government. And the power it exercises is not, as he supposes, illegitimate, for it is derived from laws which have indicated to citizens holding public office how it is to be transmitted.

And what are the attributes of the Director of Colonization? I do not know, but I do not believe that there are any attributes, for there is no such position. The title owes its origin to a projected law initiated in the Chamber of Deputies of the Federal Congress, and it was taken from there and given to Señor Híjar.[54] But as

---

Californians in Híjar's instructions, and only one mention of Indians (Article 7, in which towns inhabited only by Indians were not to be permitted). In fact, since the Gómez Farías administration was anxious to do away with the old racial distinction between Indians and whites, it was logical not to mention such distinctions in its instructions to Híjar. Governor Figueroa either did not understand this point of view or deliberately rejected it.

51. It is true that the Territorial Deputation or Provincial Deputation existed in California and owed its origins to the Spanish Constitution of 1812, but this hardly gives Figueroa the right to say that the Spanish Constitution of 1812 was in effect in California. The Mexican Constitution of 1824 was the constitution in force, and when it suited him, Governor Figueroa did not hesitate to refer to it for support. See nn. 66, 100, and 133 below.

52. See n. 28 above. The original Spanish version of the *Manifiesto* contains the error June 33, 1813, as the date of this law. This is corrected in the printer's list of errata to read June 23, 1813. The translation of 1855 (and its reprint of 1952) gives the date, incorrectly, as June 13, 1813.

53. It should be pointed out that Article 2 of the Deputation's proposals, as originally worded, reads as it appears on p. 32. This version differs from the one here in that it permits Híjar to be Director of Colonization "subject to the bases agreed upon by the Deputation." The version here changes this to: "subject . . . to the laws and regulations passed on the matter." It was the original version to which Híjar was objecting. The version here is so vague that Híjar would hardly have had reason to oppose it. It is, therefore, misleading of Figueroa to imply that Híjar objected to this revised rendering.

54. This bill of 40 articles on colonizing the former mission lands was sent to the Chamber of Deputies on April 16, 1833, but although it was

the Regulation of February 4, 1834, subjects colonies that are to be established to Political Chiefs appointed by the Government,[55] and since Señor Híjar has ceased to be Political Chief, it is clear that the appointment as Director of Colonization does not confer any civil jurisdiction on him. In spite of this, the Deputation respects him as a commissioner of the Federal Government, in proof of which I have not tried to remove him from this position, as Señor Híjar falsely states.

It is certain that the colony must be established in accordance with the bases decreed by the Federal Government, but this does not free it from subordination to the Territorial Government, nor can this subservience hinder fulfillment of the conditions offered to it. Consequently the honor of the Government is preserved, and the right of foreigners and nationals to be colonists remains intact, for no one has tried to disturb it.

[Híjar]: The third proposal orders me not to have any part in the secularization of the missions and says that mission property is not to be put at my disposal. This resolution is scandalous and, like the previous one, a crime against the Federal Government as well as being subversive. I have never tried to interfere in the secularization of the missions, and consequently do not understand the significance of the first part.

The Federal Government of the Union, empowered by the decree of November 26, 1833,[56] ordered that I should take possession of the property of the missions to invest it in a

way that suited the Government; in the proposal under discussion, that order is completely disobeyed. It is certainly scandalous that the persons charged with obeying and seeing that others obey the laws and orders of the Government should be the first to give an example of disobedience—a most unfortunate example, for it leads to the overturn of the whole social order. Where should we be if everyone disobeyed the laws as he saw fit? We should be back in the state of nature in which the stronger is the lord of the weaker. Let Your Honor consider that by the very act of approving this resolution you have authorized the right of insurrection. If Your Honor and the Deputation believe that you have a right to attack the law, any other person may make use of that same right, and then the social pact is finished. There is more to it yet: a citizen may do anything that the law does not prohibit him from doing, but Your Honor and the Deputation can do only what the law stipulates. And since your principal duty is to obey the laws and see that they are obeyed, your breaking them is all the more remarkable and your disobedience all the more scandalous, as if a double crime was being committed, for you are attacking the law that you disregard and the laws that make it your duty to see that the rest of the laws are kept. How can you reprimand a soldier for breaking a law if Your Honor yourself and the top authorities have given such a scandalous example?

I shall conclude this part by affirming that the proposal is subversive because it leads directly to subverting the social order, as I have shown. It is scandalous because it provides an unfortunate example for the ordinary citizen, and it is a crime against the Federal Government for the reasons that I have previously mentioned. Neither the Political Chief nor the Territorial Deputation can or should put themselves above the orders of the Government. The conduct of an upright magistrate and a good citizen should be to obey and to petition if faults are found; but disobedience will always be most unfortunate for society.

[Figueroa]: In his statements of October 16 and 17, Señor Híjar asks me to

approved by the Deputies on May 9, 1833, and went to the Senate on May 10, it never emerged from that body (see n. 38 above). It is evident from this passage that Figueroa had seen the bill, probably in *El Telégrafo*. For a translation of this bill, see Appendix C of my *Frontier Settlement in Mexican California*.

55. As is pointed out in n. 45 above, the Regulation of February 4, 1834, applied to States and not Territories.

56. See n. 35 above.

order the commissioners I have appointed for the secularization of the missions to operate in accordance with his instructions, he asks that the property of the missions be handed over to him, and, in short, he wants to arrogate[57] to himself the administration of the temporalities. Is not this trying to take part in the secularization of the missions? If this is not so, in what respect does he claim to govern the missions and under what title does he want to seize their wealth? Examine his cited statements and see whether the administration of temporalities is or is not connected with the secularization of the missions. It was for this reason that I consulted with the Deputation as to whether Señor Híjar was Director of Colonization and Secularization or only of the first, and it was for this same reason that the Deputation, in the expository part of its report, very properly expressed the reasons which induced it to draw up the third proposition, which made such a strong impression on Señor Híjar. It may be inferred from what has been said that there was a strong motive for saying in the first part of that proposal "that José María Híjar shall have no part in the secularization of the missions."

Señor Híjar, adding to the list of insults and diatribes which he bestows upon me, affirms that the Federal Government is empowered to dispose of the property of the missions by the decree of November 26, 1833, and that we have disobeyed its orders. In order to answer this charge, let us first examine the said decree. It reads: "The Government is empowered to take all necessary steps to assure Colonization, and bring about secularization of the missions of Upper and Lower California, and

for this purpose to make use, in the most suitable manner, of the estates belonging to the Pious Fund of those Territories, in order to provide resources for the Commission and for those families going to them who are now here in Mexico City."

I know nothing about logic, but it seems to me that Señor Híjar knows nothing about it either, for only he has understood this decree to authorize the Federal Government to dispose of the property of the missions. Persons who have considered it interpret it as empowering the Government to bring about the secularization of the missions, and depriving the neophytes of their wealth is not going to do this.[58] Secularization, according to the Spanish dictionary, "is the act or effect of secularizing. Secularization is to make secular what was ecclesiastical; to withdraw a person or thing from the regular state, etc." Besides, the law of August 17, 1833,[59] has decided the way in which secularization is to be carried out, and in none of its articles does it order the Government to take over the wealth of the neophytes; on the contrary, it exempts them from taxes, providing that the stipends of the parish priests who are to take the places of the missionary Fathers, and the expenses of the church, are to be met from the income from the estates, capital, and rents of the Pious Fund of the California missions.

The conclusion that results from all that has been said is very clear, and however much the sense of the decree

57. The original Spanish has the word "abrogate" here, which I assume must be a misprint for "arrogate."

58. It is to be noted that the Federal Government considered the mission Indians as having the right to be colonists, i.e., to settle on lands formerly belonging to their missions. From this point of view, therefore, the mission Indians were not to be deprived of their share of mission lands.

59. The text of this law is available in Dublán and Lozano, *Legislación*, II, pp. 548–549, no. 1242.

of November 26 is strained, it does not contain the authorization that Señor Híjar supposes from the Federal Government, to dispose of the wealth of the missions, for the only power that it confers is that of disposing of the estates of the Pious Fund to provide travel expenses in Mexico for the Commission and for those families destined for these Territories, but the wealth of the neophytes is not in Mexico, nor does it consist of Pious Fund property.[60] It is proven by what has been said that, far from disobeying the laws, we have forced Señor Híjar to respect and keep them.

To be sure, the Federal Government in its instructions orders that all the property of the missions be taken and distributed. Who is given the duty of carrying this out? The Political Chief; and since Señor Híjar was removed from this position by virtue of the Government order of July 25, I do not understand how he

dares to claim the right to exercise a power that under no circumstances belongs to him.

The administration of the temporalities,[61] while they remain undivided, can only belong to the Territorial Government and in no way to the Director of Colonization. The very instructions on which Señor Híjar tries to base his pretensions convince one of this, and it is expressly stated in laws whose contents he appears not to know.

Since it has been sufficiently proved that the Federal Government is not empowered to dispose of the property of the neophytes, the accusation that we have disobeyed the law is contradicted. Nor are we disobeying the order of the Federal Government, for petitioning is not disobeying. The Federal Government orders the Political Chief to take the property of the missions, to distribute a part of it among the colonists, and to sell another part of it. We are sure that the Government did not calculate the damage it was going to cause, for it would not have dictated such a measure; this error, which involves a violation of the fundamental law, was hidden from the Government by its outwardly beneficial aspects. When the Government permits and orders the appropriation of property belonging to more than 20,000 persons, it is easy to see the false ideas which were used to influence it.

The Territorial Government, caught between the obligation to obey a Federal

60. It is true that the decree specifically empowers the Government to make use of Pious Fund property in such a way that resources will be made available for the transportation from Mexico City of Commission members and colonizing families. But it is also clear that the government is to "take *all* necessary steps" (my italics) to bring about colonization and secularization, and that the specific permission to use Pious Fund money is simply one of the steps to assure that its policies are implemented. Figueroa insists, however, that the decree only provides for secularization of the missions. The crucial sentence is: "The government is empowered to take all necessary steps to assure colonization, and bring about secularization of the missions of Upper and Lower California. . . ." Figueroa presumably takes this to mean that the government is authorized to assure the colonization of Upper and Lower California and to bring about the secularization of the missions of Upper and Lower California. Even with the presence of the comma after "colonization," however, this interpretation cannot be maintained. The fact that Gómez Farías is known, from other sources, to have desired to colonize the missions leaves little doubt that it was Figueroa who was straining the sense of the decree, and not Híjar.

61. Governor Figueroa and the Territorial Deputation had provided a detailed plan for the administration of mission farming and commercial pursuits, or "temporalities," as they were called by the friars, in the *Reglamento provisional para la secularización de las misiones de la Alta California* (see n. 31 above). This was to take the place of the unsuccessful bill of April 16, 1833 (see n. 54 above).

order and that of preserving the property of the most depressed class of its citizens, sought a way to reconcile both extremes and adopted the measure of suspending occupation of the temporalities, taking from them only what was essential, which was to be repaid, to maintain the colony, and sending a petition to the Federal Government asking the revocation of so unjust and unconstitutional a provision. In this way we believed that we were respecting and fulfilling the orders of the Federal Government, taking care of its responsibility and ours before the law, supporting observance of the law, and guaranteeing the property of our unfortunate compatriots. Few if any bad effects resulted from this measure and, on the other hand, it would be very difficult and perhaps impossible to return their property to the neophytes once they were deprived of it. We were well aware that such a provision would not fit in with the interests of Señor Híjar, but we also knew that we must not subordinate the fate of more than 20,000 persons to the pretensions of a single individual, nor could the respect we owe to the Federal Government force us to bring about the ruin of so many families without bringing this to the attention of the authorities, who were perhaps not aware of it. This is the object of the following note.

Monterey
November 9, 1834

Minister of Relations[62]
Esteemed Sir:

Since receipt of the law of August 17, 1833, by which secularization of the missions of this Territory was authorized, we have been anxiously waiting for the Federal Government to put it into effect by means of a lengthy Reg-

ulation which should determine not only matters connected with spiritual administration but also include distribution of the existing property in each community.[63] After waiting a year for instructions from the authorities, and being unable to postpone any longer the effects of a law so beneficial, so greatly desired and so often urged by the neophytes themselves and by all men of good sense, the Territorial Deputation, making use of its powers, with due solemnity drew up the provisional Regulation that I sent Your Excellency last August 9, asking for Government approval.

Then and at all times the mission neophytes have been held to be the owners of mission property, for it has all been acquired by their personal work as a community under the direction of the missonary Fathers who, as guardians, have administered and saved the existing wealth after maintaining, clothing, and taking care of the necessities of the natives, who were restricted like minors whose education was entrusted to the missionary Fathers by the Government. Thus the farms, temples, real estate, cattle, and everything on the missions have been acquired by the constant work and privations of the Indians.

The public Treasury has never been used to develop this property, either directly or indirectly. To begin with, the first foundations were made at the expense of the missionaries themselves. Later they were assisted by the piety of some individuals who donated various sums with which the Pious Fund of the missions of California was formed. From this fund 400 pesos a year in alms was given to each religious, with which all their needs were met, and 1000 pesos for material equipment for the mission and for farming were given once only to each foundation. The older missions helped the newer ones with small items, and this was the only assistance they received at their beginning. Everything else was acquired by the constant work of the Indians. The Regulation of 1781 in Title 15, Article 2,

---

62. The Minister of Relations (see the Introduction, n. 15) was Francisco María Lombardo.

63. These important matters were dealt with in the abortive bill initiated on April 16, 1833 (see n. 54 above).

shows this,[64] and the Commission on the Development of the Californias was of the same opinion in the statement which it sent to the Federal Government on April 6, 1825, when it drew up a plan for regulating these missions.[65]

For this reason and because the property right that the Indians hold over the wealth that they possess under the tutelage of the Government and the immediate administration of the missionaries is unquestionable, the Deputation did not hesitate to decide that half of it should be conferred on them and distributed to them with full rights of possession, keeping the other half at the disposal of the

64. The text of these important regulations is provided in *Reglamento para el gobierno de la provincia de Californias* (1784). A translation by John Everett Johnson, *Regulations for Governing the Province of the Californias*, was published by the Grabhorn Press, San Francisco, in 1929, with a bibliographical note by Oscar Lewis.

65. Appointed at the instance of Minister of War Manuel de Mier y Terán, the Commission for the Development of the Californias, which succeeded a similar Commission appointed by Viceroy Calleja, first met on July 12, 1824, and continued to meet to discuss California affairs until the end of August 1827. During this time it numbered 20 men amongst its members—not all of them active, however, at the same time. The major reports drawn up by the Commission were published in 1827 under the title *Colección de los principales trabajos en que se ha ocupado la junta nombrada para meditar y proponer al supremo gobierno los medios más necesarios para promover el progreso de la cultura y civilización de los territorios de la alta y baja California*. In its plan for the organization of the missions and its recommendations for instructing the first Mexican Governor of California, both included in the above *Colección*, the Commission felt that selected mission Indians who showed that they could cultivate and live off their own land should be granted as much of the common lands of the mission as they could farm. But in the regulations that the Commission prepared for foreign colonization in California, it stated that mission lands belonged to the mission Indians and to Mexicans resident in California. It is misleading, therefore, to imply, as Figueroa does here, that the Commission agreed with the view that mission lands were exclusively the property of the mission Indians. For a translation of the Commission's reports, see Keld J. Reynolds, "Principal Actions of the California Junta de Fomento, 1825–1827."

Federal Government to be invested in any way it desired for the benefit of the Indians, for such things as paying the teachers who educate them, revenue for their towns, stipends for the parish priests who take care of them, church expenses, and others that will arise. This is very much in accord with justice and in line with the directions that the Federal Government prepared for Señores Echeandía, Victoria, and myself in the instructions it gave us when conferring upon us the position of Political Chief.

Based on such strong foundations, and because it considered that Señor Híjar lacked the power to dispose of mission property to the detriment of more than 20,000 Indians, who are the sole owners, the Deputation opposed handing it over, as Your Excellency will see from its decision of October 22 (a copy of which I enclose) by which it decided as follows: "That while the Federal Government is determining what it deems suitable, the provisional Regulation agreed upon by the Deputation for the secularization of the missions shall be carried out, and the Indians be put in possession of their property and lands. . . . That the Federal Government be informed with this report and notification of what has been decided upon, for its higher approval. That a statement also be sent asking annulment of the instructions in that part that deprives the Indians of their property, and asking approval of the provisional Regulation issued by the Deputation."

I have the honor of sending this to Your Excellency herewith, accompanied by a copy of the instructions by which it is ordered that the property of the missions be taken, a part of it to be given to the colonists, half of the remainder to be sold, for no specified purpose and without regulations, to guarantee the security of its crops, and the other half of the remainder to be reserved for the stipends of parish priests, teachers, church expenses, etc. No mention is made of the Indians, who are the owners of this property, and in truth this is expropriation by violence. We believe that it must be due to an oversight in the office of the Secretary, for it could never be the deliberate intention of the Government to deprive 20,000 impoverished persons of the fruits of their toil, the sole inheritance they have received from their ancestors.

Señor Híjar in his letter of October 23 maintains that the Indians are not the owners of their own property and that the Deputation had no right to order it to be distributed to them. He is of the opinion that the Indians should continue in the same position of servitude without any change except that, in the future, they should be paid for their daily work. In truth, Sir, in this case it would be better if they did not change their condition, for this would make their sufferings worse. Señor Híjar says that they will be ordered to return the property that is now being distributed to them and that that will be most unfortunate. We think that such a proceeding only exists in the mind of Señor Híjar.

Justice, good government, and humanity take offense at such false principles. Everyone knows that the Indians by their skill and hard work have acquired and preserved the property of the missions, they have subsisted on it, and they have possessed it ever since, willingly or forcibly, they became Christians. Who, therefore, can take it away from them without attacking the social guarantees? The Federal Constitution in Article 112, Restriction 3,[66] says the following: "The President cannot take the property of any individual or corporation, nor disturb them in their possession, use, or exploitation of it; and if in some instance it were necessary to take the property of an individual or corporation for an object of recognized general utility, he cannot do so without the previous approval of the Senate, or at times when it is in recess, of the Council of Government, always compensating the interested party in accordance with the judgment of good men chosen by the interested party and by the Government."

This shows, Sir, that the Federal Government has not had the right (I speak with due respect) to dispose of the slightest part of the property in question. If it is done, as the Constitution provides, "for an object of recognized general utility," it must be preceded also by approval by the Senate or the Council of Government. If this requirement is lacking, it is the duty of the lower authorities to point out the unconstitutionality of the provision. This is the situation in which the Deputation and I unavoidably find ourselves, and because of which we respectfully inform Your Excellency that, in addition to being unconstitutional, the provision is not well drawn up, for it orders that a part of the property be sold without just cause, without determining how the money is to be invested, or specifying that it is to be deposited in the Federal Treasury. It is true that part of it is to be used for the payment of the colonists, but not all. It is also true that this expense should be met with Federal revenues, and the laws of April 6, 1830,[67] and November 21, 1833,[68] so authorize the Government. But no law authorizes the property of the Indians to be seized in order to invest it in colonies.

Señor Híjar says that the Government is authorized to do so by the law of November 26, 1833, but this is an error, for the law reads literally as follows: "The Government is empowered to take all necessary steps to assure colonization, and bring about secularization of the missions of Upper and Lower California, and for this purpose to make use, in the most suitable manner, of the estates belonging to the Pious Fund of those Territories, in order to provide resources for the Commission and for those families going to them who are now here in Mexico City."

Can it be inferred that by this law the Government may dispose of the property of the Indians as it wishes? Is the seizure of the property in order to bring about secularization? The Deputation has not construed it in this way, nor does it believe that the Fed-

66. Governor Figueroa here turns to the Mexican Constitution of 1824 for support.

67. See n. 30 above.

68. The text of this law is in Dublán and Lozano, *Legislación*, II, p. 637, no. 1301.

MANIFESTO TO THE MEXICAN REPUBLIC

eral Government interprets it in the way Señor Híjar does.[69] The Deputation deduces from all this that the aforementioned instructions were either drawn up too hastily or that they took the Government by surprise, and it concludes by asking Your Excellency to be good enough to reflect with care upon this lengthy exposition and to entreat His Excellency the President[70] to give due approval to the provisional Regulation in which it was ordered that the Indians were to be given possession of their liberty, their property, and their land,[71] and to declare Articles 1, 11, 12, 13, and 14 of the instructions given to Señor José María Híjar last April 23[72] null and void, both because they are notoriously unjust and because, since he has been removed from the civil command, he cannot exercise its powers.

Finally, sir, the Deputation and I humbly obey the laws and the constituted authorities, but for that very reason we want to be sure that we are correct, both because of our own responsibility and for the honor of the Federal Government. This is what has persuaded us to dwell upon so difficult a matter. If we are in error it is because of lack of understanding, and in this case we implore the indulgence of the authorities. For this reason we beg Your Excellency to assure His Excellency the Pres-

ident of our respect and subordination, and that we shall at all times obey his orders with pleasure.

God and Liberty.
José Figueroa

I think I have sufficiently proved that we have not disobeyed the law nor the Federal Government, as Señor Híjar falsely charges. This being so, what is the bad example we have given? What overturning of the social order? What disobedience? What insurrection have I authorized? And finally, what is this multitude of errors with which Señor Híjar tries to discredit my conduct? Where are these transgressions that scandalize my detractor so greatly? Let him point out a single one, but with positive facts, not with unintelligible gabble that means nothing. Señor Híjar affirms that the proposal is subversive because it leads directly to the subversion of the social order. And on what does he base this imputation? On the fact that I did not permit the usurpation of the property of a multitude of citizens: this is my crime.

I leave this affair to the judgment of men of good sense and of the Federal Government; but meanwhile, perhaps I may be permitted to interrogate Señor Híjar as to what right he has to denounce me. What power does he have to rebuke me? Is this the duty of a citizen? Is this the way that the laws provide for demanding that public officials be called to account? May Señor Híjar disobey me with impunity? Who authorized him to disregard my authority and declare me to be a lawbreaker? It must be admitted that Señor Híjar's opposition to the directions of the Territorial Government is more scandalous than the Territorial Government's resistance to his taking over the property of the missions. Señor Híjar is,

69. See n. 60 above. That the Government headed by Vice-President Gómez Farías did interpret the law in the same way as Híjar is shown by the bill it sent to the Deputies on April 16, 1833. What President Santa Anna thought about the matter is not known, but since he was an opportunist and was waiting for the right moment to remove Gómez Farías from power, there was always the possibility that he would interpret it in a way more agreeable to Governor Figueroa. It is likely that Governor Figueroa realized this and hoped to influence the Government to change its views.

70. It is to be noted that Figueroa suggests that President Santa Anna be asked to give his approval to the Provisional Regulation, and not Vice-President Gómez Farías, who was in charge of the Executive for much of the time because of the alleged indisposition of Santa Anna.

71. See n. 31 above.

72. For the text of these instructions, see pp. 24–25 above.

in fact, insulting and disobeying the legitimately constituted authorities, and this is indeed a crime that should be punished. We prevent Señor Híjar from committing the crime of seizing, in the name of the Government, the property of citizens in violation of the Federal Constitution and of the social guarantees, and this is a virtue in the opinon of honorable men; but Señor Híjar has seen fit to accuse me because I did not tolerate his plundering and fraud.

Let us briefly examine how the funds that Señor Híjar is struggling to obtain were to be invested. Part of them were to be used to maintain and establish the colony. Another part was to be sold. And what for? Only Señor Híjar knows, for the instructions do not say.[73] Another part is to be used for church expenses, for schools, and for stipends for the clergy. And what law authorizes the seizure of the property of one group of citizens in order to favor another? No law does this. What do the laws say about the foundation of colonies? The Law of August 18, 1824, established the general bases for colonization.[74] The Law of April 6, 1830, empowers the Government to colonize those lands that seem to it suitable, making contracts for them and paying the States to which they belonged, and to spend up to 500,000 pesos on the development of colonization. The same law designates a source of income to be applied exclusively to colonization and, in sum, gives the Government other powers which it would take a long time to enumerate.[75]

The Law of November 21, 1833, also authorized the Federal Government to spend the sums necessary to colonize the Territories and other vacant lands which it has the power to colonize.[76] The Law of November 26, 1833, gave the Federal Government the power to take steps to assure colonization.[77]

The Vice-President of the Republic, acting as the Executive, making use of the power that the Law of April 6, 1830, grants him, drew up on February 4, 1834, the Regulation that colonies which are to be established must follow.[78] But no law gives the Federal Government the power to invest the property of the California missions in colonizing.

I shall say nothing about the confiscation of property that was ordered, for that is an unfathomable mystery about which much may be inferred but nothing proved.[79]

As for paying the priests' stipends and church and school expenses, no one is unaware of the usefulness and advantage of this for those concerned, and this measure is in effect, for it is a necessity, but it must be noted that the Law of August 17, 1833, orders that the stipends provided for parish priests are to be met from the Pious Fund of the Californias.[80] In that case, what right have we to encumber the estate of the neediest class of citizens? I find no legal right to justify such an action.

73. See Article 11 of the instructions on p. 25 above. While it is true that the instructions did not say what Híjar was to do with the funds he received from the disposal of this property, he was directed in Article 14 (p. 25 above) to prepare a "detailed account" of the way in which he invested these funds, at once and annually thereafter. There was, therefore, to be no secrecy about the matter.

74. The text of the Law of August 18, 1824, is available in Dublán and Lozano, *Legislación*, I, pp. 712–713.

75. See n. 30 above.
76. See n. 68 above.
77. See nn. 35 and 60 above.
78. See n. 45 above.
79. See n. 73 above.
80. In Article 15 of the law. For the text of this law, see Dublán and Lozano, *Legislación*, II, pp. 548–549, no. 1242.

[Híjar]: In the fourth proposal it is insisted that the provisional Regulation be carried out. Each time more and more violations pile up, and I cannot conceive how so respectable a body can be so obstinate not only in disobeying but in resisting the orders of the Federal Government. What right have Your Honor and the Deputation to dispose of property which has in no way been placed under your supervision? No law, no order has authorized you to provide for the investment of funds which do not belong to you, and which you have not been able to dispose of without a Government resolution. How will Your Honor and the Deputation answer the charges that will be brought against you for this arbitrary act? What guarantees will those who are to receive the property of the missions have if neither Your Honor nor the Deputation have the right to convey them to any corporation or person? If the Regulation in question is not approved as asked, what disorders there will be! The property would have to be forced out of the hands of its possessors, and dashed hopes would engender a thousand grievances and, consequently, produce a wave of discontent which would bring alarm to the Territory.

It is insisted that a Regulation be carried out which, if it is put into effect, will certainly bring about the ruin of the Territory. I pass over in silence, General, the contradictions it contains and the servitude to which the natives continue to be subject. The great difficulty in policy consists in finding a means of freeing the Indians from the slavery and primitive state which they are in, so as to bring them to a state of civilization and liberty. Neither Your Honor nor the Deputation has come to grips with this difficulty. With a facility which is frightening, decrees have been issued for the creation of towns and the instituting of town councils, just as if laws were being made for civilized people possessed of all the necessary elements for them. What will happen, then, to the new towns after such a sudden and unprecedented change? They will be lost, as has happened in all countries and in all nations where the same thing has been done, and I appeal to history. Whenever a people is violently wrenched from a state of servitude to one of liberty, it can in no wise follow the flight of its leaders; it loses sight of them and goes astray. Such is the fate that the Territory's officials have prepared for it.

I greatly regret having had to touch upon a matter that did not concern me, but upon seeing that there was a determination to carry out a Regulation which must inevitably in the course of time cause trouble, I felt it my duty to make these passing reflections on it.

[Figueroa]: The charges and accusations which Señor Híjar makes against the Territorial Government are varied, but they are all baseless, as I shall demonstrate. The first charge is: Why is it insisted that the provisional Regulation be carried out?—Señor Híjar deducing from this that more and more violations are piling up and that the Deputation persists in disobeying and opposing the orders of the Federal Government. The provisional Regulation in question is the one drawn up by the Territorial Deputation to expedite putting into effect the Law of August 17, 1833, on secularizing the missions.[81] It determines the way in which distribution is to be made, to the neophytes in each mission, of the lands that they possess and part of the property which also belongs to them—for they are the legitimate owners of everything. The Deputation has done nothing more than obey the law and propose to the Executive the way to carry it out. This action is very appropriate to its authority, and it has been legally empowered to draw up the Regulation in order to present it to the Federal Government for its approval—both because local knowledge is needed, and no one has so great a claim to such information as this Deputation, and because the Law of June 23,

81. See n. 59 above.

1813,[82] and the Spanish Constitution, which is in effect in this Territory,[83] make it the duty of the Deputation to do so. The Law of June 23, 1813, gives the Deputation authority in various ways, and by Article 14 of Chapter 2 orders it to present to the Government the plans and projects which seem to it most suitable for developing agriculture, industry, the arts, and commerce. The Spanish Constitution, in Article 335, Item 10, gives it the right to watch over the economy, order, and progress of the missions.

If this should not be sufficient, the Laws of the Indies, whose pages shine with the wisdom and charity toward the Indians with which they were drawn up, may be consulted. Under the free administration of Señor Farías, attempts have been made to deprive the Indians of even the possessions they have acquired by their own labor. The Territorial Government is not ignorant, like Señor Híjar, of the privileges enjoyed by the Indians under the rule of the Spanish Government. It has kept in mind the following Laws of the Indies: Law 9, Title 3, Book 6; Law 14, Title 4, Book 6; and Laws 5, 7, and 9 of Title 12, Book 6 of the *Recopilación de Indias*. It is ordered in these laws that the land on which the Indians live is not to be taken away from them, nor are they to be disturbed; it is to be kept as town land and distributed to them. Their property is not to be used for objects other than their welfare and those purposes for which the towns were founded. Other rules and regulations are given, but they are all in favor of the Indians, with heavy punishments for transgressors.[84] The Territorial

Government kept in mind the Laws of March 13, 1811; November 9, 1812; and January 4 and September 13, 1813; for all of them have directed that the Indians be given their lands.[85]

It was desirable, my opponent will say, to give political importance to the Director of Colonization, and no effort should be spared to achieve this. That is why he wanted to make his powers rival those of the Territorial Government, and after the widespread publicity by which public attention was drawn to them the result was . . . the mountains brought forth a mouse.

The laws which organized these establishments have from their foundation made them subject to the Territorial Gov-

---

82. See n. 28 above.

83. See n. 51 above.

84. Law 9, Title 3, Book 6, and Law 14, Title 4, Book 6, concern Indian lands and property, but they were passed in 1560 and 1565 and have little relevance to the situation in California in 1834. The "other rules and regulations" in Laws 5, 7, and 9 of Title 12, Book 6, provided that Indians were not to be condemned to give personal service to individuals, that carrying on their backs food for towns was to be considered personal service, and that Indians were not to be forced to carry goods except under certain conditions. The only one of these laws relevant to the discussion between Figueroa and Híjar is Law 5, Title 12, Book 6, prohibiting personal service.

As is pointed out below (n. 88), the Deputation's provisional Regulation for secularizing the missions stated (Article 17) that former mission Indians were to continue to provide free personal service to the missionary Fathers. This was abrogated by Figueroa after these discussions with Híjar. It seems likely that it was after Híjar had made his criticisms of the secularization proposals of Figueroa and the Deputation that recourse was made to the Laws of the Indies for support. When, as in the case of personal service, the Laws of the Indies not only gave no support but in fact prohibited what had been proposed, Figueroa had to make this change. If these laws were not consulted until after the secularization decree had been drawn up, it is misleading to say, as Figueroa does, that the Deputation kept them in mind when preparing this legislation.

85. The texts of the Laws of March 13, 1811; November 9, 1812; and January 4, 1813, are in Dublán and Lozano, *Legislación*, I, pp. 340–341 and 396–399. The Law of September 13, 1813, is in Maza, *Código*, pp. 152–153.

ernment, and no one except Señor Híjar has disregarded its authority in this respect.

He ignores or does not understand the content of the laws that I have cited, and that alone can excuse him for the audacity with which he upbraids the Territorial Government, while overlooking its powers. Señor Híjar should know, then, that the Government has lent its protective guarantees in order to preserve and grant those possessions to their proper owners. He should know that these owners have not yet left the abject state in which nature placed them, and since they are children on the road to civilization, who do not use their reason nor know their true interests, the Government must perform the duties of common father and provide them with every kind of protection. This is the duty of a just government. And can it be abused because it converts them from wretched wards into free proprietors by distributing their own possessions to them? Is not the Law of August 17, 1833,[86] indeed, aimed at bringing about this one objective? Is it not designed to withdraw them from the ecclesiastical state to which they were subject, to redeem them from the servile wardship in which they have lived? All of us are convinced of these truths.

Assuming that the neophytes are separated from the economic control of the religious missionaries, they undoubtedly remain subject to the Civil Government, and by the Law of June 23, 1813,[87] this Government is obliged to establish their local authorities in accordance with the laws on the matter. It must also distribute among them the property they have acquired as a community, because the community ceases to exist and they enter upon

the enjoyment of their rights as citizens. These are the bases which the Territorial Deputation used for planning the Regulation in question and presenting it to the Federal Government. There is nothing arbitrary in such an action, it commits no transgression nor act of disobedience, it is not contrary to any order from the Federal Government; it is, in fact, a move worthy of the unsullied zeal of this Deputation for the well-being of those whom it represents.

But despite the justice of the Deputation's motives, this measure encountered the opposition of the Political Chief who, out of delicacy, and because he expected his successor to bring with him regulations for the law, opposed the views of the Deputation and delayed for more than six months the preparation of this Regulation. I knew that Señor Híjar was to come and relieve me, and I did not want to influence his judgment as to how secularization was to be carried out. Nor did I want to undertake it, for I knew how delicate and difficult it would be to put into effect and the grievous results if it were established hastily and all at once. My opposition on these and other grounds was public and well known, but since the damage was done and it was my duty to obey the law and be responsible for its execution, I had to submit to the force of circumstances against my own convictions. I do not mention this incident in order to vindicate myself, but so that it may be determined whether I have acted with integrity and frankness.

I believe that after what I have explained, Señor Híjar will not remain in any doubt that the property of the missions is subject to our control, and that we have had to draw up the regulations for distributing it among its owners. It has been shown that the idea that no law authorizes

86. See n. 59 above.
87. See n. 28 above.

us to make use of these funds is in error. This is how we reply to charges that might in any event be brought against us on account of the supposed arbitrariness of which we are accused.

Another charge is that those to whom the property of the missions is to be conveyed will have no guarantees, because neither the Deputation nor I have the power to transmit it to any corporation or individual. If Señor Híjar is unaware of it, he should know that to transmit means "to yield or transfer what one possesses to another." Thus we are only making regulations about how the property is to be distributed among its possessors; the conclusion is inevitable, consequently, that we have not yielded or transferred anything from one owner to another, and that the possessors of the property in question have sufficient guarantees to make use of it, for no one except Señor Híjar has challenged the property rights and possession that they have enjoyed without interruption, under Government protection, since the foundation of the missions. And who, except for Señor Híjar, can doubt that the Federal Government will approve of the Secularization Regulation?

Let us agree that His Honor's prediction that the property will be removed from the power of its possessors is groundless, and that this injustice could only be committed under his auspices, but by no means under the protection of the Federal Government, which has always respected the property of its subjects, and especially that belonging to this class of citizens whom it considers minors, who live under its guardianship. How is it that the Regulation will bring about the ruin of the Territory, as Señor Híjar affirms? Can it be perhaps because His Honor is not enjoying at his pleasure the wealth of the

neophytes? They alone have the right to enjoy the fruits of their work, and this is precisely what angers Señor Híjar.

Señor Híjar mysteriously remarks that he is ignoring the contradictions involved in the Regulation and the servitude to which the natives remain subject. I should appreciate it if he would demonstrate the contradictions and the servitude of the natives which he censures,[88] so that I might answer his objections; but assuming without evidence or certainty implies fraud or bad faith.

Neither the Deputation nor I, he says, have undertaken to examine ways of withdrawing the natives from slavery to a state of civilization and liberty. With a facility which is frightening, he says, the creation of towns and the instituting of town councils has been decreed, just as if laws were being made for civilized people. In my opinion, this indicates an inconceivable contradiction, for the servitude of the neophytes is assumed and grumbled about, and at the same time there are objections against the excessive liberty which has been accorded them.[89] But

88. Híjar's remarks were: "I pass over in silence, General, the contradictions it [the provisional Regulation for secularizing the missions] contains and the servitude to which the natives continue to be subject" (p. 45 of the *Manifesto*). Although Híjar did not explain what he meant by this, it is evident that he was thinking of the statement in Article 16 of the provisional Regulation that Indians could be forced to work on the land, and the stipulation in Article 17 that they were to continue to provide free personal service for the missionaries. That Figueroa did know what Híjar meant by these criticisms may be inferred from the fact that Figueroa abrogated the less vital Article 17 on November 4, 1834, not long after his discussions with Híjar.

89. The "inconceivable contradiction" which Figueroa sees in Híjar's criticisms here may be resolved by noting that Híjar is criticizing two distinct provisions of the Regulation. First, he points out that it may force certain Indians to labor on the land; second, he doubts whether the Indi-

ignoring a multitude of redundancies which are off the point, I shall restrict myself to showing that the Deputation has only been careful to keep the natives in the precise state of dependence indispensable for preserving good order and obedience among them, so as to avoid the excesses and misconduct to which they are inclined because of their stupid ignorance. At the same time it has taken care not to invade their liberty or violate the social guarantees. These facts are evidence of our foresight in endeavoring to remove them from servitude to the state of liberty, without disregarding the difficulties that the change presents. We have had to overcome too many obstacles, and long before passage of the Law of Secularization we pointed out its disadvantages—not so that it would be suspended, but so that it should be done more slowly and piecemeal, because that would better fit the character and circumstances of the natives.

But since there has been no desire to listen to the opinion of the local authorities—and then Señor Híjar himself, who is now criticizing us, and Adjutant Inspector José María Padrés were agitating in Mexico for the passage of the law that was to have enriched them[90]—it was not seen fit to consider what the Political Chief declared. The law was passed, and

it was certainly not the Territorial Government which sanctioned it. Nor, in view of this, should it be made responsible for the resulting evils, for the Deputation has not done anything except obey the laws and see that they are obeyed—avoiding, as much as its powers permit, the going astray of men suddenly wrenched from servitude into liberty.

Señor Híjar finds it strange that towns should be created, when the Territorial Government has done no more than so name them, since they have been established for many years under the designation of missions. But have they for this reason ceased to be towns? Certainly not. Look up the definition of this word, and it will be seen that they have always been towns. In similar fashion he finds the instituting of town councils strange, it being one of the principal duties of the Territorial Government to see that they are established in places that do not have them. The Law of June 23, 1813,[91] in Chapter 2, Article 1, and the Constitution in Article 335 expressly direct this.[92] Señor Híjar should also know that if the laws that regulate the government of the towns are not similar to those of the natives, it is not the fault of the Territorial Government, for it does not have the power to change or reform these laws, and it must apply them without restricting them.

Señor Híjar also predicts that the natives will not be able to follow this leap of their guides, for they are violently wrenched from a servile state to one of liberty. He predicts that they will be lost, as has happened in all nations where this has been done. He cites history as evidence for such facts and concludes his

ans who have to become city councillors in the new towns will be able to fulfill their new tasks without having more preparation for them. By combining his attack on these two matters, Figueroa makes it appear that Híjar's views are self-contradictory.

90. There is no evidence that Híjar or Padrés "agitated" for the passage of either the Secularization Law of August 17, 1833, or the bill distributing mission property which failed to become law. It will be noted that Figueroa here launches his unsubstantiated attack on them as adventurers out to feather their own nests at the expense of the mission Indians.

91. See n. 28 above.

92. Figueroa is here referring to the Spanish Constitution of 1812.

discourse by predicting that the natives will go astray because of their agents— that is, the Territorial Government.

I shall not occupy myself proving that Señor Híjar's fears are groundless, for in his view the neophytes should not leave the wardship in which they have been kept, nor should they be given property of any kind, for they are not worthy of possessing it, nor could they then be forced to cultivate the fields of their feudal lords.[93] Such are the philanthropic ideas of his Honor. On such grounds he was planning to organize the civil government of the mission neophytes, and those whom he greatly favored he would consider as colonists so as to give them a piece of land.

Señor Híjar will permit me to remind him of these statements, which he made at several conferences that we had, and that I refuted him, completely contradicting his views. He will remember very well that I defended with the same laws the right of the neophytes to be made equal to ordinary citizens in enjoyment of their possessions, and the preference that should be given to help them so that they may be granted the land and property that they possess, which has been acquired by their own and their ancestors' labor. And I could not agree either that they should be treated as colonists, for they are proprietors who are settled on the same lands where they were born, and for other reasons that it would take too long to relate. It may well be that not all of them may be capable of following this leap of their guides, because of their present state of ineptitude, but this is no reason to neglect

the beneficent measures which have been passed in their favor. Some of them will go astray, but many will succeed, and the result is always a benefit for society and a step forward in civilization. It is not merely a matter of converting them from wards to proprietors, but of educating them and making them industrious, and if this is not undertaken, they will never emerge from the wretched condition of slavery.

It is necessary that they be permitted to make their way along this perilous road so that they may finally arrive, and this is certainly not wrenching them violently from a servile state to liberty, as Señor Híjar falsely asserts, for they are not left to themselves but remain under the protection and guardianship of the Government, subject to special laws and regulations. I do not know to which nations or what history Señor Híjar is comparing them, and for this reason I cannot reply to his argument. As is his custom, he blames the Territorial Government for the resulting evils that he predicts, without any more evidence than his own say-so, based on quibbling which in substance means nothing.

He finally admits that these matters are no concern of his, but on seeing that there was determination to carry out a Regulation which in time must cause trouble, he felt obliged to make these trifling reflections. It would have been more honorable of him to take no part in such matters, since as he frankly admits, they are not his concern. Indeed, what right does he have to object to the measures of the Territorial Government, when his commission as Political Chief has ceased? Why such acrimony against the Teritorial Government because it is promoting the distribution of property to its legitimate owners, and is opposed to its

93. Figueroa appears to be alleging here that Híjar was afraid that if the mission Indians were given property of their own, they could not be forced to work on the former mission lands for, say, the Cosmopolitan Company.

being handed over to the inalienable possession of Señor Híjar? It must be repeated that His Honor cares little or nothing about the fate of the natives, and that the only reason for his disoriented discourse is that he sees the abundant wealth over which he tried to exercise exclusive control, under the ostensible pretext of colonization—to the notable detriment of those who accumulated that wealth—slipping from his grasp. This was what the grandiose projects for happiness, which Señor Híjar and his followers proclaimed so highly that they became engulfed in the arrogant presumption of calling themselves the redeemers of the Californians, consisted of. If, since he admits that it is no concern of his to deal with these matters, he had refrained from getting involved in them, I should have had no need to make his ambitious pretensions public.

[Híjar]: The fifth proposal is aimed at providing regulations for some of Your Honor's and my procedures, and declaring, with the firmness of law, that no colony is to be settled on mission lands, since they belong to the natives. On those relating to me I have nothing to say, since I am determined to observe no other instructions than those the Federal Government gave me, as the only legitimate ones in existence up to now. I should certainly be contemptible before mankind and an unworthy son of Jalisco if I were so weak as to submit to recognizing orders made by an errant authority which, going beyond the limits of its powers, tries to usurp those granted to the highest powers of the Union. Neither Your Honor nor the Deputation has the right to regulate my procedure with regard to my assignment. The law, and not caprice or arbitrariness, governs me.

If it is believed that mission lands belong to the Indians, how is it that by Your Honor's Regulation they are only to be given as a maximum a small square of 400 yards a side, and

another[94] small amount as common pasture land? So many contradictions, General! It seems as if the intention is only to deceive the wretched natives by taking advantage of their vulnerability. This is not the place and it is not my business to investigate the right to ownership of these lands which it is sought to inculcate in the natives, totally excluding the Government's right of eminent domain, but I will be permitted to say that some day this indoctrination will be unfortunate for those who have proclaimed it, and detrimental to the prosperity of the Territory.

[Figueroa]: In order to reply to the various charges that Señor Híjar makes against the Territorial Government, it will be necessary to repeat the contents of the fifth proposal, which he opposed. It runs as follows:

The Political Chief will order that the colonists be given, from mission stocks, the implements and other assistance that the instructions provide for, as soon as they reach the site where they are to settle, the contributions to be divided up proportionately so as not to hurt any one mission. In accordance with the amount allotted to each person, he will provide seed, meat, and whatever is most necessary for subsistence. The Director of the Colony will be subject to the Political Chief and will give him a detailed list of the number of persons who are going out as colonists, and a budget of the payments to be made to them every month, so that the contributions for this purpose may be arranged proportionately. Mission lands belong to the Indians, and no colony will be established on them.

I appeal to the judgment of men of good sense to say whether these measures are

94. I have substituted "otra" for the original "esta" on page 73, line 7, of the *Manifiesto*, both because "otra" makes better sense than "esta" and because this passage is given again on page 77, line 17, and "otra" is then used in place of "esta." See the facsimile of the original in this volume.

within the orbit of the Territorial Government and whether they conform to the spirit of the laws. But in order to dispel equivocations, I shall reply briefly to Señor Híjar's objections.

This gentleman says that he is determined to observe no other instructions than those he received from the Federal Government, and that he would be contemptible if he were so weak as to submit to orders issued by an errant authority which has usurped the powers of the Government of the Union. I have already demonstrated, and Señor Híjar himself admits, that his assignment as Political Chief has ended, and along with it all the powers related to it, including those given him by the instructions which he received from the Federal Government. But he is very sensitive about relinquishing the power that raised his hopes so high,[95] and he does not fear to contradict himself about doing injury to the respect he owes authority. He has said that every man not specially privileged must be subject to the local authorities, and that it was useless to give this advice, and immediately responds that neither the Deputation nor I should regulate his proceedings. I have also shown that by the Regulation of February 4, 1834, colonies are subject to Political Chiefs appointed by the Federal Government, and they are subject to them also by civil law.[96] I have proved that the Deputation and I are empowered by the laws to regulate the proceedings of Señor

Híjar as Director of the Colony, however much it may displease His Honor. In the same way, I have proved the legitimacy of the jurisdiction we exercise, for it has been legally derived from the Federal Power, which has bestowed it upon us with the formalities prescribed by law. This being so, we do not know on what grounds Señor Híjar bases his charges of illegitimacy and usurpation. But however much he may dislike it, he must be subject to the Territorial Government and obey its orders without censuring them, for he does not have the right to do so. And even on the hypothesis that we might be exceeding our powers, he would only have the right to enter a case against us, demanding responsibility as it is determined by the laws, but never would he have the right to disobey us. For this reason I shall repeat this question: Who is Señor Híjar that he disregards my authority and declares me a lawbreaker? Is he perhaps a jurist without fault in the present case? He is certainly not more than a subject, and a subject without jurisdiction independent of the Territorial Government, as he claims.

Señor Híjar ironically says that we declare, with the firmness of law, that the colony is not to be situated on mission lands because they belong to the natives. Before going further, I shall prove to him that this is not an ordinance of the Territorial Government but a clear provision of the Law of August 18, 1824, in which the second article runs as follows: "The objects of this law are national lands which, not being the property of an individual nor belonging to any corporation or town, may be colonized."[97] The Federal Government issued regulations for that law on November 21, 1828, and in Article

95. The Spanish text on page 74, line 28, has the word "alagaba," presumably from alagar "to make ponds or lakes." This is probably a misprint for "alababa" (alabar = to praise, to magnify) which I have substituted here.

96. Figueroa continues to rely on the Regulation of February 4, 1834, but, as has been pointed out, it referred to Federally sponsored colonization in the Mexican States and was not applicable to California (see n. 45 above).

97. For the text of the law, see Dublán and Lozano, *Legislación*, I, pp. 712–713.

17 proclaimed the following: "In Territories where there are missions, the lands that they occupy may not be colonized now or until it is decided whether they are to be considered as the property of the converted neophyte catechumens and Mexican settlers." This will be sufficient to show conclusively that it was not petulance which obliged the Territorial Government to dictate such a measure, but a clear provision in a law which has not been annulled nor can it be interpreted.[98]

All the laws which I have cited give the neophytes property rights over lands which are recognized as those of the missions, a right which the Spanish Government respected during its domination and which no one up to now has disturbed. But even if this were not so, is it not certain that civil and natural possession, which no one can doubt, favors them? Will Señor Híjar deny that they were born on the land on which they reside and that they have been cultivating it under the guardianship of the Government for more than fifty years? Will they fail, despite their inertia, to comprehend and believe that they are the owners of the land they cultivate and of the wealth they acquire by their work? This is very certain, whatever attempts are made to obscure it. If mission lands belong to the

Indians, asks Señor Híjar, "How is it that by Your Honor's Regulation they are only to be given as a maximum a small square of 400 yards a side, and another small amount as common pasture land?" The Regulation is not mine, for it was drawn up by the Territorial Government, and Señor Híjar's satire is most unseemly. That small square was allotted to the neophytes, to begin with, because they are not considered to be capable of cultivating more, and because an attempt is being made to distribute the surface of the land in proportion to the number of individuals who are considered to have a right to it, leaving the door open to grant it to industrious persons who devote themselves most persistently to its cultivation. It is false that the area assigned as common pasture land for the neophytes' cattle is as small as Señor Híjar asserts, and the proof is that no fixed amount has yet been determined, for it was left to the discretion of the commissioners so that they might enlarge or diminish it, in accordance with the number of cattle and the area of land belonging to each mission. In addition to the land which is to be given to each individual with full property rights, it was proposed that common lands should be allotted and that each town should be assigned an area of public land so that revenue from it might be used for the common benefit of each town.

But Señor Híjar paid no attention to these points nor does his criticism have any other foundation than the unjust venting of his resentment. His vague exclamations are completely unsubstantiated and his insinuations are so many calumnies. It seems (he says) as if the intention is only to deceive the wretched natives by taking advantage of their vulnerability. And how will Señor Híjar prove his assertion? By keeping silent,

98. As has been noted above (n. 60), the decree of November 26, 1833, empowered the Government to "take all necessary steps to assure colonization, and bring about secularization of the missions." This decree, therefore, annulled the Law of November 21, 1828, which Figueroa cites. That this was indeed the intention of the administration of Gómez Farías is clear from the bill of April 16, 1833, which failed to become law. Furthermore, the Law of November 21, 1828, cited by Figueroa, shows that the legislators were considering at that time whether mission lands should belong to the mission Indians *and* Mexican settlers. This was the recommendation of the Commission on the Development of the Californias, as has been noted above (n. 65).

because he has no facts to present, just as he is quick to invent gratuitous slanders. Señor Híjar should be informed, then, that the Territorial Government genuinely believes that it is performing a positive good for the natives by the many measures it has passed in their favor; and indeed, how can giving them landed property and the freedom to acquire and enjoy as much wealth as their industry warrants be a delusion? And although they might not achieve these positive advantages, which have nothing illusory about them, is Señor Híjar unaware that governments, as the wise Bentham says, must elect the lesser evil?[99]

Señor Híjar reluctantly admits that it is not his business to investigate the right to land-ownership which is being inculcated in the natives, to the total exclusion of the Government's right of eminent domain, but he says that this indoctrination will be unfortunate for those who proclaim it, and detrimental to the Territory. If it is not his business to investigate this matter, by what right does he rebuke the Territorial Government? Then his scurrilous style is one of the greatest disrespect, if it is not criminal. It is not his business to make an investigation, and he has the audacity to openly deny the neophytes not only their rights to ownership of the lands that have been granted to them, but even to the possessions they have acquired by their personal labor. This is clear all through his discourse, and he related it to me more explicitly in the various meetings that he had with me on the matter. If Señor Híjar prides himself on being a gentleman, he cannot deny this truth.

And what is the eminent domain of the Government? I do not know, and I have proved by the Constitution that the Government cannot take the property of any individual or corporation.[100] Nor does Señor Híjar say what eminent domain means. He holds it very much against us that we are teaching the Indians about their rights, but shortly before that he accuses us of subjecting them to an ignominious servitude and says that neither the Deputation nor I have come to grips with the difficulty of withdrawing them from a state of servitude to one of liberty, that we are violently wrenching them from the former to plunge them into the latter so that they will go astray. He goes right on to say that we are simply trying to deceive them by taking advantage of their vulnerability, etc., etc. Here is a long series of inconsistencies that not even the author himself can explain if he leaves any room for reason.[101] And why will it be unfortunate for us to inform the neophytes of their rights? Let the selfish lament the progress of our unfortunate natives, we respect a man's rights, whatever his origin. In the opinion of Señor Híjar this will harm the Territory, but how does he arrive at such a conclusion? I do not know. He wants to be taken at his word, and this is no proof.

[Híjar]: The sixth proposal may be summarized as ordering that the instructions that the Federal Government gave me be retained. This decision has greatly surprised me; never did I believe that such advantage would be taken of the good faith in which I offered to

99. Jeremy Bentham (1748–1832), the English jurist and philosopher, whose works, in Spanish translation, were available in Mexico at this time. A search through Bentham's printed works failed to bring this citation to light, but it is entirely in line with Bentham's views. It is probably not a literal quotation.

100. Item iii of Article 112, Section 4, of the Mexican Constitution of 1824 prohibits the President from taking the property of any person or corporation.

101. See n. 89 above.

comply with the wishes of the Deputation by sending it the originals of the instructions which it requested with the greatest courtesy, even suggesting that I might present them if it were not inconvenient. By what right am I deprived of a document which belongs to me as long as the Federal Government does not relieve me of the position of Director of Colonization? I am dumbfounded, General, and I never thought that so respectable a body would attack me in a manner which offends its honor and delicacy. What is the object of holding back my instructions? In truth, I cannot understand it. If it is to send in a report against them, I would have provided a copy whenever I was asked. If it is to prevent them from being put into effect, it would have been sufficient for the Political Chief to have written at the foot of the order: "Not to be executed in this Territory." Not having, then, the power to take away from me a document which pertains to me, and since I have to fulfill my commission in other places outside the Territory under Your Honor's command, I hope that you will be good enough to return my instructions to me for the above reasons.

[Figueroa]: The instructions were retained because they were given to the Political Chief of Upper California and not precisely to José María Híjar. The document is an official one that only pertains to the Government itself and not to Señor Híjar, as he improperly claims. It should be placed in the Archives of the Government, which is the Nation's office. It must, in short, remain in the hands of the Political Chief, who is the only one charged by the Constitution and the laws with executing those instructions and the decrees of the Federal Government. Without stopping to discuss all the directions on the matter, I shall cite only Articles 1 and 17, Chapter 3, of the Law of June 23, 1813,[102] which runs as follows:

1. Since the Political Government of each Province, according to article 324 of the Constitution,[103] is in the charge of the Political Chief appointed by the King in each one of them, superior authority within the province resides in him to take care of public tranquility, good order, security of the persons and property of its inhabitants, execution of the laws and orders of the government, and in general everything pertaining to the public order and prosperity of the province. And just as he will be responsible for misuse of his authority, he must also be respected and obeyed scrupulously by everyone. Not only can he carry out by act of government the penalties imposed by police laws and decrees for good government, but he will have the power to impose and demand fines from those who disobey him or are lacking in respect for him and those who disturb the public peace or order.

17. Only the Political Chief will circulate through all of the province all the laws and decrees issued by the Government, publishing them in the capital of the province, acquainting the Provincial Deputation with them, and taking care to send them to lower-level political chiefs, if there are any, so that they may circulate them in their territory, or to mayors in district capitals, for the same purpose. It being the responsibility of the Political Chief to circulate the laws and decrees, he will require receipts from those authorities to whom he communicates them.

This being understood, can the Territorial Government carry out the orders of the Federal Government without having knowledge or certainty of them? Or can Señor Híjar, on his own, carry them out independently of the Political Chief? What kind of authority does he have? What basis does he have for saying that his instructions belong to him? If public employees claimed in the same way that they were the owners of the laws, orders,

---

102. The text of the law is in Dublán and Lozano, *Legislación*, I, pp. 413–424.

103. The Spanish Constitution of 1812.

and documents they receive, there would be no Archives and everything would be in confusion. In addition to the reasons put forward, the Territorial Government suspected that bad use would be made of the instructions, and indeed its fears were later justified, and for that reason it ordered them to be withheld with no other object than compliance, as far as possible, and to avoid the abuses of the Director of Colonization. The Territorial Government had to act in this way because it had not received any other orders which would cover its responsibility, for there had been communication with Señor Híjar only during the time he was designated Political Chief. But that function having ceased, no jurisdiction remained to him as Director of the Colony, with whom the Political Chief was to communicate for his compliance with the orders of the Federal Government included in the instructions.

How could Señor Híjar comply with those orders in any other way? Would he operate completely independently of the Territorial Government? Then let him demonstrate the source of those powers that he wishes to exercise. But his silence confirms my opinion and vindicates me against the insults lavished upon me. In spite of what has been said, his instructions were returned to him so as to show him our willingness to go along with whatever is compatible with our duty, and what use have they been to him? None whatever, for he has come right to the Political Chief for support of his authority and orders to carry it out. This is a fact that Señor Híjar cannot deny.

[Híjar]: The seventh proposition may be summarized as various petitions which the Deputation believes it proper to direct to the Federal government, and I have nothing to say about them. But since it appears that they are

asking that the part of the instructions which deprives the Indians of their properties be revoked, I believe it is my duty to point out that such an idea could only arise out of some mistake or because of the different views we have formed of the property of the missions. The Government, far from depriving the Indians of property, orders me to make them landowners and give them possessions that up to now they have not had. They were to enjoy real, actual property the moment I was in a position to carry out my commission. But Your Honor and the Deputation did not consider this desirable. Consequently the responsibility will not be laid upon me.

[Figueroa]: This is certainly a delusion, Señor Híjar. Have you forgotten so soon that you are only trying to get possession of the property of the missions in order to divide some of it among the colonists and sell the rest?[104] Is it not evident that there is not one single word favorable to the neophytes in the instructions?[105] Is it not true that the first article in the instructions provides that all the property belonging to the missions be occupied, making use of military force? Is it not true that by this article the property that the neophytes have acquired by their personal labor, and are enjoying in peaceful possession,[106] is to be taken from them? Is it not true that they are being subjected by this act to robbery with violence? Will Señor Híjar deny that, on the different occasions we discussed this affair, he maintained that to make the neophytes happy it was sufficient to set them free, and in future pay daily wages to those occupied with the work of the missions? Is it not true that

104. Mission Indians, however, were to be considered as colonists. See the Introduction, pp. 12.

105. See n. 50 above.

106. It is hardly accurate of Figueroa to state that the mission Indians were "enjoying peaceful possession" of mission lands.

in order to extricate himself from the remarks that I made in favor of the rights of the neophytes, he answered that, at most, those who claimed land for cultivation should be considered as colonists? And does he have the temerity to assert with emphasis that he was going to make them landowners, when he is trying to deprive them of the property and lands they possess? And is not this abusing even the true sense of the words? Such inconsistencies spring from the heated fantasy of Señor Director of Colonization.

[Híjar]: The eighth proposition is essentially that the Deputation's decision be published. Let it be published at the proper time, although I regret that some of the facts have been misrepresented and, what is more deplorable, to the discredit of the Federal Government, which we both ought to uphold. Some day the whole of this affair will come to light: all men will be acquainted with the motives of each party, they will make a judgment between the two and render their verdict.

[Figueroa]: The day foretold by Señor Híjar has now arrived. The public is going to find out about these clamorous events, and it will pronounce judgment in favor of the one who has justice on his side. If making a petition to the Federal Government against one of its measures, which attacks the Constitution in violation of the social guarantees, discredits the Government, it is not the fault of the lesser authorities, who are obliged either to point it out or to become accomplices in the violation if they execute it without question. There can be no dishonor for the Secretary who signed the measure if he revokes it because he is convinced that it is unconstitutional, for he is not infallible and could very well make a mistake.

[Híjar]: I would like to know how it came about that the decision on my relinquishing

the civil government became mixed up before the Deputation with the special commission for colonization. But Your Honor has not judged it appropriate to tell me. I would have appreciated it in order to correct any errors which they may have made; otherwise I do not see how they could have passed measures which are so anarchical, blatant, and far-reaching for the social order.

[Figueroa]: What does Señor Híjar mean by anarchy? The Spanish dictionary says that it is "a state which does not have a head to govern it." This definition is very badly applied by Señor Híjar in the present case, for the measures which Señor Híjar calls anarchical are dictated by the constitutional Government of the Territory, whose authority is legitimate, as I have shown. The power that it exercised when it passed the measures under discussion is properly one of its attributes, and they are designed to call Señor Híjar, who is trying to take actions in defiance of the laws, to order. This is what Señor Híjar calls anarchical and blatant measures; such terms apply only to the noise that the novelty of such strange pretensions has caused among the public.

[Híjar]: In view, therefore, of all that has been put forward, I beg that Your Honor, after listening to the voice of your conscience and of reason, see fit to change your mind, for duty and the laws demand this, and I hope you will be good enough to return my instructions to me without the necessity of further requests, since this return is just in every respect.

[Figueroa]: I have already mentioned that the instructions, in spite of their belonging to the Archives of the Territorial Government, have been returned to Señor Híjar, but in no other respect was the decision changed because, far from clearing things up, his vague protests provoked a lengthy examination of the laws by means of which the Territorial Government confirmed its proceedings and carried them out.

[Híjar]: I conclude, therefore, by begging Your Honor to please let me know your final decision, so that I can make further arrangements, and I hope that you will pardon the harsh language of a republican who demands fulfillment of the laws.

[Figueroa]: The language that Señor Híjar has used is not for demanding fulfillment of the laws, because I have proved the opposite. The public will decide whether republicans have the right to repudiate social principles and disobey the authorities.

[Híjar]: In conclusion, I heard the decision of the Deputation was published, and from what I perceived in the expository part of the Committee's proposal, all grounds for not complying with the Federal Government's orders consist in regarding the instructions at issue as associated with the office of Political Chief. Your Honor will permit me, out of moderation, not to mention what I think of such a remarkable misconception. The official letter which was addressed to me with these instructions, and which Your Honor returned to me, says, word for word: "By order of His Excellency the Vice-President, I am sending with this letter the instructions by which you must proceed in the fulfillment of your assignment relative to the colonization of California, and at the same time I inform you that through the Secretary of the Treasury the order is being given to the Commissary of Jalisco to place at your disposal whatever sum of money he may have received from General Joaquín Parres, so that you can carry out all the orders given in these instructions."[107]

107. General Joaquín Parres was the Government administrator of the former Jesuit hacienda of Ciénaga del Pastor near Guadalajara, one of the rural properties belonging to the Pious Fund of the Californias. (Minister of Relations to Joaquín Parres, April 1, 1834, *Californias*, vol. 20, in Archivo General de la Nación, Mexico City.)

Ask schoolchildren whether these instructions are addressed to anyone other than the Director of Colonization. My assignment also extends to Lower California, according to my orders, and for that Territory I had no political role.[108] It seems, therefore, beyond all doubt that the special commission was entrusted to me as Director and not as Political Chief.

I have the honor of repeating to Your Excellency the assurances of my appreciation and high regard.

God and Liberty.
José María de Híjar

[Figueroa]: After having loaded us with reproaches and insults, he is trying to show modesty and moderation. In this vein he asks that he be excused from mentioning what he thought about so remarkable a misconception. If this is his intention, why does he sarcastically say that we should ask schoolchildren whether the instructions were given to the Political Chief or to the Director of Colonization? I, on the contrary, appeal to the judgment of reasonable men to decide to whom are addressed instructions which begin as follows: "Instructions in accordance with which José María Híjar, Political Chief of Upper California and Director of Colonization for Upper and Lower California, is to regulate his conduct."

It is of no particular significance that the official letter with which they sent him these instructions orders him to regulate performance of his colonization assignment in line with them because, as I have shown, it is inherent in the position of Political Chief, with which he was also invested; and by the act of removing him from this latter post, he was dismissed

108. His instructions gave Híjar the title of "Political Chief of Upper California and Director of Colonization of Upper and Lower California."

from the former as well. For this reason the Deputation, when it advised me that he could continue to direct the colony, made it conditional upon his being subject to the Territorial Government. But the stratagem of maintaining some authority suited Señor Híjar's ulterior motives better, so as to lend an appearance of validity to the specious pretensions of his supporters. Such is the perspicacious policy of the Director of Colonization.

I have fought Señor Híjar's libel with the weapons of reason, and although I invited him to demonstrate for me that the laws, orders, and regulations on which the Territorial Government based its measures were annulled, I did not get the satisfactory answer that I sought. Everyone who attended the conference can testify to the truth of this. Lawyers Luis del Castillo Negrete and Rafael Gómez,[109] on being asked their views, both corroborated the opinion that I had expounded and added arguments, doctrines, and laws of great weight which completely coincided with what had been done by the Territorial Government, so that Señores Híjar and Padrés had nothing with which to destroy such well demonstrated truths. Then, pretending to be surprised, or perhaps they were genuinely surprised, they asked for time to consider and answer satisfactorily or admit they were convinced, and thus put an end to heated and violent discussions. As our aim in suggesting the meetings was none other than to avoid public scandal and ill will, we assured them we would defer as long as it was compatible with our honor and duty, and we agreed that we would meet again on the following day to continue the conference.

That is what happened; but before we met again I received this note from Señor Híjar:

October 26, 1834

My General and friend:

I believe it is important that we have a secret interview before the meeting. See if you can walk over here after lunch or indicate a place to me.

Your most affectionate friend,

Híjar

My response was to present myself to Señor Híjar at the house of Don José Joaquín Gómez[110] where, in spite of my requests and entreaties, he had taken lodging two days before, disdaining my friendship and my home, in which I had put him up; but without mentioning such matters I offered him my services in whatever way he thought I could help. Then—oh fatal moment, could I but blot you out from time!—he proposed that if I handed over to him the property of the missions, he would protect my private interests with the same mission property, with assets that he had in Mexico and Guadalajara and with his credit and connections that he would apply in my favor in the way that would best suit my affairs; and finally, he would place at my disposal a credit of twenty thousand or more pesos that he would request from Mexico City or Jalisco, if I so desired, provided the missions be handed over to him. If I wished to do this it would be as good as done, because the Deputation would follow my advice without demur, since the cause of its opposition was myself; for that body would only do my bidding, and it was in my power to make the

109. For Luis del Castillo Negrete and Rafael Gómez, see n. 44 above.

110. José Joaquín Gómez was a Mexican merchant who settled at Monterey, where he became a customs officer and member of the City Council; for a thumbnail sketch of his career, see Bancroft, *California*, III, pp. 758–759.

fortune of everyone. Since he invoked friendship and secrecy in proposing this accommodation to me, I used the same confidence to demand that he convince me with justice, and that that alone would make me desist from the plan I had formed; for money is not a legal or decent arbiter, nor one that would make me sink so low as to sell the interests of innocent persons whom I felt obliged to protect, and which I would only hand over to him by express order of the Federal Government, after I had pointed out to it the damage that would be done to the neophytes.[111]

We had a lengthy discussion on the right of the neophytes to property, and Señor Híjar restated his opinion, maintaining that the neophytes have no right to the property and land of the missions, and that the Government could freely dispose of everything as it thought best. But all this is based on his own statements and nothing more. I upheld the contrary as well as I could, and I even dare to assert that I convinced Señor Híjar; but being so deeply committed and involved, he was preoccupied with the chimerical projects that Señor Padrés, who did not even look after his own reputation, suggested to

him, and as a last resort he proposed to me that I should hand over to him the mission property, under guarantee that he would not proceed to sell any of it until the Federal Government had made a decision on the report being sent to it on the matter. He would formally pledge himself to comply with this offer if his proposal was agreed to.

After a sufficiently lengthy discussion, I offered to Señor Híjar that if the Deputation agreed to his last proposal, I, out of courtesy, would not oppose it, provided the property of the neophytes was not disposed of, but neither would I support his claims, for that would force me into very notable inconsistencies. Thus ended our secret conference, which Señor Padrés knew about although he did not take part, and immediately we met again to continue the conference left unfinished the previous day.

Señor Híjar began by making the proposal I have mentioned above, but the members of the Deputation and the lawyers brought forth against it convincing reasons which left no room for its realization. Thereupon both Señor Híjar and Adjutant Inspector José María Padrés appeared to be convinced, declaring that the Deputation had operated within the orbit of its powers in entire agreement with the laws and resolutions of the Federal Government. They said that the instructions on which Señor Híjar solely based his authority were neither so clear as was necessary to remove all doubt[112] nor did they possess the validity required in such a case, since they were contradicted by the Government order of July 25, which removed Señor Híjar from civil power, and were opposed to various measures of the Government. That because of this he was not insisting on his claims,

111. It should be noted that Figueroa, who had hitherto been quick to resent real or fancied insults from Híjar, took this alleged attempt to bribe him with relative equanimity. It is also worth noting that Figueroa does not call the alleged attempt bribery, but rather an "accommodation." Furthermore, although Figueroa does not hesitate to accuse Híjar and Padrés of numerous crimes, such as robbing the missions, in the course of his *Manifesto*, he makes only one further use of this incident (on the next to the last page of the *Manifesto*), when he admits that there is no direct proof of Híjar's attempted bribery that he can bring forward, and suggests that the reader must rely on his own opinion of Híjar and Figueroa in coming to a conclusion about the matter. This is begging the question, however, and it can lend little credence to the story, which may, in fact, have been no more than an attempt by Híjar to interest Figueroa in buying some of the shares of the Cosmopolitan Company.

112. For a translation of the instructions, see pp. 24–25. above.

although he was determined to take the Colony to Old [Lower] California, where he thought he could establish it more easily, because there his commission as Director of Colonization remained in force without the contradiction it had suffered in Upper California. Señor Padrés maintained the same, adding that it was certain that the instructions were very brief and written in a style that necessarily gave rise to various doubts, but that this arose from the excessive confidence placed in them by His Excellency the Vice-President of the Republic,[113] who had given them orally the other orders and instructions of great interest that they were to put into effect.

The affair was settled, and we occupied ourselves persuading Señor Híjar to remain in Upper California directing the colony. We pointed out how difficult it would be to move the colony to Old California because of the lack of resources to maintain it during the journey back that it would have to make, and the far-reaching political effect of failure of the undertaking that was primarily directed at Upper California. We added that the colony would not have in Old California either lands on which to establish itself, because of the natural aridity of the soil there, or means by which to support itself, for the missions there have very few cattle, which do not produce even enough for the missionaries. We pointed out to him that his determination would merely worsen the lot of the colonists, which was bad enough, because of the lack of funds with which to support them. We said that they would overwhelm Old California with calamities by the sudden immigration of so many people, who could not be supported without harming the inhabitants there, who can scarcely survive except at the cost of great labor and vigilance. We said that because of the sterility of the soil and the lack of laborers, even articles of prime necessity for life are lacking there, things that are obtained at great cost from Sonora and Sinaloa, and there is never as much as is needed. We said that the National Treasury there has less resources than it does in Upper California to take care of its needs and, in brief, that he could not even move from this point because of the lack of funds and ships to get the expedition under way. We begged him to put aside his resentment and remain with us on good terms. We said he might establish the colony he had brought out under his care, and that he would receive the same four thousand pesos that the Federal Government, which would be consulted and given a recommendation to obtain its approval, had assigned to him.[114] We said we would give him effective assistance so that he could carry out the enterprise, and we would do whatever was compatible with our duty to oblige him.

Convinced that his idea of going with the colony to Old California was impracticable, he agreed with everything we suggested and straightaway we discussed the measures we should adopt.

As a consequence of what we agreed upon at the conferences, I passed the following note on to the Deputation:

Monterey
October 29, 1834

I communicated to Señor José María Híjar the eight propositions agreed upon by Your

113. Vice-President Gómez Farías, acting as President.

114. Actually, the Government had assigned Híjar 3000 pesos for his salary as Governor, and 1000 pesos as Director of Colonization. (García to Híjar, July 16, 1833, State Papers, Missions and Colonization, BL, vol. 2, p. 209.) Figueroa could justifiably have limited Híjar's salary to 1000 pesos, since he was no longer Governor. Figueroa's offer in this case may either be considered generosity or attempted bribery.

Excellencies on October 22, and since he did not agree, he replied in his note of the 23rd, the original of which I enclose. The exaggerated ideas with which he tries to ridicule the powers of the Territorial Government could be overcome with the pen, but as I wish to preserve harmony and reconcile public and private interests, I thought it more prudent to settle the question by means of conferences, so as to avoid all animosity and public scandal.

Consequently, Señor Híjar met with me, and after a thorough discussion on the various points mentioned in his note of the 23rd, convinced by the evidence of the just foundations on which the Territorial Government based its decisions, we agreed to the following:

(1) That Señor José María Híjar will discharge the special assignment of Director of Colonization, subject to the political Government of the Territory, and to the laws and regulations that bear on the subject. This is to be the true meaning of the second proposition agreed upon by the Deputation, because this is the sense that it had in mind when it said "the bases agreed upon [by the Deputation]," and for this reason it authorizes this interpretation.[115]

(2) That the instructions given to Señor Híjar by the Federal Government, which it was ordered should be held, are to be returned to him; only a copy of them is to remain in the Archives of the Territorial Government.

That being in agreement with everything else contained in the abovementioned eight propositions, he yields and states that he will discharge his special assignment until the Federal Government of the Union decides whatever it may believe to be proper.

Señor Híjar commends to Your Excellencies' consideration the individuals who have come in his company with the object of being teachers,[116] on which matter he explains that

he received verbal instructions from the Federal Government for their placement.

May you decide on all the above whatever you believe to be proper and most just.

God and Liberty.
José Figueroa

The Deputation, after having heard a committee of its members, at its session on November 3 approved the decision and propositions in the following communication:

Monterey
November 4, 1834

The Territorial Deputation, as of yesterday's date, approved the report of the Committee on Government and agrees to the following propositions:

The Committee on Government has examined the letter of October 23 by José María Híjar in answer to the one sent him by the Political Chief, dated October 22, informing him of the eight propositions agreed to by Your Excellency on that day. It consists of a mass of erroneous ideas, unfounded imputations, and gratuitous reproaches against the Territorial Government. In order to vindicate Your Excellency's highly insulted honor, the Committee could draw up a lengthy analysis to correct the mistakes and repudiate the slander with which its just proceedings are opposed. But having decided to offer once again proof of moderation, politeness, and urbanity, it ignores the acrimony in which this document abounds and rests on the testimony of its conscience and honor.

Your Excellency, on considering the measures refuted by Señor Híjar, had at hand the laws and regulations in effect on the subject. It is of no importance that an attempt is made to twist the genuine meaning of them, it is necessary to observe them. Those who take offense at it may use their rights, and the

115. See n. 53 above.
116. The following came as teachers: Alvina Alvarez, Carlos Baric, José Mariano Bonilla, Luis Bonilla, Jesús Castillo, Guillermo Coronel, Ignacio Coronel, Manuel Coronel, Petra Enríquez, Dionisio Fernández, Francisca Fernández, José Zenón Fernández, Loreta Fernández, Manuela

Fernández, Máximo Fernández, Sabas Fernández, Antonio Noreña, José María Oviedo, Ignacia Paz, Victor Prudon, José Mariano Romero, Francisca Rosel, Florencio Serrano, and Ignacia Zárate. (Legislative Records, BL, vol. 2, p. 260.)

proper authority will decide in favor of the one who is within the law. Your Excellency as an authority fulfills your duty by going ahead with your measures and interpreting those that offer some doubt. Señor Híjar, although he tried to disavow your authority, has made assurances that he will obey it after realizing his mistake, following private conferences with the Political Chief. This is a tacit confession of his error and a proof of his conviction.

Having concluded in this way the questions which have so greatly occupied us, we must bring to an end all public scandal and bury all personal resentment in silence. The superior authorities will make the appropriate clarification, and the results will justify our procedure. The individuals who compose this body are just as good republicans as Señor Híjar, they use stern language like His Honor, but they avoid insults and diatribes. They could make a just reprisal, but they profess principles of liberty, moderation, and tolerance, and the only rule of their operations must be the laws and orders of legitimately constituted authorities. This body is satisfied that it has not overstepped its powers and that it has not usurped powers that the laws do not impart to it. In view of this, the Committee presents for Your Excellency's deliberation the following propositions:

(1) In order to explain the true meaning of the second proposition approved on October 22, for the words "and the bases agreed upon by the Deputation" there will be substituted the following: "and to the laws and regulations that bear on the subject."[117]

(2) That the instructions given by the Federal Government are to be returned to Señor Híjar, with one copy of them remaining in the hands of the Political Chief.

(3) That presuming that Señor Híjar is in agreement with everything else drawn up by the Deputation on October 22, this decision and the former propositions be submitted to him so that he may express in writing whether or not he is in agreement with everything de-

117. See n. 53 above.

cided by the Territorial Government. In the first case, the Political Chief will order that he be granted the salary of four thousand pesos and will report to the Federal Government to request its approval.

(4) The Political Chief is authorized to resolve, in accordance with the laws, whatever doubts there may be with regard to this resolution and to the one of October 22 in those cases in which the Deputation has the right to intervene.

Monterey
November 4, 1834

José María Híjar
Director of Colonization

The enclosed [copy of the Deputation's resolutions] is in answer to your note of October 23, and is accompanied by the instructions given you by the Federal Government.

I should be obliged, if some doubt occurs to you or if you have any objection to make, if you would take the trouble to have a conference with me first on the matter, so as to agree on the most prudent course to be followed or the measures that I should take. If there is no other difference in our views, will you please be good enough to let me know.

With this object in mind, I repeat assurances of my due appreciation and consideration.

God and Liberty.
José Figueroa

Señor Híjar replied with the following letter:

Monterey
November 6, 1834

General José Figueroa
Political Chief

I am in receipt of Your Honor's note of November 4 in which you enclose the resolution of the Territorial Deputation on my communication of October 23, and I consider any dissent on the points which we have discussed useless, since we are not in agreement on the way in which we see things.

Your Honor will permit me merely to correct a mistake. It is stated in the expository part of the resolution which you send me that I tried to repudiate the authority of the Deputation. I have never had any such intention. What I have done is to deny its power to put itself above the laws, but that is not to repudiate its authority. I have the greatest respect for the legitimate authorities and I know how I must act when they go astray. I do not believe, therefore, that I have made any mistake, as is stated.

In the conferences which are mentioned, only reasons of utility, convenience, philanthropy, and humanity toward the Indians were brought up, but no express power to act in the way proposed. There is no law, and consequently no right either, for Your Honors to have deliberated as you did. That is my opinion, for although some Spanish laws were cited, these have been annulled by our own, because they are opposed to our system of government.

In the third proposition which is enclosed, it is demanded that I say in writing whether or not I am in agreement with the resolution of the Territorial Government, and that in the former case I am to be assigned four thousand pesos in salary. I regret very much that the Deputation has formed so poor an opinion of me that it perhaps thought that money would make me give in to everything that has been decided upon. No sir, not only am I not in agreement, but I protest against what Your Honors have proposed in all of those parts in which the regulations and laws of the Federal Government are attacked, as I informed you in my communication of the 23rd.

Since the questions that have occupied us are concluded, it only remains for me to inform Your Honor that I am determined to continue with the colony until it is established at the place the Government desires, for the following reasons:

(1) The personal desires of the families which compose the colony made them decide to throw their lot in with mine and follow me. Consequently, if I should abandon them, the colony would be stranded, with grave injury to its members.

(2) If the colony should fail, it would be a discredit to the Government, since it would be believed incapable of carrying out undertakings of this kind, having uprooted these families from their homeland to cast them off in a remote country and, finally, it would never again succeed in persuading any man to leave his home and go forth to be a colonist.

(3) The desires of the Government would remain unfulfilled, and the important northern frontier, threatened by the Russians and Anglo-Americans, would remain unprotected, and the heavy expenses that have been paid for the colony would be lost. All these considerations, General, have made me decide to put aside all my resentments and wounded pride so as to preserve the national interest and decorum and assure the well-being of the families entrusted to me. I have not been able to resist the tears of gratitude that my traveling companions have on various occasions shed in my presence. I decided, and I remain decided, to sacrifice everything, even though I am not recompensed by an ungrateful Government which has outraged me so capriciously. I am, therefore, going to establish the colony and wield a hoe myself if it is necessary to survive. But the pleasure of having fulfilled the duties of a good citizen, maintaining the national decorum, and working for the happiness of the families who put their trust in me, will remain with me.

I conclude, therefore, with the hope that Your Honor will see to it, as you have agreed, that nothing that the Federal Government offered the colonists is lacking, and I put my trust in your probity so that everything may be done punctually and at the appropriate time, so that no colonist shall have any reason for complaint.

The instructions that you returned to me are in my possession, together with your note, to which I have the honor to reply with assurances of my appreciation and high regard.

God and Liberty.
José María de Híjar

Señor Híjar insists on clinging to several errors that I have pointed out and combatted. For this reason I avoid answering at length the opinions he presents in this last letter, in which it will be seen that this gentleman always understands things in a different way from other men. He says that he knows how he must act toward the authorities when they go astray, and it is useless to point out to him the errors which abound in his own writings. Let us leave his disillusionment to time and follow the course of events. Note the importance that he tries to give to his own person even against the Federal Government, because it had suspended him from the position of Political Chief, which it had granted to him. He cannot hide his resentment, in spite of those solemn assurances that he will sacrifice himself for the sake of the colony and national decorum. Would that his deeds had corresponded with his words.

The Territorial Government, pleased at having arranged these affairs in friendly fashion, publicly congratulated Señor Híjar and treated him with the courtesy due friendship. Inspired by the best feelings, it agreed to various measures and acts of assistance so that Señor Híjar could establish the colony. Half of the colony was at San Gabriel and San Luis Rey, 630 miles from San Francisco Solano [Sonoma], which is the closest point to the place it was to occupy. After overcoming many obstacles and causing heavy expense to the nation, because they had disembarked at San Diego, arrangements were made to transport them. The plans of the Federal Government were finally to be put into effect, however, and to this end the Territorial Government directed its exertions.

While it was most enthusiastically occupied with these tasks, the news arrived that First Lieutenant of the Navy Buenaventura Araujo[118] had called the

pagan savages (Cahuillas)[119] together for a meeting. They attacked the ranch of San Bernardino, belonging to the mission of San Gabriel, and committed various robberies and other excesses. Because of this, a party of 20 armed men was dispatched to observe them and if necessary force them to order. But the insolence with which these unfortunates had been imbued[120] made them rash enough to attack this party, and it was necessary to defeat them. At the same time Francisco Berdusco, one of the colonists, wanted to win over the neophytes of San Luis Rey in order to take by surprise a small detachment stationed there, but his conspiracy was discovered and the plot thwarted.[121] The Cahuillas again attacked the same ranch of San Bernardino, where they committed various murders and major robberies. A party of 50 men went out after them and punished their insolence by killing several who

record of Buenaventura Araujo in Archivo Histórico Militar de México, Mexico City.)

119. Híjar had instructed the colonists to inform the non-Christian tribes, of which the Cahuillas were one, that the Mexican Government would protect them provided they cooperated with it. They were to be informed that they would be given lands and could live where they liked without fear of molestation. Lieutenant Araujo was presumably going to inform the Cahuillas of these matters at his proposed meeting with them.

120. Figueroa appears to be implying here that Buenaventura Araujo was to blame for the disorders of the Cahuillas. There is no evidence that Araujo was responsible, however, and it is possible that the Cahuillas, who were in touch with the independent Colorado River tribes, may have been encouraged by them to start an uprising, or they may have had some old scores to wipe out against the white man.

121. Berdusco was accused of trying to obtain weapons to arm two companies of colonists, seize the property of the missions, run them for a year or two, and leave with the booty before the mission Indians rose in revolt. His defense rings truer than the accusation against him. (Berdusco Criminal, Beinecke Collection, Yale University Library.)

118. Buenaventura Araujo was a Mexican naval officer who had fought against the Spaniards in naval battles at Callao, Peru. He was being sent to California to strengthen the navy there. (Service

resisted. Romualdo Lara, another colonist who accompanied Señor Híjar on his journey from San Diego to Monterey, tried at several missions through which he traveled to induce the neophytes to join his party. This is clear from the diary that he kept himself, which by chance reached my hands.[122] All these attempts inspired in the Government the natural lack of confidence that it should have of their perpetrators, but it did no more than dictate some precautionary measures to avoid an upheaval, without even taking steps against the promoters, since it believed them capable of listening to the voice of reason and desisting. The very reverse happened: they worked under cover to put Señor Híjar by force at the head of the Civil Government and dispose of the wealth of the missions under his auspices.

I watched from a distance the storm that was going to break over my head and I could not dispel it without exposing myself to the bitter criticism of my antagonists, who only seek the shelter of the law in order to insult the authorities with impunity.

José María Padrés—who the moment he disembarked had asked me to hand over to him the military command, by virtue of the Government order of July 12, 1833, who protested to me, after I turned down such a pretension, that he would not take over his post of Adjutant Inspector because he did not want to depend on the military government, and because it was incompatible with his commission as Assistant Director of the Colony—after a few days tried to get me to make him Military Commander of the northern frontier. This inconsistent changeability of

mind made me distrust him, and I rejected his request. This insubordinate officer, before he reached the Territory, had boasted that he was coming, according to what he said, at the head of a people in arms. Everyone knew that he brought 200 rifles and a considerable supply of munitions of war, and far from complying with his duty to inform me of these weapons, either as Military Commandant or as Political Chief, he tried to hide them from me.[123] He gave orders to the colonists that no one was to see me or transact any business with me, for they were to deal only with him. I had noticed that he had a dominant influence over the mind of Señor Híjar, and that he persuaded him to do whatever he wanted.[124]

All of this, his propensity toward disorder that I already knew about, his previous interest in devouring the property of the missions, the maneuvers and intrigues he used so that the Deputation should disooey the order of the Federal Government, and other considerations which would take a long time to relate, made me believe that Padrés was the prime mover of all the conspiracies, and that I should observe his conduct with more care.[125] The order that Padrés cites, for me to hand

122. This diary appears to have been lost, so that there is no way of verifying Figueroa's statement. It is possible that Lara was simply following Híjar's instructions to make friends with the mission Indians by informing them that Híjar was going to give them land, cattle, and protection.

123. For a discussion of the career of José María Padrés, see the Introduction, p. 9. The rifles had been given to the colonists by the Mexican Government, presumably so that they could protect themselves against the Indians at the dangerous site where they were supposed to settle.

124. The documents do not bear Figueroa out on this claim. In fact, when Padrés first arrived at Monterey and Híjar was at San Diego, Figueroa commented in a letter to Vallejo (Sept. 28, 1834, Cowan Collection, BL) that Padrés did not want to make any decisions and that they were awaiting Híjar so as to discuss things and determine what should be done.

125. Figueroa's unfavorable views of Padrés probably went back to his briefings in Mexico City by Foreign Minister Lucas Alamán, who accepted former Governor Victoria's highly unflattering opinion of Padrés.

over to him the Military Commandancy, I shall insert here so that the public may learn that it is not so peremptory as is needed to fulfill Padrés' desires.

Mexico City
July 12, 1833

General José Figueroa
Commandant of Upper California

Under this date I am informing Adjutant Inspector José María Padrés as follows: "His Excellency the Vice-President, exercising the Federal Executive Power,[126] is pleased to order that you proceed to the Territory of Upper California in order to take over as Military Commandant, in case General José Figueroa should continue to be ill and wish to resign." I am informing you of this by the same Government order, for your compliance and related purposes.

I have the privilege of sending this to Your Honor for this objective, with the idea that if your illness makes it desirable for you to return to Mexico City, you may do so.

God and Liberty.
Herrera[127]

In spite of what had happened up to then, I took the most determined steps to reunite and establish the colony, at the cost of great sacrifice and hardship, because its Directors had divided it into two groups. But as much as I made efforts in favor of it, the speculators kept on promoting disorder and preparing for a revolution which was to remove me from the civil government and put Señor Híjar in my place.

This was the objective of all the maneuvers of José María Padrés, Francisco Berdusco, Francisco Torres, and Romualdo Lara, who were the men who played the principal roles on the scene. It can be understood that each one had his

followers and all of them were conspiring with the same end in view. So from various quarters I received reports that the colony was attempting to conspire against the Government, according to the statements of several of its members. On January 18 and February 12 of this year [1835], two different trustworthy persons communicated with me from the mission of San Antonio that the plan for a conspiracy was certain. Several individuals from the colony secretly revealed to me the disorders into which they were to be plunged. Others tried to withdraw from the colony, alleging various pretexts. The sedition was to be tried in different ways in various parts of the Territory, and in the very capital, where the most important plans were being made. Under these circumstances, Señor Híjar preserved a passive conduct and a simulated indifference which removed him from suspicion. But the principal instigators of the revolution paid court to him, and it was with them alone that he discussed his affairs and only they received his highest confidence, and it is virtually impossible that he should not know about the plans that they were to carry out under his auspices and in his name.

When I could no longer doubt the decision they had taken, motives for intense suspicion which coincided with the seditious plans appeared daily. Then the winter, which hinders any occupation, conspired against the unfortunate colonists who, accustomed to a more benign temperature, could scarcely bear the rigor of the season. And under these circumstances they were forced to travel great distances and double their sufferings, with the sole object of bringing them together to subvert the social order after they had sacrificed the wealth of the nation in useless expenses. These results were brought on by the incompetence or

---

126. Vice-President Gómez Farías, acting as President.

127. Minister of War José Joaquín de Herrera.

depravity of the Directors of the colony, for they never consulted either its comfort or the good of the country, nor the success of an enterprise worthy of better results. They directed everything without any more foresight or planning than the fantastic frenzies of José María Padrés and his uncontrolled greed to seize the property of the missions. But such is the blindness of passion that it seems that they all let themselves be guided by his influence, and this man, infatuated by his arrogant presumption, wanted to play the part of Minerva. Behold the Mentor[128] of the colony, whose vote outranked all the others.

Some of the colonists had reached San Francisco Solano, others in the course of their march were at different places. Founding a town requires strong, hardworking people, men accustomed to work in the fields and to a simple, frugal life. The colony directed by Señores Híjar and Padrés is in its majority composed of delicate persons worthy of a better fate. They are families suddenly uprooted from Mexico City, where they were born and brought up in the midst of wealth and pleasures. However slight their fortune was there, they had established a system of life adapted to their strength, their character, their inclinations, their customs, their temperament, and their taste. In proportion to their industry and their connections, they enjoyed comfort and pleasures that they would have difficulty in obtaining elsewhere. Many of them profess some mechanical or liberal art which in Mexico City would bring them some income but in California is useless.

128. Minerva was the Roman goddess of wisdom and good counsel who is identified with the Greek Pallas Athena. Mentor was a friend of Odysseus and the tutor of his son Telemachus. It was in the guise of Mentor that Pallas Athena often appeared to Telemachus.

Let the tinsmiths, silversmiths, trimmings makers, embroiderers, painters, etc., bear witness. Compare the difference between handling the instruments of the arts and grasping the handle of a plow, a hoe, an axe, and the other implements used for cultivating the fields. Compare the difference between working indoors, sheltered from the sun, from wind and water, to working in the fields exposed to bad weather and the hazards of a life filled with privations, discomforts, and dangers. Could it be possible that the girls, ladies, and delicate young men who saw from the roads that they traveled the first fields they had ever seen—could it be possible, I repeat, that these individuals would be able to overcome the fatigue, the difficulties, the privations, the necessities, and the mass of afflictions and accidents to which the undertaking of founding new towns is subject? Let those involved answer this for me, and impartial-minded men will justify the measures of the Territorial Government in putting a stop to the sufferings of the colonists and freeing them from the harsh obligation into which their Directors were leading them to make their fate more unfortunate.

There is no doubt that the colony recruited by Señor Padrés is lacking in the qualities that constitute a good colony, not because of any defect in its individuals but because of the ignorance and malice of the Directors, who only sought in the enterprise to enrich themselves at the expense of the neophytes on the California missions and the unfortunate colonists, who let themselves be duped by the false promises and fantastic pictures of prosperity with which they had been deceived in order to persuade them to come to this country. Several individuals arrived with the belief that they could freely dispose of the horses and cattle they needed without having to do more than take them out in the country where cattle were common property. Others anxiously asked the way to the beaches, where they thought they would be able to kill as many sea-otter[129] as they wanted with clubs. Some were searching for pearl beds[130] to fill their pockets and, finally, others thought they owned the farms and other more important mission buildings that had been offered to them. These were the base methods used by Señor Padrés to recruit families, who should have been protected from his iniquitous schemes. These events have just happened; I speak in front of the actors themselves, they will contradict me if I do not speak the truth.

Let it be assumed, therefore, that the colony, because of its natural incapacity, could not found a new town, which was the objective of the Federal Government's policy to protect the northern frontier against foreign aggression; that the political beliefs of its Directors were openly at variance with the sane principles of every settled society; that their subversive plans would have caused positive harm to the average inhabitant; that the Political Chief was blamed for the wants, privations, and hardship suffered by the colonists, which they could not even bear with resignation, because they were being urged every day to avenge supposed insults in order to compensate for their sufferings; that in order to incite their anger, they were being read every day at San Francisco Solano the nonsensical letter with which Señor Híjar answered me on October 23, on whose

contents the Mentor of the colony made lengthy commentaries, which generally ended with him showering insults on my person and using invective unworthy[131] of the lofty personage he took himself to be. All these factors were so many other combustibles that were being prepared for the general conflagration. I looked upon them as being obvious and calmly watched the approach of the day of the explosion. No one will believe it, but under such circumstances I simply kept on the defensive and stayed that way from the month of September, when the expedition reached the Territory, to the month of March, when they withdrew their masks and forced me to take the offensive.

Since summer was approaching, the season when they should have been completing the work 'of regeneration which they had planned, they pretended to busy themselves with totally different affairs. Francisco Torres[132] professedly went off to Mexico City on a commission from Señor Híjar, who did not have the courtesy to communicate to me, as he should have done, the object of his trip, for no colonist may leave without the express knowledge of the Political Chief. In spite of this, I granted him a passport without making any objections, knowing that the real object of his journey was to go to Los Angeles on the pretext of seeking passage in some ship, in order to promote a revolution there. By chance he met the Spaniard Antonio Apalátegui, a man of naturally restless disposition who has nothing to lose and is devoted to any kind of revolution. I had refused him

129. This North Pacific coast otter (*Enhydra lutris*) was hunted for its valuable fur.
130. The pearl beds were along the Gulf of California coast of Lower California.

131. The original Spanish has "invective worthy (*digno*) of the lofty personage," i.e., Mentor; but assuming this to be an error for *indigno*, I have changed it to "unworthy."
132. Francisco Torres was a physician from Guadalajara who had come as a member of the colony.

a position he wanted and he was on the lookout for some lucky venture. So he readily joined in with Torres' plans, and they left Monterey together.

Señor Híjar prepared to march to San Francisco Solano in company with Berdusco, Lara, and Araujo to join Padrés and the colony, which was still scattered, because of several obstacles which had prevented its getting under way. The real object of this gathering must have been revolution, but Señor Híjar feigned ignorance of it. I hinted something about it to him so as to persuade him to avoid the upheaval and the consequences that any revolution brings with it. But he ignored my hints, and instead told me that he had decided to return to Mexico City, and that as soon as he had arranged the affairs and accounts of the colony with Padrés he would set off on his journey. On this pretext he left for San Francisco Solano at the end of February. I set out for the same place, with no other object than to keep a watch on him and discover his plans. We met again at San Francisco de Asís, where we had a conference in which I demonstrated to him that his followers and friends wanted to involve him in deceiving the Government and most particularly myself, that I knew from various sources about the plans that they were making, that the revolution was to break out soon, that I was under the necessity of defending myself, and that I should perhaps have to take action which would be regrettable for him. I told him who the principle movers were, I pointed out to him the harm that it was going to do to the Territory, and that it was within his power to avoid it, if he wished, out of regard for tranquility and his own reputation. I assured him that the whole affair would be kept quiet if they remained peaceful, because I was not persecuting them, nor was I

afraid of them. But whether because he felt victory was certain or because he scorned my offers, he was as cold and indifferent toward me as he is toward the most important affairs. Then I found myself forced to prevent the colony's reuniting, to keep it out of the revolution for which they were summoning it. Several individuals had tried to do this, to prevent the ruin which was inevitable if they submitted to the caprice of the Directors, who even tried to monopolize their personal labor under the pretext of the Cosmopolitan Company. For they had done nothing useful, nor could they because of their physical incapacity, as I have demonstrated, and especially because I had no funds available to pay their daily expenses, as Señor Híjar wanted. I adopted the measure of leaving them free to establish themselves at whatever place suited them best for undertaking some line of business on which to live. This is recorded in the following correspondence between us:

San Francisco de Asís
March 1, 1835

General José Figueroa
Political Chief

I am about to go to San Francisco Solano for the purpose of determining the site at which the colony must be established. But since Your Honor informed me at various private conferences that it is impossible to provide for the colonists what the Federal Government offered them when they were recruited in their homeland to come to the Territory, I should be obliged if Your Honor would tell me once and for all whether the Government is or is not able to keep its pledge, so that I can make my arrangements and have all the colonists transported to the site where they are to be settled, if Your Honor provides the resources offered; or in case this is impossible, so that I can inform them and they can decide what to do if the Government fails to keep the conditions of the contract which it made with the families who were entrusted to me, and whom I am distressed to see in the depths of misery.

I feel it is useless to point out to you the harm that will follow from the dissolution of the colony, which has caused the Federal Government such great expense and effort, and the political results which must ensue, in which the honor of the Federal Government is clearly involved. Your Honor knows as well as I do the consequences of this decision, and I hope that your prudence will enable you to solve it in the best possible way, without losing sight of its political influence, the honor of the Federal Government, the individual interests of the colonists, and the public interest of the Territory.

God and Liberty.
José María de Híjar

San Francisco de Asís
March 2, 1835

José María Híjar
Director of Colonization

The Federal Government has given me no previous instructions concerning the colony. The instructions given to you, when you were appointed Political Chief, are the only official document authorizing the measures dictated on the subject; this document is in Your Honor's hands. It is true that it contains the order to take the wealth of the missions and to invest it in the colony, but this provision attacks the property of the Indians, and as I have informed Your Honor at various conferences, this is unconstitutional. I have pointed this out to the Government, and it can be appropriately seen in Article 112, restriction 3, of the Federal Constitution,[133] which runs as follows: "The President cannot take the property of any person or corporation nor disturb him in the possession, use, or enjoyment of it. And if in some case it might be necessary to take the property of an individual or a corporation for an object of known utility, the President cannot do so without pre-

133. The Mexican Constitution of 1824.

vious approval of the Senate or during its recesses, of the Council of Government, always compensating the interested party according to the judgment of good men chosen by the interested party and the Government.[134]

This is the basis on which the Territorial Government has founded its defense of the property of the missions, which it has always recognized as belonging to the mission neophytes. But in spite of such serious obstacles, and with the solemn assurance that it will claim due indemnity, it agreed to provide the colony with all the assistance necessary for its establishment and support, for it never believed it was just to abandon so many persons worthy of its appreciation and respect to their fate, nor has it regarded their sufferings with indifference.

Your Honor is aware that in conformity with the decision of the Territorial Deputation on October 22, 1834, I ordered that all the articles you had listed for the establishment and support of the colony be put at your disposal. Your Honor knows that only some of these things have been supplied and that most of them are lacking, that the season of the year and the lack of resources of all kinds is slowing down or paralyzing the enterprise. You are aware that I am surrounded with difficulties and that, because of the secularization of the missions and other complicated matters, my attempts to provide for the colony are frustrated at every step. You know that the burdens newly imposed on the property of the missions, and the losses they are suffering

134. If it be agreed that mission property belonged to the Indians, Governor Figueroa has a case here, but his able argument is seriously weakened by the fact that in the regulations drawn up by the Territorial Deputation, and approved by Figueroa, for the provisional secularization of the California missions, the nation is made the original owner of mission lands, not the Indians. See Articles 18 and 19 of "Provisional Steps for the Emancipation of the Mission Indians." (A manuscript copy of these regulations is in Legislative Records, BL, vol. 2, and there is a translation of it in Zephyrin Engelhardt, *The Missions and Missionaries of California*, III, pp. 523–530. Bancroft in his *History of California*, III, pp. 342–344, n. 4, has a synopsis of the decree.)

because of the innovations that are being introduced, are further obstacles which are daily placed in the way of the resources on which I can reckon. I have shown you the communications I have received from the officials in charge of the missions regarding the help which they have to give to the colony, and they mention several unavoidable deficiencies.

I am determined to overcome all these hindrances in whatever way I can, and with this object in mind I have told Your Honor that I shall spare neither labor nor efforts. But expenses are growing to an extent impossible to bear without serious injury to the public, for the notorious decadence the missions are in, the great debts they have contracted and which must be met from their effects, the emancipation of the native families, who amount to more than 20,000 persons, who have to be given property for their establishment and support, the heavy burdens newly imposed for stipends for the missionaries, salaries for the teachers, stewards, and other employees who formerly did not exist, the daily wages of the laborers who are employed in the upkeep of the farms, everything, everything is borne by the properties of the natives and threatens their rapid destruction without being able to completely fulfill every requirement.

In spite of everything I have said, I repeat to Your Honor that I shall make every effort necessary to provide the colony with the assistance essential for its survival, but I cannot promise to pay its daily expenses punctually, for there is no currency nor is it easy to acquire it. Nor could the sum of 35,000 and more pesos, which is what the daily expenses amount to, be met in a short time with any other articles, without bankrupting the missions.

Because of all that I have said, because several persons from the colony have asked me by word of mouth and in writing to let them establish themselves where they like; because it is well known that most of the individuals who compose the colony, although they are very commendable and useful at various callings, are not fitted for work in the fields, which they have never done before;[135] because six months have gone by and the colony has not been established, nor has it undertaken any useful work; because Señor José María Padrés, without the knowledge of Your Honor nor of this Government, is getting some individuals and families who are already resident in the Territory to join the colony, which only results in an increase in expense; because transporting the cattle and other property to the other side of San Francisco Bay will be very expensive and slow, in addition to the losses that will be suffered in the course of it; because it is very difficult to concentrate at one point all the property of the colony; because there is general dissatisfaction among the colonists, which might relapse into disorder if their sufferings became worse; and, above all, because Your Honor has informed me of your decision to leave the office of Director of the Colony, and you have informed the Government of this and are thinking of withdrawing to Lower California to await orders—all this made me consider a conciliatory measure, and I suggested to Your Honor that, in my opinion, it is advisable to permit the colonists to establish themselves in the place that suits them best so that, aided by their industry and their trades, together with the assistance that the Government is giving them, they may provide a more comfortable life for themselves, the hardest-working among them acquiring advantages that they could not otherwise obtain.

In thinking of this measure, I am bearing in mind not only the comfort and preferences of the families but the savings for the public Treasury, the general tranquility of the Territory, the greater ease in providing assistance

135. Híjar drew up a list of colonists and their occupations dated November 8, 1834. (State Papers, C-A53, BL, vol. 2, p. 187; see the Introduction, p. 13.) For an official list of the colonists, see my article, "An Official List of the Members of the Híjar–Padrés Colony for Mexican California, 1834."

for the colonists and giving them free rein so that they can find useful employment at their trades. This is the only way, in fact, that I can do my part to lessen their sufferings and fulfill at the same time the promises the Federal Government has made them. In this way, also, in my opinion, they can be more useful and beneficial to society, since they cannot manage it in the hard labors of the fields. In spite of this, if one of the colonists or all of them are willing and ready to settle on the frontier, Your Honor may select the site that suits you and I shall assist you there with all the resources in my power.

National honor, the dignity of the Government, and public convenience are taken care of by the measure I have indicated. The colonists will be provided with their allowances proportionately and perhaps with less delay, with less burden on the Treasury, and more satisfaction to themselves.

I have thought a great deal about this affair, and every day experience convinces me that there is no other solution more suited to our circumstances nor one which better reconciles private interests with public ones. This is my opinion, and I should appreciate it if the colonists were acquainted with it, so that they may come to whatever decision they wish. I assure you that I shall gladly give my care and close attention, as I have up to the present, to see to it that they receive as much assistance as I can give them, for the shortages that some have suffered are due either to the inconvenience of the season or to the exhaustion of the Treasury or some other chance. But Your Honor and Señor Padrés are satisfied with the frankness and equity with which national funds have been distributed amongst all of them, and with my good will in ordering all the requests they have asked me for, since the moment they disembarked, to be fulfilled.

Following my offers and Your Honor's request, I am sending you on this same date the respective orders so that you may collect and distribute to the colony the sum of 2000 pesos in necessary goods, since there is no currency.

All of which I have the honor to inform you in reply to your note of yesterday's date which deals with this subject.

God and Liberty.
José Figueroa

San Francisco de Asís
March 3, 1835

General José Figueroa
Political Chief

The measure which Your Honor proposes, to leave it up to the colonists to settle wherever they wish, does not take care of my responsibility. And if the Federal Government can fulfill the pledge that it made to them, they should go to the site that the Government intended for them, to fulfill the objective proposed, since leaving four or five persons at each of the populated centers of the Territory would not have made the Government willing to bear the heavy expenses that they have. Your Honor must be convinced that a political objective, aiming, among other things, at preserving the integrity of the Territory of the Republic, was what persuaded the Government to make extraordinary sacrifices amidst the most difficult circumstances.

If the Federal Government can fulfill its pledge, the colonists should not complain that they are forced to go to an uninhabited region, for they contracted to be taken wherever it was suitable.

Because of this, and because the fate of the colony presently depends entirely on Your Honor's orders, I entreat you to tell me finally whether the Federal Government is in a position to fulfill its contract or if, as you have informed me on several occasions, it is not possible for it to keep its promise. I believe my responsibility will be covered by this final answer, and then the colonists will settle where they wish and collect their daily allowances when this can be done.

Your Honor is well aware that pro-rata requisitions from the missions on my requests for the colony have not been realized, except for a small amount, and it will be difficult to collect these because of the obstacles placed in the way. Although Your Honor has given orders to assist the colony, the fact is that they have not been followed, except in very small part. On every hand there have been difficulties and hindrances which have held up the establishment of the colony, difficulties which forced Your Honor to give orders that the colonists should pass the winter scattered among the missions, where as transients they have not yet been able to undertake any kind of work.

Everything points, General, to the need to take a definite step, and I would like Your Honor to tell me categorically to allow the colonists to settle where it suits them best, so that each one of them may devote himself to what he likes, counting only on the assistance that may conveniently be given them, as Your Honor offers, and not on what they are owed on their contract. In this way the colonists would emerge from tiresome uncertainty, and my responsibility would be over. If after a few days they are to be told that there is no way of fulfilling the contract it would be better to say so now, and less damage would be done to the unfortunates who came with me. It is proper that you should know that the colonists cannot precisely demand currency, because they have been told since they were in Mexico City that it was very scarce here, but that they will be paid in goods of equivalent value.

I will conclude by informing Your Honor that if Señor Padrés has received some individuals resident in this region as colonists, this does not burden public funds, because they will only be given land and nothing else that was offered to those contracted in the interior. I shall also add that even though I leave the colony, as I have petitioned the Federal Government, this must not affect in any way the future fate of the colony, much less the aims that the Government had in mind when it sent it.

All of which I have thought it proper to tell Your Honor in reply to your note of yesterday, without becoming involved in the question of ownership of the funds with which the colony is to be assisted, since this is a matter that does not concern me.

God and Liberty.
José María de Híjar

San Francisco de Asís
March 4, 1835

José María Híjar
Director of Colonization

On repeated occasions I have informed Your Honor how difficult it is to pay in full the expenses that have to be made for establishment of the colony, due to lack of funds, and because the expenses daily grow larger, while the resources available are diminishing notably, for reasons that it is not in my power to avoid. In view of this, I believed it necessary to leave the colonists free to establish themselves where they think best, so that, aided by their industry and by what can conveniently be given them for their daily allowances, they can live without being in want.

Your Honor has realized the difficulties and is convinced that it is impossible to carry out the enterprise, but in order to discharge your responsibility you urge upon me in your note of yesterday a final decision, and I hereby inform you that it is impossible to provide in full everything that the Federal Government offered the colony because the funds in my power are not sufficient. Consequently, I order that the colonists remain at liberty to establish themselves within the boundaries of the Territory at whatever place pleases each one of them, and they will be assisted there in accordance with the resources I have available.

I have the pleasure of informing Your Honor of this in answer to your note cited above. I request that you be good enough to inform me of your decision, for my future plans.

God and Liberty.
José Figueroa

In spite of the treachery with which I was being treated, I endeavored to endure my sufferings to the end and help the colony in whatever ways I could. So I did not molest anyone or charge them with their crimes, in the hope that they would withdraw from their extravagant pretensions. With this intention I withdrew, after placing 2000 pesos at the disposal of Señor Híjar so that he might help the colony. I stopped a few days at the missions of Santa Clara and San Juan Bautista to make inquiries to discover who were the leaders of the revolution. I had made considerable headway when, on March 13, I received by special messenger the news that a revolutionary pronouncement had been made at Los Angeles on the 7th of that month, led by Juan Gallardo[136] at the head of 50 adventurers from the State of Sonora. These men had been incited and involved in the revolt by Francisco Torres and Antonio Apalátegui[137] under various pretexts and tricks, but in trying to extricate themselves they revealed the depravity and cunning with which they had acted, and the revolutionaries themselves handed them over to the Alcalde so that they should be judged in accordance with the law. All of them claimed obedience to the Government, in whose name they had been called together by Torres and Apalátegui, and for this reason they were handing them over to the authorities, before whom they offered to lay down the arms they had unwisely taken up, saying that they would not again disturb public order under any pretext. The City Council of Los Angeles sent me the following message and plan:

Los Angeles
March 7, 1835

A leaderless band of Sonorans rose in revolt early this morning for the plan, a copy of which we are sending you. In substance, and regarded in a true light, it consists of nothing more than personal views which have also not been beyond the consideration of this City Council, which prudently decided to assemble for an extraordinary session, and I also send you herewith a copy of the minutes of that meeting.

It has seemed very strange to most people in this town that a mob of Sonorans, for reasons of their own, should try to make changes in the regulations established in this Territory. It is true that it can be seen from Article 6 of the plan in question that the rebels peacefully consent to obey justice, but they contradict themselves in the same article by saying that they will not put down their arms until they see that their objectives have been realized. They consider themselves protectors of the laws, and they are the first to break them. They proclaim order, and have even used force to surprise a member of the City Council who had the key of the jail, so as to seize the stores and equipment in it. Faced with the dangerous extremes of repelling that force without having the means to do so, or of giving way to the objectives of the rebels, it was necessary to take a middle course, and this may be seen in the resolution that the Council made at its second meeting.

In conclusion, the rebels remained in arms until three o'clock in the afternoon, and the one who appears as a representative of the group, Juan Gallardo, brought in as prisoners to the jail Antonio Apalátegui and Francisco Torres, and Felipe Castillo[138] presented a statement, a copy of which I send herewith. Apalátegui and Torres were put in a secure prison, and charges are being drawn up against them.

I assure Your Honor in the name of this

136. Juan Gallardo was a shoemaker and carpenter.

137. Antonio Apalátegui was a Spanish clerk who had asked Governor Figueroa for a position but had been turned down.

138. Felipe Castillo was a cigarmaker and merchant from Sonora.

City Council of my feelings of appreciation and respect.

God and Liberty
Francisco J. Alvarado
Manuel Arzaga, Secretary
City Council of Los Angeles

In the Pueblo of Our Lady of the Angels [Los Angeles] on March 7, 1835, a multitude of citizens met with the object of agreeing upon the most suitable means of saving the Territory of California from the evils that it has suffered and is suffering under the administration of General José Figueroa, and considering, first, that this leader has not complied with various orders that the Federal Government of the Union has sent him to improve the lot of the inhabitants of this country; that, taking advantage of their docility, he has exceeded the limits of the powers that the laws grant him by illegally reassuming both the civil and military commands against the Federal system and against express laws that prohibit this combination of powers; that out of the law of mission secularization he has made a scandalous monopoly by reducing its products or crops to an exclusive trade, taking advantage of the good faith of the Territorial Deputation so that he might set up at his own desire a general law; by infringing upon the regulation of the Commissariat, he disposes of the soldiers' pay as he wishes, without the knowledge of the official in charge of the Treasury, and without regard to the formalities which several laws and regulations provide for such cases.

Second, since the Territorial Deputation does not have the power to regulate or make additions to a Federal law, as it has done with the law on the secularization of missions.

Third, since the missions are going, as indeed they are, to total ruin with giant strides because of the blatant measures that have been passed for the withdrawal of the natives and the distribution of their respective property.

And fourth, that some commissioners, either because of their gross ignorance of how to manage this type of business, or because of their evil conduct, have proposed to further their own private interests by ruining the property of the missions, to the notable harm of the natives, who, by their personal labor have acquired them—the citizens have come to agree and have agreed upon the following:

Article I. General José Figueroa is declared to be unworthy of public confidence. Consequently, the first constitutional Alcalde of Monterey[139] will provisionally take over civil control of the Territory, and Captain Pablo de la Portilla,[140] as the oldest and highest-ranking officer, will take over the military command according to army regulations.

Article 2. The resolutions of the Territorial Deputation with regard to the regulations which have been passed for administration of the missions will be declared null, void, and completely invalid.

Article 3. The missionary Fathers will take exclusive charge of the temporalities of the respective missions, as they have done up to now, and the commissioners will hand over the documents concerning their administration to these same religious, who will make the appropriate observations.

Article 4. The previous article is not to be used to hinder the power of the Director of Colonization to act in accordance with the instructions given him by the Federal Government.[141]

Article 5. The present plan is to be entirely subject to the Federal Government for its approval.

139. The "first constitutional Alcalde" at Monterey in 1835 was David Spence. (Bancroft, *California*, III, p. 673.)
140. Captain Pablo de la Portilla was Captain of the Mazatlán Cavalry Company long stationed at San Diego. From 1831 he became nominal Commandant at San Diego. There is a brief review of his career in Bancroft, *California*, IV, p. 782.
141. An apparent inconsistency in the plan will be noticed here. Article 3 gave charge of the mission temporalities to the missionaries, whereas the instructions, which Article 4 said were not to be hindered, gave the Director of Colonization orders to take over all mission property. Figueroa points this out on pp. 80–81 of his *Manifesto*.

Article 6. The forces in insurrection will not put aside their arms until they see the above articles in effect, and they set themselves up as protectors of the honest administration of justice and of the respective authorities.

Signatures here[142]
Juan Gallardo
Manuel Arzaga, Secretary

[Copy—Los Angeles, March 7, 1835]

This defamatory libel has no more foundation than slander. If Torres and Apalátegui were not so despicable and cowardly that they deny being the authors of the plan, I should have demanded damages from them as false slanderers, apart from the criminal case that is being prepared against them as conspirators, disturbers of the public order, and promoters of sedition. But since I cannot use this recourse that the law allows me to chastise the insolence of these wretched fellows, I shall denounce them before the inexorable tribunal of public opinion, contradicting with the language of truth the catalogue of lies that they fashioned in their contemptible farrago.

First they assert that a crowd of citizens met with the object of agreeing upon means to save the Territory from the evils that it is suffering under my administration. This is the first political blasphemy of these fools. The citizens who they say met are some adventurers who have just arrived in the country from the State of Sonora to seek their fortunes, because they had no employment at all. Torres and Apalátegui were the same. They have just arrived in the Territory, and they do not know or understand how it is governed. Fools! Could they not even realize that the Californians obey me more from love and with pleasure than because of

142. The names of the signers are not given in the *Manifesto*.

the authority I exercise? Do they not realize the scorn and general hatred in which they are held? Are they not aware of the fact that no Californian took part in their riot, in spite of the fact that they incited them to do so for seven months, counting from September to March? Are they not aware that those they did win over returned to order without the necessity of using force? Have they not themselves experienced the lenience with which I have treated them, in spite of their crimes? Do they not know that since they rebelled against my military authority it became my duty to judge them and I have renounced this right, so as not to find myself obliged to pronounce judgment, although legally, against my declared enemies? Can these be the evils that the Territory is suffering under my administration? Idiots; if they had a shred of integrity they would not lie so shamelessly!

And what right do citizens have to hold disorderly meetings, break the laws that regulate society, and attack public authority? In the writings of which legal commentator has Señor Torres read such doctrines? Is he going to try to apply in politics the knowledge that he possesses of pharmacy or the specifics that the pharmacopoeia describes? Did he perhaps think that his plan would be obeyed as exactly as his prescriptions at the druggist's? Well, he made a grievous mistake, and it is to be hoped that this event will make him take warning and return to helping suffering humanity by again joining the throng of physicians from whose ranks he deserted.

Continuing the description of the famous plan, its authors assert that I have not fulfilled various orders which the Federal Government sent me to improve the lot of the inhabitants here. Liars; they talk like parrots! If they spoke with some basis and said what the Federal orders are that I have left undone, I would reply; but the fact that the fault is not mentioned proves it is calumny.

The second clause of consideration number one in the preamble to their plan claims that, exceeding the limits of the powers that the laws grant me, I illegally reassumed the civil and military commands against the Federal system. Barbarians; in what way have I gone beyond the limit of my powers? Do they not know that joining together again the civil and military commands was a power granted to me by the Federal Government of the Union and that it has been able to do this without breaking any law, for it is expressly authorized in the law of June 23, 1813, Article 5, Title 3?[143] And how does this measure oppose the Federal system? Not at all; for if it did two Presidents of the Republic would be needed, one military and the other civilian. Do these two commands correspond to the provisions of any of the three powers into which the sovereignty of the nation is divided? Certainly not, for both are part of the executive power. Then we must infer that the authors of this invective are fools who do not know what the Federal system is.[144]

The third clause of consideration number one in the preamble to the plan is that I made a scandalous monopoly out of the law of secularization, reducing the products of the missions to an exclusive trade, and that I took advantage of the Deputation so that they should establish the law according to my desires. Imposters; how will they prove such atrocious calumnies? What does the monopoly consist of, or what does Señor Torres mean by monopoly? Where is this exclusive trade? It has only existed in the fantastic plan of Torres, and if he had any sense of shame he would not lie with such effrontery before the nation. How did I take advantage of the Deputation? I have already mentioned that, far from seeking the drafting of the secularization regulation, I opposed it and openly held it back for more than six months. But against this indisputable evidence the Apothecary wanted to show off, but he did not want to subject himself to giving any proof of what he said, because it seemed enough to him to give credence to his calumny by simply writing it down.

The fourth clause in consideration number one in the preamble to the plan is limited to affirming that I am breaking the regulations of the Commissariat, that I dispose of the soldiers' pay as I wish without the knowledge of the officer in charge of the Treasury, and without the formalities established by the laws and regulations. Señor Apothecary, in what way or why have I broken the Commissariat regulation? Is it because I have taken care to see that it is fulfilled exactly, and that the Subcommissariat and

143. The section of the Spanish Law of June 23, 1813, which Figueroa wishes to cite is in Chapter 3, Article 5. It runs as follows: "The office of Political Chief will as a general rule be separated from the military command in each province. But at places which are threatened by the enemy, or in any case in which the preservation or reestablishment of public order and general tranquility and security require it, the Government, which is charged by the Constitution with the internal and external security of the state, will be able to reunite the military and political commands temporarily, reporting to the Cortes the reasons that it has had for doing so." For the Law of June 23, 1813, see Dublán and Lozano, *Legislación*, I, pp. 413–424.

144. Governor Figueroa appears to be asking here whether the civil and military commands are part of more than one of the three powers, executive, legislative, and judicial, which have to be kept separate under the Mexican Constitution of 1824. He answers that both are part of the executive power—and therefore, he implies, joining them together does not violate the Federal system.

Custom House are regulated according to the system of accounting and reckoning prescribed by the laws? Is it because I have not left these important offices in the confusion and disorder that they have been in since they were created, until my appointment to the command of this Territory? Is it, finally, because I audit the payment of sums and do not permit them to be misapplied? Let the imposters say how I have broken the regulation. The official in charge of the Treasury and the commanders and paymasters of the military forces under my orders can say if I have ever interrupted their work; they can say whether, before I was in command of this Territory, there was the same care in settling and liquidating the accounts of the troops as there is now; they can say whether at any time before I took command there has been such order and method in the fair distribution of money, and above all, here is what the present Subcommissary says:

Monterey
June 30, 1835

I certify that during the time I have had this position, from October 7 of last year until today, the management and direction observed with regard to this office under my charge by Brigadier General José Figueroa, Commandant and Political Chief of this Territory, have been only the supervision provided in the laws and regulations of the administration of the public Treasury. And so that it may be a matter of record, and for whatever purpose it may serve, I give these presents at the request of the party concerned in Monterey on June 30, 1835.

José María Herrera

I defy Torres and Apalátegui, and anyone else who wishes, to prove that I have committed the slightest fault in the management of the federal Treasury or the pay of the corps. It would be enough for me to reply to such an atrocious accusation

that the responsibility belongs to the Subcommissary and the paymasters, in whose charge the sums are; but in spite of this I wish, and it is my desire, to submit to an examination of my responsibility whenever someone attempts it with positive facts.

The second consideration in the preamble to the plan can be summarized as stating that the Deputation does not have the power to pass regulations on a law as it has done on the law of secularization. I have proved that the Deputation could and should have proposed the secularization regulation because it is one of its attributes according to the law of June 23, 1813, Articles 1, 14, and 16, Chapter 2.[145]

Another cause that brought on the plan is the decadence of the missions because of the withdrawal of the natives and because mission property was going to be given to them. This indeed is a powerful motive for Torres' revolution, because distributing the property amongst its owners will result in their not allowing it to be taken from them, and then the Cosmopolitan Company would be left without funds at its disposal. For this reason the wise Torres, as a large share-

145. Article 1 of Chapter 2 of the Law of June 23, 1813, states that the Provincial Deputation has the duty of establishing town councils in towns lacking them if certain conditions, such as size of the population, are met. Article 14 states that the Provincial Deputation is to furnish the Government with suitable plans for the development of agriculture, industry, trade, and commerce. Article 16 instructs Provincial Deputations overseas to bring inhabitants living scattered "in valleys and mountains" together in towns and to suggest methods of providing them with land and the means of cultivating it. This article clearly refers to the long-established desire of the Spanish Government to settle nomadic and scattered Indian tribes in towns. None of these articles, however, would appear to support Figueroa's point that the Territorial Deputation had the right to propose secularization regulations for the missions.

owner, wanted to get hold of the property of the missions by means of a revolution. An excellent idea but a vain one, for it did not work.

Also noted as a cause is the fact that the commissioners, by advancing their own private interests, are ruining the property of the missions to the detriment of the natives, who have acquired it by their labor. And does not Señor Torres immediately admit that the natives are the owners of this property? We shall soon see, however, how he tries to seize it from them. And how does he describe the damage that the commissioners have done to the missions? By making use of the terrible weapon of calumny. The commissioners will give proof of their conduct by their results, and it is not time yet to analyze them.

Taking the above causes for granted, they approved the plan, whose first article was to declare that I am unworthy of public confidence, in order to remove me from civil and military control, transmitting the military command to Captain Pablo de la Portilla and the civil command to the first Alcalde of Monterey. It is a fact that the rebels Torres and Apalátegui declared me to be unworthy of public confidence, but the public—that is, all the inhabitants of California except for a very few Cosmopolites—honored me with more confidence than I deserve. It would be ridiculous for me to take up my time by criticizing Torres' filthy scheme. I shall only make an analysis of the distribution of commands. The civil command was to be given to the Alcalde, for although in no case does the law call for this, it was desirable to disorganize the Government completely in order to open the way for Señor Híjar, who was to be called after the triumph, on the pretext of having been appointed Political Chief and

of being the only man capable of making the Territory happy. The senior member of the Deputation, who in the absence of the Political Chief is to carry out his duties, according to the law of May 6, 1822,[146] was not suitable, according to the shrewd foresight of the Apothecary, and for this reason he tacitly declared him to be unworthy of public confidence. The military command was given to Captain Portilla so as to deceive him, keep him occupied, and involve him in this way; meanwhile, there appeared on the scene Engineer, Lieutenant Colonel, Adjutant Inspector, and Assistant Director of the Colony, etc., etc., José María Padrés, who was to have taken over the military command by order of succession and because General Figueroa was to have been ill and ready to march to Mexico. There is no doubt that the plan was marvelously worked out! A production worthy of Torres!

The second article of the plan declares the resolutions of the Deputation referring to the administration of the missions to be null, void, and invalid. This gets to the root of the matter, Doctor. What will Señor Híjar say about this method of legislating? I am sure that he would not be worried, as he was when the Deputation passed the resolutions that Lawmaker Torres is annulling.

The third article orders the return to the missionary Fathers of the administration of temporalities. Who would believe that there is a sinister intent here? I am going to show that there is. If Torres knew,

146. The senior member of the Territorial Deputation in 1835 was José Antonio Carrillo, who was representing Upper California in the Mexican Congress at this time. The second in seniority was José Antonio Estudillo, who was apparently too sick in August 1835 to take his place in the Deputation. For the Law of May 6, 1822, see n. 34 above.

as I do, the probity of the missionaries, he would not have insulted them by encouraging them with the tiresome inducement of administering the temporalities, which they have spontaneously renounced on numerous occasions. It is not sufficiently attractive to get them involved in a disastrous revolution, even if the offer were genuine, but besides the affront he does to the probity of the Fathers, he is trying to deceive them, as if they were children, by making them into the passive instruments of his depredations. Perfidious hypocrites; they do not fear to offend sound reason and therefore make a pretense of offering what they are least thinking of carrying out. How can they offer to restore the administration of temporalities to the missionaries when, according to Article 4, which follows in the plan, they are not to obstruct the powers of the Director of Colonization, according to the instructions he received from the Federal Government? Do not these instructions provide in their first article for the taking over of all mission property? In that case, what will the Fathers have to administer? Is not this openly attempting to deceive?

Do these fools think that we do not understand their game? Have I not clearly proven that the instructions given to Híjar by the Minister of Relations were obtained by taking him unawares, so as to strip the California Indians of their property?[147] Have I not made a petition to the Federal Government on the unconstitutionality of that measure, so that it may be revoked? Have I not demonstrated with facts and figures that the real aim of the colonizing expedition is to seize the property of the

missions? Are the plans and schemes of the Cosmopolitan Company unknown, by any chance? Is not the contract by which the missions are condemned to pay for the brigantine *Natalia* public and notorious? Is it not certain that the country property belonging to the Pious Foundation of these same missions is going to pay for this ship, because the Director of Colonization and his gang wanted it that way?[148] Is it not certain that in addition to this burden, and the fact that national funds have been used to fit out the *Natalia* expedition, the nation is being asked to pay the passage of the colonists who came in it and the freight for their baggage? And have the missions or the Federation received any benefit or can they hope for any benefit from so many exactions? None . . . absolutely none. But after all, Torres and Apalátegui would say, it does not cost anything to take advantage of and deceive the Fathers if they allow it, by offering them the administration of the temporalities. They will contribute to the overthrow of the Government and later they will fall themselves. Such is the extravagance of their pretensions.

I could go on to make other observations on the third article of the plan, but it would tax the patience of the public. It should be noted that in this article they offer the missionary Fathers the administration of the temporalities, and further on they contradict themselves in the following way: "4. The previous article is not to be used to hinder the power of the Director of Colonization to act in accordance with the instructions given him by the Federal Government." Ah, villains, here the whole secret of your unbridled greed is laid bare. I have already mentioned, as is recorded in several places in

147. The proof advanced by Figueroa and the Deputation may be found on pp. 41–42 of the *Manifesto*. It would appear to be no more than statements of their convictions.

148. For the details on this transaction, see n. 42 above.

this statement, that the instructions that they want to put into effect are contrary to the Federal Constitution, and that, under the pretext of executing them in the name of the Federal Government, the Cosmopolites wish to enrich themselves on the ruin of more than 20,000 persons, who are the legitimate owners of the mission property. This is the inevitable result if these instructions are put into effect by Señor Híjar. They are the only objective of the revolution, the only means by which the rebels could get hold of the property they want, since they have been unable to acquire it by honorable means.

In the fifth article, they submit their plan to the approbation of the Federal Government. This is a fiction to deceive the public, because the rebels have not taken the Government into account, nor would the Government in any case approve of attacks against authority, whatever the pretexts put forward by the promoters of sedition. Where has there been a Government that would approve of its own destruction by a despicable handful of frenzied demagogues? Who has confided to them the fate and governance of the citizens? Who has given them the power to pass judgment on or look into the accountability of the legally constituted authorities?

The sixth article is no less absurd. In it they make assurances that they will not lay down their arms until their program is put into effect, and they constitute themselves as protectors of the administration of justice and of the authorities. Who can make anything out of nonsense like this? Not even the wisest knight of the woeful countenance[149] would be capable of such bragging and political dexterity. They say they will not lay down

their arms until their program is put into effect, and at the moment that they issue their *pronunciamiento* they conceal themselves from the sight of the profane, leaving their squires to defend their oaths. Obviously, the cowards had to put on their show, and they were not to have to expose themselves to public expectations. And how is the part about the protection of justice and of the authorities to be understood, when a mortal blow is made against the body politic by cutting off its head, which is the Government? According to the way of thinking of knight-errants, that is the reason of unreason. Do we then have righters of wrongs? There is no doubt that there are some, indeed there are. The fact is that they have become annoying. Protectors of justice, imitate Sancho in the government of his island.[150]

I have stopped to analyze the plan that failed in Los Angeles because my honor is atrociously attacked, and although the criminals who proclaimed it are at the disposal of the Tribunal which is to judge them, I want the public to know the depravity of its authors, who came to the tragic end that can be seen in the following statement.

Pueblo of Los Angeles
March 7, 1835

To the Constitutional Alcalde

Juan Gallardo and Felipe Castillo, in the name of the armed force that appeared today, representing the rights of the people, come before you with due respect and say that: having been invited by citizens Antonio

149. A reference to Don Quixote.

150. Sancho Panza governed his island in *Don Quixote* with honesty and discretion. He was, as Cervantes put it, "the Flower and Mirror of all island-Governors." But possibly Figueroa is thinking of Sancho's decision to resign after a brief rule. "A Spade does better in My Hand than a Governor's Truncheon," Sancho remarked. See *Don Quixote*, Part II, Chapters 45, 49, 51, and 53.

Apalátegui and Francisco Torres to cooperate with our physical forces for the good and prosperity of the Territory of Upper California, as is shown by the plan they presented to the City Council, which was not adopted; and satisfied that that body must have considered the matter with greater judgment and maturity; and considering, at the same time, that it is the best and only means of avoiding an outbreak—we have agreed to bring forward, as indeed we do bring forward, the promoters of the affair, so that if their undertaking is reasonable they may justify themselves before the law and affirm their rights as designated by law. It being well understood that if the step taken is a criminal one, both your authority and a vindicated public will take into account the good intentions with which it was done and judge the case on its merits.

For this reason, we unanimously beseech you to absolve us by decreeing indulgence, a justice which we implore, asserting our respect for the laws.

For himself and those who are alarmed.

Felipe Castillo

[A copy—Alvarado]

The following documents are the reply that I sent to the City Council of Los Angeles, and a proclamation to the public:

San Juan Bautista
March 13, 1835

City Council of the Pueblo of Los Angeles

By your official communication of March 7 I am informed of the disagreeable occurrences that have taken place in your community and of the audacity of Francisco Torres and Antonio Apalátegui who, not content to live peacefully under the protection of the laws, are constantly conspiring against the society that nourishes them. I have examined their plan, and however much they have disguised their ambitious objectives they cannot conceal how passionately they want to devour the property of the unhappy mission natives. For this reason, and because they regard my person as an obstacle to their schemes, they seek my removal from the civil and military command. For this reason they are annulling the resolutions of the Territorial Deputation, which prevented the robbery of the property, and finally, for this reason, in the fourth article of their plan, they decide to put the Director of Colonization in possession of mission property in accordance with the Government's instructions. Here is the deadly poison with which those adventurers want to sacrifice the Territory. The real and only objective of their plan is to get hold of the property of the missions to satisfy their greed, at the cost of the sweat of the Californians. I, who have resolutely defended this property, am the target for their shots; but it does not matter, I shall do my duty even though I am sacrificed, so that the Californians are not defrauded.

I defend the justice, liberty, security, and property of citizens; my cause is that of the people and the laws, they speak for me. I support the Government that I have been given. If I abuse my authority or commit some crime, let me be accused before the Government itself, or before the court which is to judge me. If I have been unworthy of public confidence I am ready to leave power, but into the hands of a competent authority and one whom the law has empowered in such a case. However, I shall never leave it in the hands of an unruly mob, who only call on order to subvert it and on the laws to break them.

I have offered to the Californians to leave my command, and I am ready to do so. I have sent in my resignation to the Federal Government, and the Territorial Deputation has interposed its respectable influence so that a successor may be appointed Political Chief. The decision will soon come and desires will be satisfied; but in the meantime it is the duty of every citizen to respect and support my authority.

Although you have realized how monstrous the plan is, and the end it is aimed at, it has been necessary for me to make these observations in order to confirm your judicious opinion, and to make the persons who became involved in the revolt understand it, by informing them that their prompt return to order gives me an understanding of their worthy intentions, and that they were only taken advantage of and deceived by the perfidious Torres and Apalátegui, who are enemies of the happiness of the people and of any government. Those who returned to order have given me evidence, which assures me of their good conduct in future, by turning their corrupters over to the hands of the authorities to be tried in accordance with the laws. All those individuals involved in the *pronunciamiento* who desisted the same day are pardoned in the name of the Federal Government, which I shall inform, provided they do not again become mixed up in revolution or riots disturbing the peace. They should return to live in peace in their homes under the guarantee of the laws and protection which is hereby offered them, and they should denounce any person who, under any pretext, tries to disturb public order.

It remains for me to render to your City Council and honorable citizens the due homage of my gratitude and respect for your heroic conduct and the noble firmness with which you refused to take part in the movement, which might momentarily have disturbed public tranquility. I therefore offer Your Honors for such eminent service my most heartfelt thanks, and recommend that you redouble your care and vigilance for public safety, and not permit order to be disturbed under any pretext invented by slander.

I recommend very strongly that the persons of the criminals Torres and Apalátegui be well secured, and that the case against them be substantiated as soon as possible, for although jurisdiction over it comes within the military branch, I suppose that the Alcalde has prepared the trial and must substantiate the case until sentence is passed.

If Your Honors should need the assistance of further armed force for this or other objects in the public service, you may request it of Lieutenant Colonel Nicolás Gutiérrez until the division which is marching to your area, to make certain that tranquility is assured, arrives.

I have the pleasure of informing Your Honors of all this in reply to your note of March 7 with which you sent me the plan of the rebels and the replies exchanged in this respect.

God and Liberty.
José Figueroa

Monterey
March 16, 1835

The Commandant General and
Political Chief of Upper California
to the Inhabitants of the Territory

Fellow Citizens:

The genius of evil[151] has appeared among you, spreading the deadly poison of discord. The enemies of order, jealous of the happiness that this people has enjoyed, and not satisfied with the blood of their compatriots that they have spilled in the interior of the Republic, brought to the Californians the baneful gift of anarchy. The repeated proofs they received that the Californians are not giving way to their iniquitous projects has irritated their presumptuous pride, and they wish to sacrifice them at whatever cost. This is the sum and substance of the benefits that Híjar, Padrés, Torres, Berdusco, and others brought to California; they want to remove its tranquility from a country that was progressing in the shade of peace and confidence, in order to sink it in the disasters of civil war.

Citizens, these are the grandiose projects that engage the heated imagination of those men. From the time they landed on the beaches of the Territory they have been secretly plotting its ruin, until, on the 7th of this month, they removed the veil from their excessive ambitions. In the community of Los Angeles a number of individuals from Sonora, corrupted by Francisco Torres and the Spaniard Antonio Apalátegui, issued a plan of conspiracy against the Territorial Government. That famous miscarriage of calumny abounds in atrocious and cunning scandals and falsehoods, attempting to delude the people so as to lead them on into disobedience, destroy the

151. The expression "genius of evil" was frequently used in Mexico at this period when referring to the political turbulence of the times.

prestige of authority, and attack the persons who exercise it. This is the sum of all the accusations which they lavish on me, and which I propose to refute by means of a manifesto as soon as my public duties permit me to do so.

In the meantime, however, I shall point out their pretensions: They ask for my separation from power because I was opposed to their squandering the mission property, and because Señor Híjar wants to put himself in my place. They use the trick of electing the first Alcalde of Monterey as Political Chief, without remembering that in the absence of this officer, the law calls upon the senior member of the Deputation,[152] but in order to conceal the ambition of the aspirant it is necessary to disorganize the Government completely so as to open the way for him. They invite Captain Portilla to be Commandant, in order later to substitute Señor Padrés, who wants the position. They annul the resolutions of the Territorial Deputation, because these guarantee the Indians' enjoyment of the properties which they wish to take away from them. They suspend the secularization of the missions, apparently returning to the missionaries the administration of the temporalities, because they believe they can deceive them into becoming involved in the revolt. And, finally, they put the Director of Colonization in possession of mission property, so that he can dispose of it according to the instructions that the Federal Government gave him, as if the public were not aware that that measure is unconstitutional because it leads to depriving more than 20,000 persons of their property.

In brief, all of this is desired by force, which is the law of highwaymen; the Constitution and the laws are directly attacked in it, all the guarantees of society are broken, the pact is dissolved, leaving the fate of the people to the whim of the daring usurpers, who want to be dominant even against the will of the Federal Government, which they pretend to respect, and of the citizens whom they wish to subdue.

152. See n. 146 above.

I have briefly related the object of the revolution, which fortunately expired in its cradle. As soon as they realized the crime they were about to commit, when the City Council of Los Angeles disapproved of their conduct, and when no son of California took part in their erring, even those who were involved in it gave up the affair, submitted to the Government, and handed over the conspirators; justice will classify their crime so as to apply the punishments that the laws they have broken impose.

The tranquility that momentarily could have been disturbed by these events was immediately reestablished. But the attorneys of anarchy do not cease to preach discord, nor will I lose sight of their death-dealing plans against liberty.

Fellow citizens, this is all that has happened. As far as my own person is concerned, the public will pass judgment on what I have done, the Government will call me to account if perchance I am responsible, and the court which has jurisdiction will apply the law to me if I have committed a crime. I have resigned from the position of Political Chief, and the Territorial Deputation has interposed its good offices so that my successor may be appointed. The decision will soon come, and you will see me obediently deposit into his hands the power that the President of the Republic delegated to me in order to govern this Territory. Meanwhile, fellow citizens, do not believe the deceitful proposals of the enemies of order and of the Government who, blinded by ambition and greed, invoke the sacred name of justice in order to dishonor it, and squander your blood and treasure. Continue peaceful and united in the enjoyment of your social rights. That is true happiness and the only reward to which my ambition aspires.

José Figueroa

Although the revolution appeared and expired on the same day in Los Angeles, it had ramifications headed by the leading participants. Under the pretext of establishing a colony, they sought to organize a force with which to support their claims.

In fact, they brought with them from Mexico City a large number of rifles and cartridges which the Government provided for them.[153] They tried to conceal this and various other preparations from me. I had discovered their schemes, and only tolerated them in the hope that they would reveal their crime more publicly or that they would give it up. I did not succeed in this, in spite of giving repeated proofs of my good will and patience, for the more I endeavored to persuade them to turn away from their crooked designs or the more I overlooked their plans, the more insolent they became, perhaps because they took my moderation to be weakness or cowardice.

So it was that, given encouragement by this confidence, they daily went ahead with their preparations, and even Señor Híjar himself, in spite of his seeming modesty, could not conceal the part he played in these movements. It was for this reason that he went to San Francisco Solano on a pretense of bringing the colony together, when he had always looked on it with the greatest indifference.[154] It was also for this reason that he sent to the Reverend Father President Narciso Durán, in February, under his signature, a copy of the nonsensical letter with which he replied to me on October 23.[155] It was for this reason that he concealed the activities of Berdusco and Lara who, in his name and under his immediate protection, were fomenting revolution. It was for this reason that Señor Híjar himself, without having received the command, made speeches to the Indians in the missions through which he passed,[156] exhorting them to defend the liberty which nobody was attacking. It was for this reason that he met with Torres, Berdusco, Lara, and Araujo at secret conferences at Bonifacio's house.[157] Finally, it was for this reason that he regarded with such scorn the proposals for peace that I made to him on various occasions, begging him to restrain his protégés so that I should not be forced to punish them, since I had already discovered their plans and was suspending all my moves out of consideration for his person. Whether, therefore, Señor Híjar was definitely protecting the revolution or whether he was the blind instrument of its authors, the fact is that his adherence to it was clear, and after I acknowledged, in friendly fashion and in various ways, his attachment to my enemies, he could inspire no confidence in me—for even doing him the favor of believing him to be innocent of the scheming of his henchmen, he is of so apathetic

153. Figueroa claimed (*Manifesto*, p. 66) that the colonists brought with them "200 rifles and a considerable supply of munitions of war." When they were finally disarmed at Sonoma, however, only 41 rifles were found, and of these only 25 were in working order. With the rifles were discovered three boxes of cartridges and a few other odds and ends of weapons. These weapons seem to have been provided by the Government for defense against the Indians at the exposed site where the colonists were to establish a town.

154. Figueroa's assertion that Híjar regarded the unification of the colony with indifference may be contrasted with Híjar's own words on the matter, reported in Figueroa's *Manifesto* (p. 64): "I am determined to continue with the colony until it is established at the place the Government desires."

155. Híjar's letter of October 23, 1834, is printed in Figueroa's *Manifesto* (pp. 34–37, 45–58), interspersed with Figueroa's comments, in the manner of the Mexican pamphleteering of the day.

156. When Híjar made speeches to the mission Indians on his way to meet Figueroa at Monterey, he was not aware that he was not going to be Governor, so that there is no justification for mentioning the fact that he was making speeches "without having received the command."

157. Possibly Juan B. Bonifacio, probably of Italian origin. Bancroft (*California*, II, p. 723) records that he died about 1834, leaving a widow and three children.

and insensitive a character that even his own existence would be a matter of indifference to him.

In view of this, and the outbreak of the revolution in visible fashion, what should be done with Señor Híjar? Is he not the rival whom my emulators put before me so as to hide their crimes and deceive the public? Should I permit him to make a mockery of my patience any longer? Should I endanger public tranquility more than I have done, because of an imprudent tolerance? I believed it was my duty to keep away any reason for disturbance, and this could not be done by letting the causes remain active. I was not in a position to wait until charges had been previously drawn up, because, in addition to the fact that it is difficult to prove precisely the secret crimes of revolutionaries in such matters, they are only waiting for a favorable moment to launch their attacks. The small military force that I have under my orders, and the numerous matters it must attend to in an area of over 1387 square miles, is another motive that forced me to act with more energy. For all of these reasons I ordered Lara and Berdusco arrested, I suspended Híjar and Padrés from their positions as Directors of the Colony and made them return to Mexico City at the orders of the Federal Government, and wrote the following note to Híjar:

San Juan Bautista
March 13, 1835

The revolution that Francisco Torres went to promote—as I informed Your Honor in friendly fashion, telling you that your friends wanted to involve you so as to flout the government—has finally taken place. This occurrence, which was revealed to me ahead of time, and other antecedents which I told you about, all of them designed to conspire against public order and against the laws, make it my duty to issue orders to assure public tranquility, which is constantly threatened. For the prudent behavior which I have used with all of them and the frankness with which I have revealed their mistaken demands to Your Honor, so that you might keep them within the boundaries of duty, have not been sufficient to restrain the audacity of your followers. In spite of the fact that the projects which they were plotting to obtain their ends came to my attention previously, I have kept silent so that in no case might I be blamed for being violent. But now that the curtain has been drawn aside, they have very quickly received a severe disappointment. The reckless fellows whom Torres managed to corrupt by surprise admitted to their mistake, and they themselves handed him over, and his associate Apalátegui also, as prisoners to justice.

As a consequence of these events, I have arranged that Your Honor and Adjutant Inspector José María Padrés are to be suspended from the assignment that the Federal Government confided in you, and that you are to hand over the arms, munitions, property, and everything that you have in your charge to Ensign Mariano G. Vallejo, and that you are to march immediately, at the disposition of the Federal Government, before which you will answer the charges that result from your conduct from the time of your entry into this Territory.

I have the honor of informing you for your information and compliance.

God and Liberty.
José Figueroa

Señor Híjar replied with the following communication:

San Francisco Solano
March 17, 1835

Political Chief General José Figueroa

Your Honor informs me in your letter of March 13 that finally the revolution which Francisco Torres went to promote, as you informed me privately, has broken out, and that the promoters of it have been arrested and that this forces you to take steps to assure tranquility. That you have arranged, in fact, that Adjutant Inspector José María Padrés and I are to be suspended from the assignment which the Federal Government entrusted to us, and are to hand over to Ensign Mariano G. Vallejo the arms, munitions, property, and everything we have in our possession; and, finally, we are to march immediately, at the disposition of the Federal Government, to answer charges against us as a result of our conduct from the time of our entry into the Territory.

In regard to the first point, Your Honor will permit me to inform you that the revolution of which you speak seems to be purely imaginary. I shall never be able to persuade myself that Señor Torres, who was passing through bearing important papers for the Federal Government, should have begun an aimless revolution in a country in which he has no connections or acquaintances. I do not see more in all this than a mystery which time will clear up; if the veil has been drawn back for Your Honor, it still remains opaque enough to me, but I hope that it will soon be rent, that things will appear as they are in reality and that everything will become as clear as day.

I must suppose that some hot-headed and justly resentful colonists may have wanted to revolt, but I do not understand how this could be of great importance to me, as if I had incited them or taken part in the revolution. Nevertheless, Your Honor has me suspended, striking me the most terrible blow and wounding me to the quick. Your Honor has contrived to sully my reputation, which I value more than all of life. I am made to appear as if I had committed crimes or offenses that I have certainly not committed, but I solemnly vow that I shall drag my persecutor, whoever he may be, before the competent courts, where I shall demand suitable satisfaction.

Your Honor is well aware that if I stayed in this Territory it was only because of the repeated entreaties and pleas of Your Honor, of a Committee of the Deputation, and of other persons whom Your Honor knows. You also knew that I was about to leave the Territory within a few days, and that consequently I

had no interest in continuing to direct the colony. I am making this slight digression so that Your Honor may understand that the deep emotion which is devouring me did not arise because I have been suspended from a position that I was about to leave, but because of the insulting way in which it has been done.

I have always performed with distinction many delicate and important assignments and the various governments which have made use of my modest services have been satisfied with my conduct, which has never merited the slightest reproach. My public career, well known in the interior, had not been given a single blemish, and this was my one glory, but it seems that Heaven had reserved Your Honor to inflict the most atrocious insult upon me. Yes, General, if I did not hope to vindicate myself, I would have shot myself, so as not to drag out an opprobrious existence, and so as not to appear an object of scorn before the eyes of my fellows.

I do not find that Your Honor has the power to suspend me, but it is necessary to yield to force; consequently your orders will be obeyed in full and I am ready to leave as soon as Your Honor furnishes the means for me to do so (I wish it were tomorrow). I shall present myself before the Federal Government with the serenity born of a tranquil conscience, and there I hope to confound my accuser.

I shall bring this communication to a close by informing Your Honor that we have suffered unheard-of outrages, we have been treated in a scandalous manner, one which would not be used with a band of outlaws, the inalienable rights of man that our Constitution guarantees being rudely attacked. It would all have been avoided, and I would have had the arms, munitions, and everything else handed over, without the necessity for pushing anybody about, if Señor Vallejo had shown me Your Honor's communication. But he purposely wanted to make us feel the full weight of arbitrary power, treating us more like fugitives from justice than like Mexicans. Patience, General; perhaps one day the laws will take command.

I have transcribed Your Honor's communication for the Adjutant Inspector's information, and I believe that with all of this I have answered your letter of March 13.

God and Liberty.

José María de Híjar

Señor Híjar's confusion is so great that he tries to obscure even the public acts of his protégés by doubting them, as if I were a play actor who occupied myself with trifles, or by supposing that the event that I officially inform him about is a diversion. Note how he says that Torres was taking important papers to Mexico, unequivocal proof of the great confidence this adventurous Aesculapius inspired in him. And so he adds that he can never be persuaded that Torres would have started a revolution without object and in a country where he is unknown. What hypocrisy! It is already clearly proven that Torres was the immediate agent of the rebellion and that it had its objective worked out. Why did it not break out before Torres reached Los Angeles? What was the objective of his untimely friendship with Apalátegui, with this crony of the Sonorans? And why did these same Sonorans, repenting their punishable uprising, point to Torres and Apalátegui as their seducers and principal instigators and hand them over as prisoners to the authorities?

However much Señor Híjar uses fallacious arguments and evasions, he will never be able to persuade the Californians that he had no part in this affair, which I myself informed him about beforehand through the reliable information that I had of their treacherous schemes. By throwing stones and keeping his hands hidden or shielding himself behind straw men, he thinks he can evade the severity of the laws, but he is mistaken; every step he takes condemns him, as we have seen.

He predicts that he will drag me before

the courts. All of the necessary antecedents will now go to the courts, and I am ready to appear and confound with reason, the law, and justice the man who tried to trample my authority under foot. The probity of the judges cannot be less than favorable to one who has preserved the integrity of the Republic and maintained peace and the law in this Territory.

Señor Híjar was never asked to stay in the country.[158] I was only interested, as were the other gentlemen at the conferences, that he should not lead the tired colonists to Lower California, as their Directors imprudently or supposedly wanted.

If the services of which Señor Híjar boasts have been useful elsewhere, here his concealed indifference and underhanded plans to attack the civil government by surprise have been detrimental. And if the minds of the Californians had not been so discerning and my confidence in them had proved vain, the Cosmopolites would undoubtedly have been victorious, because their leaders are skilled in the art of intrigue and know how to take advantage of their flowery and empty rhetoric. But their energy and open and loyal valor is so slight that they do not have enough even for the cowardly action of shooting themselves—as Señor Híjar, with his anglophile mania,[159] says that he would already have done if he had not hoped to vindicate himself.

He denies me the power to suspend

158. This statement contradicts Figueroa's own narrative of what took place (*Manifesto*, p. 61), where he says: "We begged him [Híjar] to put aside his resentment and remain with us on good terms."

159. By the expression "anglophile mania," Figueroa may be referring to the belief in eighteenth-century Europe that suicides were undertaken more willingly in England than elsewhere. Voltaire speaks of this in his article on Cato in his *Philosophical Dictionary* (in the 1824 edition [London], this article is in Vol. II, pp. 93–104).

him, and previously he has given assurances that he submits to the Civil Government and recognizes its authority.

The unheard-of outrages of which he complains were none other than the absolutely necessary measures to collect the arms and munitions which Señor Padrés was hiding, and to prevent him from calling out the colonists and making it necessary to use force. Thus no one was injured or even bruised through the tact and military prudence with which Ensign Mariano G. Vallejo discharged this assignment. Now it can be seen that the attack on the inalienable rights of man was nothing more than having prevented the improper use of arms, but it was a resounding phrase which could not be omitted. I say no more about the note.

Received aboard the Sardinian frigate *Rosa,* which was in San Francisco Bay, Señores Híjar, Padrés, Berdusco, Lara, and some others were taken to San Pedro and transferred to the Anglo-American schooner *Loriot,* on which they left in May with Señores Buenaventura Araujo, Francisco Torres, and Antonio Apalátegui for San Blas, at the disposition of the Federal Government.

The colonists have improved their position since their leaders, who were enslaving them and leading them to their total ruin, have been separated from them. Now settled where it suits them best, assisted as much as possible by this Government and sheltered by the Californians, they are not in need of subsistence, nor do the industrious lack something to do, and the advances that some of them have made are already noteworthy.

Peace has been strengthened and, with it, its inestimable benefits. It seems unnecessary to mention that the Cosmopolitan Company was dissolved, of its own accord, and because it was essentially founded on the triple representation of Híjar and Padrés as its founders and first shareholders, Directors of the colony, and leaders of the Territory. The colony and the civil and military governorships were, therefore, the foundation of the Company and the most powerful support for the grandiose speculation they had devised, violating the laws which prohibit Government employees from being merchants.

José María Padrés has been the most underhanded and active agent of this enterprise. I have already mentioned that with his projects for the missions, which were not under his control, and his devious conduct, he disturbed the peace of the Territory in 1830, and was the cause for the disavowal of the legitimate administration of Lieutenant Colonel Manuel Victoria by some rash citizens, for which he received the disapproval of the Federal Government. But in spite of this, he managed by intrigue to return with the colony, with the title of Adjutant Inspector, to this Territory, from which he had been expelled. I have touched on this matter so that it may be seen how long he has been concerned with commercial schemes for California.

It is to be presumed that this same officious gentleman, with the influence that he had on the mind of Señor Híjar, and the influence he prided himself on enjoying over His Excellency Vice-President Gómez Farías, would be the one who intrigued in Mexico City so that the Federal Government should not ask for information from this Territorial Deputation, nor from me, about the resources available here for the settlement and support of colonists, who came out with wages to be paid until after they had been finally settled for a year—having to be supplied, as I have said, with grain, cattle, and implements. For all of this, very heavy sums had to be spent, which could not be paid by the public Treasury of the Territory, which does not even take care of half of its ordinary requirements, and which did not have, nor does it yet have, a Federal order for such supplies. But since a report from this Civil Government could not be favorable to the aims of those who in Mexico City speculated with the property of these natives, it was not asked for. Meanwhile, they concocted a pretty scheme of destruction, which consisted in secularizing the missions in order to remove the guardianship of the natives from the missionary Fathers and leave the Indians defenseless, while the Director and Assistant Director of the colony, with civil and military control in their hands, and under the pretext of helping and settling the colonists, disposed of the property of the Indians as they wished—for with the shepherds away, it is easy for the wolves to devour the flock.

But Providence frustrated such misguided projects by a series of events that the Directors, who from the time they left Mexico City encountered difficulties in their ill-considered enterprise of the colony, and their vaunted Cosmopolitan Mercantile Company—as poor in funds as it was rich in hopes, and notable for the pedantry of its name—were unable to foresee. This Company had the misfortune to have its brigantine *Natalia* wrecked on this coast a few days after it had anchored in this port[160] because it was not well enough tied up, and because of lack of skill and the carelessness of its owners.

We have seen that Señor Híjar, on the pretext of his assignment, and relying on some unconstitutional, unwise, and possibly surreptitious instructions, wanted to take possession of the wealth of the missions and attack the indisputable property rights of the natives. And we have seen that he disavowed the legal authority of the Deputation over communal property, and the supervision and vigilance that I had as Political Chief, charged with preserving the social guarantees from danger and with keeping the laws and seeing that they are kept. And I have related how he tried to make use of my authority as Commandant to degrade the national armed forces by making them serve his unjust pretensions by giving their aid and authority to the iniquitous plunder of property which was being plotted against the helpless Indian.

It is surprising to see the Directors of Colonization so set on their lamentable determination to seize other people's property that they are constrained to drag in by the scruff of the neck what they call the eminent domain of the Government, and to allege that the missions have no right to their property because they are moral bodies, and as such, incapable of acquiring property and even less of holding it.[161] What sublime philosophy and what very illusory theories revolutionaries have for getting hold of other people's property! More cowardly than bandits, they employ sophistry and empty and high-sounding words, and put on masks of patriotism and piety, when they out-

160. On December 21, 1834, the cables holding the *Natalia* broke in a strong north wind. It ran ashore and became a total wreck, with the death of three crew members.

161. The argument that the missions were "moral bodies" was put forward by the contemporary Mexican writer José María Luis Mora in his *Dissertation on the Nature and Application of Ecclesiastical Income and Property*, which first appeared in 1833. Mora held that institutions such as hospitals, colleges, missions, etc., administered the funds in their charge, but that these funds belonged to the public and consequently should be controlled by the Government, which represented the public. (Mora, *Obras sueltas*, I, pp. 223–224.)

rage their country and mock their religion. Once their school is open and they have proselytized the unwary and have sufficient power, there is no barrier that will stop them; they overcome everything with legal formulas and nothing is respected, nothing is sacred, except what belongs to their party. Can these gentlemen not see that if moral bodies cannot acquire or retain property, as they say, neither can the Government acquire it or retain it?[162] And do they not infer from their principles that the eminent domain of the Government is null in the case in which they invoke it here, for no one can give what he does not have? How many contradictions in eagerly trying to pass oneself off as learned and wanting to be rich by means of philosophy!

Whose attention would not be called to the fact that Señor Híjar says in his note of November 6 that the Spanish laws that protect the property of the Indians are at variance with our system? It should be said, rather, that they are at variance with the system of depredation that they had adopted. He wanted to undermine the wise Spanish law on the books which directs that sovereign enactments which tend to dispossess anyone of his property, without his being previously heard and defeated in a judgment against him, are to be obeyed but not executed.[163] And in spite of this, he claimed that the Indian, still ignorant, needy, and half wild, should be absolutely and identically equal in effective political rights to other citizens, perhaps in order to delude him better, or more easily to surprise him when he is off-guard. According to these principles, we should strike out from our codes laws that regulate the powers of parents over children, or that provide for the dominance of husband over wife in marriage, or those that discuss guardianship and tutelage of minors, fools, the insane, wastrels, and several others.

Carried to such an extreme, legal equality would unhinge society. Such is the fatal persistence in making everything equal in appearance, so as to render it unequal in substance, in order to destroy it, and so that only the intolerant and despotic fanaticism of pretended philosophers will prevail. This is the way our politicos and purveyors of sophistry are going, this is the course of these same gentlemen who deny the Indians their property rights over the holdings of the missions. But the plan was to overwhelm them with rights and deprive them of their possessions; this is the kind of philanthropy that was going to be applied to the California Indian.

Fortunately, the theories and high-sounding promises of the Directors of the Colony with their garrulous, proselytizing spirit, had no following whatever among sensible Californians and, despairing of being able to rely upon them for their revolutionary projects, they had recourse, as I have said, to winning over through their emissaries some immigrants from Sonora who had come to seek their fortunes in this Territory and were at Los Angeles. And, in truth, only in the minds of wretched adventurers could the aims of Torres and Apalátegui, who left here (from the very house where Señor Híjar was staying) with that special objective, find a welcome. But leading them astray and issuing a pronouncement was a mo-

---

162. Figueroa apparently did not understand Mora's views.

163. The traditional method of Spanish New World authorities, including Viceroys, of putting off the enactment of legislation from Madrid that they deemed unworkable was to declare "I obey but do not execute." Governor Figueroa's attitude toward the Government in Mexico City over secularizing the missions appears to follow this precedent.

mentary affair, and only served to bring down upon its authors and promoters general adverse criticism, so that public opinion would end by condemning them, and their immediate leaders would suffer the degrading humiliation of finding themselves taken prisoner and handed over to the inexorable arms of the law by the unwary Sonorans themselves, who quickly realized their error and the perfidy of those who had taken advantage of their position and abused their misplaced confidence.

The Directors of the Colony have denied having had any part in the criminal uprising I am talking about, which was promoted by their followers Torres and Apalátegui. But who in Monterey is ignorant of the fact that Torres was Híjar's favorite, and that he was one of those who, with Lara, Berdusco, and others, were the staff officers of the colony? Who can doubt that this quack doctor was one of Híjar's daily counselors, and that because of his great talent, his medico-political knowledge, his sly, cool disposition, and his hypocritical and underhanded character, he merited the high appreciation of his superiors? Híjar himself proves it when he confesses in his letter of March 17 that he had sent him to Mexico City with papers of the greatest importance. But there is more to it: in the lawsuit in the civil court of this capital, which was instituted against the Sonoran Miguel Hidalgo, as the carrier of certain letters sent by Torres from Los Angeles to Berdusco and others, it comes out that in the preliminary meetings which were held in the house of Antonio Trujillo[164] to arrange the pronouncement against my authority, it was clearly sug-

gested by Torres himself that the principal object of the rebels was to place Señor Híjar in control of the Civil Government and Señor Padrés in control of the Military Government. No one in the Territory has had any doubt about it—public opinion unanimously affirms it—and for this same reason, a very few days after Torres left for Los Angeles, Híjar and his followers left to join Padrés in San Francisco Solano in order to second in the north, with the colonists whom they could count on, the movements of the Sonorans in the south.

This was the strategic plan that they judged most suitable, but it failed them and they were completely disconcerted and confounded by public opinion, my vigilance, and the zeal and energy displayed by the worthy officers who serve under my orders, especially Ensign Vallejo, Commandmant of San Francisco Solano. And undoubtedly the Federal Government, at whose disposition I sent them with the other supporters of the rebellion, will bring serious charges against them.

Since the great question dealt with in this manifesto is of national, not local, interest, and because also it is the side on which my antagonists the speculators will attempt to stain my reputation, which I have managed to preserve unsullied, I could not avoid setting forth at length the narrative of the events and the exposition and refutation of the antisocial doctrines which they have tried to use to corrupt virgin California, so as to bathe her peaceful, fertile fields in blood, destroy the wealth of her missions, promote anarchy, and raise up on the ruins of the Territory these hypocritical politicians, patriarchs of revolution and disorder, with the abundant wealth of the Indians, which was acquired by their personal labor under the

164. Antonio Trujillo is not mentioned in Bancroft's *Pioneer Register*, but it is known that there were several Trujillos at Los Angeles.

direction and evangelical patience of their venerable missionary Fathers.

My constant duties and my very broken health must excuse me in the eyes of the public if I have inadvertently failed to touch upon any point necessary to form a complete judgment. I do not believe I have omitted anything essential. There are many impartial, on-the-spot-witnesses informed about this series of events, who can correct my mistakes and my inaccuracies, and discuss my errors and omissions, if I have involuntarily committed such faults.

Above all, my declared rivals, the Director and Assistant Director of the colony, José María Híjar and José María Padrés, are free to answer me and publish their substantiated accusations against me, and their imputations against the people of California, whom they have openly berated. We have freedom of the press, they pass for highly refined literary men and politicians, they have therefore the knowledge and the freedom to attack my manifesto rationally, defend their doctrines by lawful means, and clear their conduct, which in the opinion of many, and as is proved by the narrative of events and the picturesque and ridiculous creation of the Cosmopolitan Company, is more crooked, more commercial and monopolistic, than it is patriotic. How far removed are these feeble republicans, proud of their austerity, from the virtue, the disinterestedness of the Porfumios, the Cincinnati, the Papirii, and the Fabii.[165] Their words

are belied by their conduct and, in the midst of their pretended liberalism, these reactionary, despotic, and grasping men dissipate with their actions the illusion of their promises, and gradually lose the prestige which their ominous theories succeeded in introducing in the heedless childhood of our country.

Now is the time to be persuaded that these men were born to be common or garden poets, writers of romances and novels, and not directors of an enlightened and sober people. Men of this kind have caused Mexican blood to flow in torrents; their names stain the pages of our history. Anarchy, disorder, confusion, and ruin are the fruit of their efforts and the result of their theories, which are brilliant on the surface and thoroughly corrupt underneath.

Men steeped in revolutionary schemes and partisans of anarchical doctrines landed in this Territory at the head of wretched colonists whom they caused untold unnecessary suffering and privation by their wastefulness and bad management, as is notorious.

At their arrival I was at the head of the civil and military administration of the country, and I believe I did what I had to do in such critical circumstances. I restrained their pretensions, drew aside the curtain from their aims, revealed their imprudence, resisted their doctrines, confounded their presumptions, thwarted their projects, humbled their arrogance, destroyed their plans, curbed their audacity, extinguished the revolutionary torch that they had lit, saved the properties of the Indians and the wealth of the missions, and rescued the unfortunate colonists from the precipice to which they

---

165. Possibly Porfumios is an error for Porphurios or Porphyrius, a Greek Neoplatonist philosopher who edited the works of Plotinus and is mentioned in some of Bentham's writings (*Works*, VIII, p. 266). Lucius Quintus Cincinnatus is the hero of the early Roman Republic who left his plowing when called upon to save his country and, after conquering the enemy, returned forthwith to his farm. The Papirii and Fabii were both distinguished Roman *gentes*, which included many outstanding families going back to the earliest times.

were being led. And I preserved the peace, order, and well-being of this California, of this important part of the Republic, which requires particular care and a highly sensitive guardian, so that the suggestions of the many native and foreign adventurers who, like flashes of lightning in a stormy night, criss-crossing amongst us on all sides, do not launch it on a career of disorder.

From my childhood I have served in the ranks of those who fought for independence from its beginnings. With my slight talent and less instruction, with all my strength, with my blood and my health, I have contributed, so far as it has been possible for me, to the glories of the nation. The names of my rivals are only known in the annals of fratricidal strife, in civil disorders, in the farcical notions of the anarchists—that ominous sect, abominated in America and Europe,[166] which is the disgrace of our century. Permit me to put forward this comparison as a relief for my sense of honor, which has been so unjustly and scandalously maligned: there is a point in this manifesto which is so lacking in immediate and conclusive proof that only the personal opinion that everyone privately has of me and of Señor Híjar can sway the balance of opinion—I speak of the secret conference to which that gentleman invited me in his note of October 26.

I have tried to express myself, holding

166. It is to be noted that Figueroa is talking about anarchism before Pierre Joseph Prudhon is credited with making it into a conscious mass movement. The term anarchism had been in use since the middle of the eighteenth century. It was frequently used in Mexico at this time by conservatives to refer to liberals or federalists. Bentham, with whose works Figueroa appears to be familiar, was a vigorous opponent of anarchism.

strictly to the truth, and without paying back insult with insult. If in any part it is noticeable that my style is overly harsh or forceful, bear in mind that I am defending myself from slander, and that I am a soldier, who has passed his life in the hardships of arduous campaigns and in offices that were also military, and that consequently I am not accustomed to the flattering expressions and flowery rhetoric with which other writers, of more literary merit than I could possibly have, garnish their productions.

But this inadequacy of mine does not intimidate me. I am not a rhetorician or a politician. I am a Mexican soldier and I make no pretense at being a literary man. In a martial and plain style, at the same time exact and well considered, and as clearly as I can, I have tried to set down in writing the crafty schemes of the Directors of the colony and their turbulent Cosmopolite followers from every aspect.

I am not afraid of the malevolence of the stubborn, I speak before the public, at the theater of events, to my contemporaries, before all the on-the-spot witnesses. Everything is visible, I omit nothing essential, I produce all the correspondence and relate the events accurately. Pass judgment on my conduct, compare it with that of my adversaries, and bear in mind all the circumstances which I have brought out. This is what I beg of my readers; while I rest on the soundness of my intentions and the purity and justified legality of my procedures, I hope that THE SENSIBLE MEXICAN PEOPLE will do me justice and favor me with their unbiased opinion.

José Figueroa
Port of Monterey
September 4, 1835

Note

While this Manifesto was being printed, Brigadier General José Figueroa died on the 29th of this same September. As a consequence of this sad event, the Territorial Deputation decided that the following resolution should be inserted in this publication:

RESOLUTION

To perpetuate the memory of the deceased Brigadier General JOSE FIGUEROA, Commandant and Political Chief of Upper California, the Deputation of this Territory moved:

Monterey
October 9, 1835

Our Chief has died, the protector of the Territory, the Father of our California, our friend, our mentor, General José Figueroa. The citizens surround his deathbed and with their eyes fixed on his rigid corpse they are silent and sigh, weeping for the great man whom death has carried away from us. The sad, unfortunate news spreads rapidly, grief seizes everyone, and sorrow is general.

The doleful echo of the bells and the gloomy detonations of the guns bring forth the heart's most repressed tears; all is bitterness, all is grief. Californians weep for a beneficent father who has given incalculable encouragement to their prosperity, and who with unprecedented care and by dint of constant and unequaled labor promoted all the branches of public welfare. They weep for the man who extinguished the torch of discord and prevented this virgin land from being drenched in the blood of its sons; he who planted the olive of peace and cultivated in its shade all manner of virtues which are progressively unfolding in the loyal breasts of these inhabitants; he to whom our agriculture owes its security and advancement and our commerce its protection; he who knew how to repulse anarchy when it dared to land on our peaceful beaches; he who consoled the widow, sheltered the orphan, and helped the soldier; he

who protected merit and encouraged learning—in a word, he who labored to regulate our social order.

Even foreigners show by their grief the affection in which they held him and the high opinion they had formed of the superior genius who presided over us. The child of the wilderness, the unsophisticated Indian, shows us, although in primitive fashion, the sorrow he feels at so great a loss.

The name of General Figueroa is heard everywhere, his merits are recounted, his political judgment, his zeal and effective work for the public good, and his winning manners, with which he knew how to capture men's goodwill, are praised. His honesty and probity are recognized by the public, which declares him to be an eminent patriot and a highly worthy son of his country. Everyone commends and recognizes the great merits of General Figueroa; shall the Deputation of the Territory not show how much it joins in this feeling? I see in the worthy members who compose it unequivocal signs of the grief that the premature death of our beloved Chief is causing them. This sorrow is just, yes, it is just, it is laudable. The whole world should know it and see that in Upper California true worth is appreciated.

And now that we, worshiping the inscrutable decrees of Providence, have beseeched at the foot of the altar divine clemency for the man whom the right hand of the Omnipotent has taken from us, and now that all civil and military honors due him have been rendered, let us, worthy Deputies, give a public and eternal testimony of our love for General Figueroa. Let us lavish our esteem on his memory and do whatever we can in his name and honor. Let us make his glory and our regard immortal and gird his brow with a crown of evergreen. Yes, gentlemen, may Your Honors hear and approve the following proposals:

1. The portrait of General José Figueroa shall be placed in the Hall of Sessions of this Deputation as a proof of its appreciation for his great merit.

2. In order to perpetuate our grateful memory of Figueroa and the gratitude of this body, a durable monument will be raised, with a suitable inscription, in one of the most public and unobstructed sites in Monterey, and so that it may be done, the City Council will be appealed to by sending it these proceedings so that everything will be done under its direction and care, as may be expected from its unsullied patriotism, its noble feelings, and the love that it has professed for the man we mourn.

3. Three more copies will be made of this resolution, one to be given to the executors of our late General and Chief, another to be sent to his widow and children, and the third to go to the press so that it may be printed and published as a continuation of his manifesto, which is in the press.

Juan B. Alvarado

Monterey
October 10, 1835

At a session on this day, the Deputation was given a report on this proposal and it was ordered to be passed to the Committee on Government.

[José] Castro, President
Manuel Jimeno, Member Secretary

Monterey
October 14, 1835

The Committee on Government has examined the proposal of Señor Alvarado, in which he reports the unhappy news of the death of José Figueroa, Commandant and Political Chief of the Territory, and in which it is moved that this Deputation do in his memory and name whatever it can. First, it is proposed that the portrait of General José Figueroa be placed in the Hall of Sessions of this Deputation. Second, that in order to perpetuate our grateful memory of him, a durable monument with a suitable inscription be raised in one of the most public and unobstructed sites in Monterey, appealing to the City Council so that everything may be done under its direction and care. Third, that three copies of the resolution be made, so that one may be given to the executors of our late General and Chief, another may be sent to his widow and children, and another be given to the press, so that it may be printed and published as a continuation to his manifesto, which is in the press. The Committee believes no objection can be made to the purposes voiced by Señor Alvarado, since they are public and well known, for the name of General José Figueroa is mentioned everywhere. Everyone commends and recognizes his exceptional merits and his long and distinguished services to his country. He always obeyed the laws and saw that they were obeyed, and sacrificed himself to fulfill his public duties. It was he who planted the olive of peace when he landed on the beaches of this coast; it was he who safeguarded agriculture; it was he who watched over the establishment of education and schools for the young;[167] it was he who encouraged all objectives for the welfare of the Territory; it was he who extinguished the torch of discord; and finally, it was he who by his example and hard work cultivated all manner of virtues, meriting for these reasons the name of Father of our Territory. Yes, gentlemen, the Committee would think itself unworthy in the eyes of the citizens if it tried to oppose sentiments so natural as those demonstrated by Señor Alvarado, and therefore it concludes by presenting the following proposals for the deliberation of the Deputation:

1. That the three proposals of Señor Alvarado be approved and immediately carried out.

2. That beneath the portrait of General José Figueroa, the title of Benefactor of the Territory of Upper California be placed.

Manuel Jimeno

At a session on this day the Deputa-

167. While it is true that Governor Figueroa did not oppose the placement of the 24 teachers who came out with the colony, the credit for establishing elementary schools in California should go to Vice-President Gómez Farías and the Direction of Public Instruction in Mexico City.

tion approved the previous report with its two proposals.[168]

> José Castro, President
> Manuel Jimeno, Member Secretary

[Copy, October 14, 1835—
Manuel Jimeno]

NOTE

The foregoing proceedings were sent to the City Council, which is at the present time occupied in putting them into effect,

168. This seems to be as far as the Deputation went, however, for the portrait apparently remained unpainted and the monument unbuilt. But countless streets in California cities, not to mention a mountain near Santa Barbara, bear Governor Figueroa's name.

and it seems that the following inscriptions are to be placed on the monument which is being contracted for:

> To the Eternal Memory of
> General José Figueroa
> Political and Military Chief
> of Upper California,
> Father of the Country,
> The Provincial Deputation
> And the City Council of Monterey
> Dedicate This Monument
> At Public Expense
> As a Mark of Gratitude.
> He Died in This Capital
> On the 29th of September, 1835,
> At the Age of 43.

Manifiesto a la República Mejicana

FACSIMILE

MANIFIESTO
A LA
REPUBLICA MEJICANA

QUE HACE EL GENERAL DE BRIGADA

JOSE FIGUEROA,

COMANDANTE GENERAL Y GEFE POLITICO
DE LA
ALTA CALIFORNIA,

Sobre su conducta y la de los Señores
D. Jose Maria de Hijar y D. Jose Maria
Padres, como Directores de Colonizacion
en 1834 y 1835.

MONTERREY 1835.

IMPRENTA DEL C. AGUSTIN V. ZAMORANO.

NOTA DEL IMPRESOR.

Se suplica a los Señores lectores se sir-
van disimular la falta de acentos que notaran
en esta obra, originada por no haber venido
aun el surtido completo de letra que se esta esperando: asi mismo se suplica presten su
indulgencia por cualquiera otro defecto tipo-
grafico que adviertan en la referida obra, teniendo en consideracion que es la primera en
su clase que se da a luz en la unica imprenta de esta alta California.

ERRATAS,

Pagina.	Linea.	Dice.	Lease
5.	10.	recibiron	recibieron
6.	8.	recibibo	recibido
9.	2.	eon	con
id.	23.	imprevicion	imprevision
11.	4.	de Colonia	de la Colonia
21.	21.	ofresco	ofrezco
23.	18.	deseba	deseaba
28.	30.	progenitores	hermanos
40.	2.	33	23
id.	id.	titulo	capitulo
44.	id.	apodrarse	apoderarse
51.	19.	posecion	posesion

MANIFIESTO A LA REPUBLICA

MEJICANA.

El aparato que en toda la Republica se ostento sobre la empresa de colonizar los Territorios de las Californias y los sucesos que siguieron a la ecspedicion que con tal objeto emprendieron los Señores D. Jose Maria Hijar y D. Jose Maria Padres me obligan a revelar al publico una breve pero ecsacta noticia de los acontecimientos. Como la empresa no tuvo el ecsito que se propusieron los Directores, se pretende atribuirme la culpa de sus ecstravios cuando solo son debidos a su falta de calculo, mala combinacion y manejos obscuros. El publico en vista de los acontecimientos juzgara de las personas.

En el mes de Abril de 1832 me nombro el Supremo gobierno Gefe politico y Comandante general de la alta California a cuyo destino llegue en Enero de 1833: en el mes de Marzo del mismo año me vi gravemente enfermo por cuyo motivo pedi se me relevara: como en aquellas circunstancias acababa de salir el territorio de una crisis pe-

ligrosa, y aun no consideraba ecstinguidas las causas de la revolucion que habia mantenido divididos a sus habitantes, opine, que no era tiempo de separar los mandos politico y militar en dos distintas personas como se habia pretendido, sino que un solo individuo debia desenpeñar ambos encargos: asi lo represente oficialmente al Supremo gobierno al tiempo de pedir mi relevo por que asi me parecio conveniente, en circunstancias que ni remotamente pensaba permanecer en el mando por que mi salud estaba bastante quebrantada y solo ansiaba por regresar al seno de mi familia.

El Ayudante Inspector D. Jose Maria Padres el año de 1830, aparentando un grande interes en mejorar la suerte de los indigenas aunque no con muy buenas intenciones, segun se ha divulgado, proyecto secularizar las misiones de este territorio, de conformidad con lo dispuesto por la ley de 13 de Setiembre de 1813: a la sazon gobernaba este territorio el Teniente coronel D. Jose Maria de Echeandia a quien Padres comprometio facilmente presentandole un proyecto que a renglon seguido mando publicar por bando y poner en ejecucion, en circunstancias que acababa de llegar a relevarlo el Teniente coronel D. Manuel Victoria; y tanto por este incidente como por que no se consulto al Supremo gobierno, se frustro la empresa que mando con-

tener el citado Victoria. Como Padres habia comprometido subrepticiamente a varios patriotas que de buena fe deseaban la secularizacion, tuvo muchos colaboradores que despues tanto por la ecsageracion de los principios que les habian inculcado, como por la severidad con que se quiso gobernarlos, fueron otros tantos contrarios de Victoria en la revolucion que se formo contra su persona acaudillada por Echeandia: revolucion que sean cuales fueren las causas, ella puso en consternacion al territorio, ya por que quedo destruido el gobierno y se dejaron sentir sus consecuencias, y ya por que se dividieron y enemistaron los ciudadanos en general. Asi es que cuando llegue a tomar el mando, el territorio estaba en completa anarquia de la cual aun no acababa de convalecer. El Supremo gobierno desaprobo altamente la conducta de Echeandia y de Padres, y me ordeno que si encontraba en practica el bando de secularizacion lo mandara suspender reponiendo las misiones a su antiguo estado sin perjuicio de informar si estaban o no en el caso de secularizarse, para emprenderlo con la circunspeccion debida; y sin perjuicio de ir paulatinamente repartiendo entre los neofitos terrenos de las misiones, para insensiblemente convertirlos en propiedades particulares. Padres fue lanzado de este pais por el espresado Sr. Victoria, pero dejo sembrado el

germen de la revolucion que despues aparecio y que debe su origen al proyecto de secularizar las misiones.

Como la distancia de aqui a Mejico es
tan dilatada, me restableci antes de saber la
resolucion que tomaria el Gobierno y le manifeste que estaba en aptitud de desempeñar
mi empleo. El Gobierno me ordeno entonces
que continuara en ambos encargos como lo
estaba haciendo no obstante que, al recibir
mi primera comunicacion mando al Ayudante Inspector D. Jose Maria Padres, que mar-
chara a California y se encargara del mando
militar „en el caso" de que yo siguiera enfermo y quisiera marchar a Mejico.

Cuando se libro este despacho, gobernaba el Sr. Gomez Farias, de quien el Ayudante Inspector D. Jose Maria Padres merecio
muy distinguidas confianzas, segun el mismo
ha publicado, y aprovechandose de esta co-
yuntura influyo eficazmente para que se san-
cionara la ley de 17 de Agosto de 1833,
contraida a secularizar las misiones de las
Californias: para que se emprendiera colonizar ambos territorios: y que se nombrara al
Sr. D. Jose Maria de Hijar Gefe politico de
la alta California y Director de Colonizacion.
Facil era persuadir la utilidad y conveniencia
de esos proyectos si no envolvieran otras miras que el tiempo ha descubierto; pero el
Gobierno animado de los mejores deseos por

la felicidad y progresos de este pais tomo
bajo su proteccion tan grandiosas empresas.
Padres, se lisonjeaba al ver realizados los planes que habia premeditado desde el año de
1830 y le valio el nombramiento de Subdirector de Colonizacion.

Se hacen los preparativos para el viage
y se reclutan a nombre del gobierno gentes para colonizar: ignoro los aucsilios que
recibiron, pero es publico que el gobierno
erogo grandes gastos hasta embarcar la ecspedicion en el puerto de San Blas.

El mes de Febrero de 1834 recibi la
suprema orden que sigue.

„ Primera Secretaria de Estado. Departamento del Interior. — El Ecsmo. Sr. Vice
Presidente en ejercicio del Supremo Poder
ejecutivo, se ha servido ecshonerar a V. S.
del encargo de Gefe Politico de ese territorio, y nombrar para este destino a D. Jose
Maria Hijar a quien desde luego entregara
V. S. el mando. — Al mismo tiempo me
manda S. E. dar a V. S. las gracias como
lo verifico, por el celo con que ha desempeñado dicho encargo, y espera S. E. continue sus servicios en favor del orden. Lo que
comunico a V. S. para su inteligencia y cumplimiento. — Dios y Libertad. Mejico Julio 15
de 1833. — Garcia. — Sr. General D. Jose Figueroa, Gefe politico de la alta California."

Mi contestacion es la del tenor siguiente.

6

„Gobierno Politico de la alta California.=
N.° 7. = Ecsmo. Sr. = Tan luego como el
Sr. D. Jose Maria Hijar se presente en este
territorio le entregare el mando del Gobierno
politico que ha estado a mi cargo, como previene el Ecsmo. Sr. Vice Presidente y V. E.
se sirve comunicarme en carta oficial de 15
de Julio del año procsimo pasado que he re-
cibibo con mucho atraso. = Quedo sumamen-
te reconocido al Ecsmo. Sr Vice Presidente
por haberme ecshonerado de este encargo tan
superior a mis escasos conocimientos, y por
las distinguidas ecspresiones con que se manifiesta satisfecho de mi comportamiento en
el desempeño de mis funciones; pues aunque
no pueda jactarme de haber llenado los deseos de la Superioridad, tengo a lo menos la
satisfaccion de haber restablecido la tranquilidad y el orden constitucional, que encontre
relajado en todos los ramos de la administracion a mi ingreso a este territorio. Por fortuna, hoy se disfruta union y paz en cuya
consecucion, nunca he omitido sacrificio ni
trabajo alguno: protesto continuar lo mismo
hasta el momento que llegue mi sucesor,
esperando que los resultados den testimonio
de mi buen, o mal comportamiento. == Mas
entre tanto dignese V. E. hacer presentes
mis sentimientos al Ecsmo. Sr. Vice Presidente, a quien tributo respetuosamente el ho-
menage de mi gratitud y reconocimiento.--Dios

y Libertad. Monterrey 18 de Mayo de 1834=
Jose Figueroa. =Ecsmo. Sr. Secretario de Estado y del Despacho de Relaciones."

Ecstraoficialmente llego a mi noticia que
con el Sr. D. Jose Maria de Hijar venia
una multitud de familias colonizadoras soste-
nidas por el gobierno, y aunque este ni el
Sr. Hijar contaron con las autoridades locales para tal empresa, me parecio prudente
hacer algunos preparativos para su establecimiento: con este objeto hice una ecspedicion
a la frontera hasta el presidio de Ross, que
es el establecimiento de los Rusos mas inmediato a nosotros: reconoci aquellos campos
y escogi el que mejor me parecio para situar
la Colonia: estableci en la misma frontera un
destacamento para resguardo de dicha Colonia y regrese a esperarla a la capital.

El 11 de Septiembre, un dia antes de
llegar recibi un ecstraordinario del Supremo
gobierno venido por tierra desde Mejico con
la suprema orden siguiente.

„ Primera Secretaria de Estado. Departamento del Interior.= Dada cuenta al Ecsmo.
Sr. Presidente con el oficio de V. S. de 18
de Mayo ultimo en que contesta a la orden
que se le remitio ecshonerandolo del encargo
de Gefe politico de ese territorio, y dice entregara el mando luego que se presente el
Sr. Hijar; ha dispuesto S. E. conteste a V. S.
que no entregue el citado mando y continue

desempeñando la Gefatura. ══ Dios y Libertad. Mejico Julio 25 de 1834. ══ Lombardo. ══ Sr. Gefe politico de la alta California D. Jose Figueroa."

Por el mismo conducto recibi las primeras comunicaciones que me dirigio el Sr. Hijar desde el puerto de San Diego donde desembarco el 1.º de Septiembre con parte de la Colonia. El 25 arribo a este de Monterrey la Corbeta de guerra Morelos conduciendo a D, Jose Maria Padres, varios empleados y el resto de la Colonia.

Desde este dia comenzaron mis compromisos y era facil pronosticar los consiguientes. El Sr. Padres me oficia pidiendome aucsilios para los colonos que habian llegado en su compañia y es la primera noticia que me comunica de su comision: el Supremo gobierno nada me previno relativamente a la empresa de colonizacion; ni a los empleados de la hacienda publica les ha ordenado por ningun conducto que eroguen gastos en la ecspresada colonia: ni aun siquiera se me comunico que habia dispuesto de la persona de D Jose Maria Padres para Subdirector de la Colonia, siendo un militar que viene a servir su destino bajo mis ordenes. Asi es que en todo me parecio ecstraña la conducta de Padres y aunque me quiso satisfacer manifestandome un oficio que le dirigio el Ministro de Relaciones por el cual le conferia la comision

de Subdirector de Colonizacion, ni es ese el modo con que debio ejecutarlo, ni Padres era el conducto por donde se me debia comunicar una orden suprema, ni el Ministro de Relaciones debio disponer de un militar sin que precediera orden comunicada por la Secretaria de Guerra. Esto no obstante me parecio prudente guardar silencio y darle a entender que no estaba a cubierto mi responsabilidad.

Ningun pago se debe ejecutar en las oficinas sin que preceda orden suprema comunicada por los conductos establecidos, determinado por alguna ley, y aprobado por las Camaras de la Union en el presupuesto general del año economico; y contra estas prevenciones ecspresas a pesar de las grandes escaseces que padecen los empleados civiles y militares, mande se socorriera la Colonia por no ecsponerla a perecer, entre tanto se ocurria a la Superioridad por las ordenes respectivas. Este es un testimonio irrefragable de la impericia, imprevicion o falta de calculo de los Directores, que debieron prevenir todo lo necesario para las gentes que traian a su cargo para no comprometerlas a sufrir miserias; pues debian saber, que hace mas de veinte años que no se pagan por completo los sueldos de los pocos empleados militares y civiles del territorio por falta de numerario, y que a mas de reagravar las necesidades de

estos, comprometerian la responsabilidad de los encargados de la hacienda publica por no tener ordenes para hacer pagos a la Colonia.

Como desde San Diego a Monterrey median ciento ochenta leguas, no llego el Sr. Hijar a este ultimo punto hasta el 14 de Octubre.

Lo recibi con demostraciones publicas de amistad y respeto: lo distingui y obsequie con el mayor esmero, y lo hospede en la casa de mi morada. Pasados los primeros cumplimientos, le manifeste la orden del Supremo gobierno y la precision que tenia de obedecerla aunque con bastante sentimiento mio por lo que debia influir contra su honor e intereses: le ofreci con sinceridad y buena fe mi corto valimiento, y que interesaria los respetos de la Ecsma. Diputacion territorial para que el Supremo gobierno le volviese el empleo de Gefe politico y que entre tanto desempeñaria la comision especial de Director de la Colonia: por ultimo le ofreci que si encontraba un arbitrio legal para entregarle el mando sin comprometer mi responsabilidad, lo haria con gusto por que no tenia ambicion en conservarlo.

Persuadido el Sr. Hijar de mi buena disposicion, convencido quiza de que no podia aspirar al mando, se redujo a la comision especial de Director de la Colonia sobre lo cual, no hacia ecspresa mencion el gobierno.

Yo aunque dudoso sobre si debia considerarlo con esa investidura despues de haberlo destituido del gobierno politico, no encontraba peligro en que fuera Director de Colonia y de pronto convine en que desempeñara dicha comision a reserva de darle cuenta a la Superioridad. Entonces me ecsige que le entregue los bienes de las misiones como cosa inherente a la citada comision: le conteste que ignoraba el fundamento de tal pretension, y acto continuo me presento el pliego que contiene las instrucciones siguientes.

„Primera Secretaria de Estado, Departamento del Interior, ══ Instrucciones a que debera arreglar su conducta D. Jose Maria Hijar Gefe politico de la alta California y Director de la Colonizacion de esta y de la baja. ══ Articulo 1.º Dara principio por ocupar todos los bienes pertenecientes a las misiones de ambas Californias y el Comandante militar bajo su responsabilidad prestara, siempre que fuere requerido, los aucsilios necesarios para la ecspresada ocupacion. ══ Art. 2. Por el termino de un año contado desde el dia en que lleguen los Colonos al lugar que hayan de poblar, se les ministrara a cada uno de ellos cuatro reales diarios, si fuesen mayores de cuatro años, y dos reales si fuesen de menor edad. ══ Art. 3. Los gastos de viage por mar y tierra seran por cuenta de la federacion, se daran en plena propiedad a los

Colonos las monturas que se compraren o hubieren comprado para su trasporte. = Art. 4. Las poblaciones se formaran reuniendo el numero de familias que sean bastante para vivir con seguridad, eligiendo parages a proposito por la calidad del terreno, por la abundancia y salubridad de las aguas, por la bondad de los vientos. = Art. 5. Se procurara en cuanto sea posible poblar a la mayor brevedad los lugares fronterizos. = Art. 6. Se levantaran planos topograficos en que se designen y figuren las manzanas de que haya de constar la poblacion. La ecstension de cada lado de la manzana será de cien varas, y todos sus lados seran iguales; la anchura de las calles sera de veinte varas, y no se permitira ningun callejon en ellas. Las plazas se repartiran a lo menos cada diez calles ademas de la plaza mayor que se situara en el centro de la poblacion. = Art. 7. Se cuidara muy especialmente de reunir a las poblaciones los indigenas mezclandolos con los demas habitantes, y no se permitira poblacion compuesta de solo ellos. = Art. 8. En cada una de las manzanas de las poblaciones, se repartiran solares a las familias para que levanten sus casas; pero no se les permitira hacerlo fuera de la linea trazada para formar la calle. = Art. 9. Fuera de las poblaciones a cada familia de Colonos se daran en pleno dominio y propiedad,

cuatro caballerias de tierra, si esta fuere de regadio, ocho si fuere de temporal y diez y seis si fuere de abrevadero. Se daran tambien cuatro vacas, dos yuntas de bueyes, o dos toros, dos caballos mansos, cuatro potros, cuatro potrancas, cuatro cabezas de ganado menor, dos hembras y dos machos, y ademas dos arados habilitados. = Art. 10. Entre suerte y suerte de tierra de los particulares, quedara una ecstension baldia equivalente a dos suertes. Los terrenos comprendidos en ella podra venderlos el gobierno cuando lo crea oportuno, y el Director de las Colonias, preferira en este caso y en el de igualdad de circunstancias a los Colonos colindantes. = Art. 11. Hecha la distribucion de los bienes muebles pertenecientes a las Misiones de la California, se procedera a vender de la manera mas ventajosa hasta la mitad de los sobrantes. = Art. 12. No se podran vender a una misma familia mas de doscientas cabezas de ganado de una misma clase. = Art. 13. La mitad sobrante de los bienes muebles o semovientes, se conservara de cuenta del gobierno general, y se aplicara en su caso a gastos del culto y congrua de los misioneros, a los sueldos de maestros de primeras letras, a los socorros de utiles de los niños de ambos secsos en las escuelas, y a la compra de los instrumentos de labranza que se han de repartir gratis a los Colonos. = Art.

14

14. El Gefe politico y Director de la Colonizacion dara por esta vez y anualmente cuenta circunstanciada de los productos de bienes de las misiones, de su inversion, de los que queden ecsistentes despues de verificado el reparto de muebles y semovientes entre los Colonos. = Art. 15 Dara igualmente parte a lo menos una vez cada año del estado de los Colonos, de los motivos de atraso si lo hubiere, y de los medios de hacerlos progresar. = Mejico 23 de Abril de 1834. = Lombardo."

Respondi que por mi parte serian obsequiadas esas disposiciones, aunque en mi concepto era una injusticia despojar a los neofitos de los intereses de las misiones que reconocian como una propiedad. Con esto termino la conferencia privada que tubimos la noche del 15 de Octubre, y al amanecer del 16 recibi el oficio siguiente.

"Direccion general de Colonizacion en Califonias. = En las ordenes e instrucciones del Supremo Gobierno general que he manifestado a V. S. como Director de Colonizacion se encuentra el articulo siguiente. = Art. 1 º Dara principio por ocupar todos los bienes pertenecientes a las misiones de ambas Californias, y el Comandante militar bajo su responsabilidad, prestara siempre que fuere requerido los auscilios necesarios para la espresada ocupacion. = Siendo pues de la mayor importancia

el dar principio a mi comision, tanto por evitar el desfalco que estan sufriendo las misiones, como por mejorar la suerte de los indigenas y establecer a las familias colonizadoras que me acompañan; suplico a V. S. se sirva dar sus ordenes a los comisionados que ha nombrado para la secularizacion, a fin de que obren segun mis prevenciones; y a los Comandantes militares de todos los puntos del territorio para que a mi o mis encargados respectivos se presten los auscilios que puedan necesitarse al objeto indicado. = Reitero a V. S. las protestas de mi aprecio y distinguida consideracion. = Dios y Libertad. Monterrey Octubre 16 de 834. = Jose Maria de Hijar, = Sr. Comandante General D. Jose Figueroa."

Conteste con este otro.

"Gobierno politico de la alta California. = Hare como V. S. solicita las prevenciones conducentes a los comisionados de las misiones para que obren segun las ordenes que V. S. les dirija, y a los Comandantes militares para que auscilien en los casos necesarios, todo de conformidad con lo dispuesto por el Supremo gobierno en el articulo 1 º de las instrucciones que V. S. se sirve transcribirme en su nota de esta fecha qué tengo el honor de contestar. = Mas me permitira V. S. que previamente consulte a la mesma Diputacion territorial a fin de recabar su deferencia y ecspeditar de mejor modo las funciones de V. S. en esta comision. = Dios y Libertad. Monterrey 16 de Octubre de 1834. = Jose Figueroa. = Sr. Director general de Colonizacion D. Jose Maria de Hijar."

Reprodujo el Sr. Hijar con este otro.

"Direccion general de Colonizacion en Californias. = Por la nota de V. S. fecha de ayer me he impuesto con satisfaccion de su buena disposicion para secundar las disposiciones del Supremo Gobierno general, consultando previamente a la Ecsma. Diputacion territorial sobre mi comision de Colonizacion. = Yo suplico a V. S. que si es posible, este asunto quede hoy mismo terminado. El ruinoso desorden en que se encuentran muchas de las misiones por donde he transitado: el procsimo tiempo de las labores de trigo, de que los misioneros parecen olvidados, seguramente por que temen dejar el mando de las temporalidades: los clamores de los indigenas que hasta ahora sufren infinitamente: la Colonia, que no puedo establecer sin que esto se resuelva y lo angustiado del tiempo para emprender labores que deben formar su subsistencia en todo el año: todo, todo Sr. General esta manifestando que no debe perdonarse un momento. = Por ultimo yo me dirijo a V. S. como autoridad militar para impetrar

paracion por el articulo 2 titulo 1.° me autoriza para convocarla a sesiones ecstraordinarias. = En uso de esta facultad, determine su reunion, que hoy miro con placer verificada. La causa que la motivo esta ecspuesta: voy ahora a manifestar los objetos que deben ocupar la atencion de V. E. = El Supremo gobierno con fecha 15 de Julio de 1833 se sirvio ecshonerarme del encargo de Gefe politico de este territorio nombrando en mi lugar al Sr. D. Jose Maria Hijar: con fecha 13 de Mayo de este año, conteste que estaba pronto a entregarle el mando luego que se presentara; y con fecha de 25 de Julio ultimo por ecstraordinario violento me ordena dicho Supremo gobierno, que no entregue al Sr. Hijar y que yo continue desempeñando el encargo de Gefe politico. Todo consta de los documentos que tengo el honor de presentar y pido que se lean para mayor inteligencia de la Corporacion. = El Sr. Hijar fue tambien nombrado Director de la Colonia que acaba de llegar, segun consta de la suprema orden que igualmente tengo el honor de presentar para conocimiento de V. E. = El Supremo gobierno al prevenirme que no entregue el mando al Sr. Hijar, se desentiende de la otra u otras comisiones que le ha confiado. = Asi es que como la de Director

los ausilios de que habla el artículo 1.° de mis instrucciones, que le transcribi en mi comunicacion anterior y sentiria sobre manera que gravitasen sobre su responsabilidad los trastornos y perdidas irreparables que la tardanza puede ocasionar. = Dios y Libertad. Monterrey Octubre 17 de 834. = Jose Maria de Hijar. = Sr. Comandante general D. Jose Figueroa."

El decidido y tenaz empeño que se manifesto en apoderarse de unos bienes cuyos dueños son unas gentes abyectas e inermes, las noticias que se habian divulgado por los mismos Colonos y sus Directores, sobre las grandiosas especulaciones de la rumbosa Compañia mercantil Cosmopolitana, de quien era el Bergantin Natalia que las misiones debian pagar con siete mil arrobas de sebo: y sobre todo, el haber mandado el Supremo gobierno un ecstraordinario con solo el objeto de que no entregara yo el mando, me indujo a desconfiar de las pretensiones sobre intereses y consulte a la Ecsma. Diputacion lo que contienen las comunicaciones siguientes.

"Gobierno politico de la alta California. = Ecsmo. Sr. = La ley de 23 de Junio de 1813 en su articulo 15 capitulo 3.° previene, que en casos señalados y graves oiga el consejo de la Diputacion valiendome de sus luces." = El Reglamento interior de esta Cor-

de la Colonia, tiene un enlace por decirlo asi con la de Gefe politico dudo, si destituido de este empleo podra ejercer aquella comision y bajo que respecto, pues aunque no es incompatible el uno con el otro, carezco de antecedentes por que nada me ha prevenido el Gobierno relativamente a la Colonizacion. El Ecsmo. Sr. Presidente en virtud de la ley de 6 de Abril de 1830, puede nombrar comisionados para establecer Colonias y en mi concepto el Sr. Hijar debe llevar al cabo la empresa de que esta encargado; mas deseando acertar y no comprometer mi responsabilidad bajo ningun aspecto, he creido necesario oir el consejo de V. E, prometiendome de su integridad y luces que meditara una medida consiliadora y decorosa. = El Sr. Hijar con fecha 16 del presente me ha dirigido la nota que original tengo igualmente el honor de acompañar: contiene inserto un articulo de las instrucciones que recibio del Supremo gobierno y segun este, pide, que los comisionados nombrados a virtud del articulo 20 del Reglamento provisional de secularizacion, obren segun sus ordenes. = He aqui una duda que se ofrece al ecsamen de V. E. el Sr. Hijar es Director de Colonizacion y de Secularizacion, o solo de lo primero? Su nombramiento dice que es Director de las Colonias: ¿sera una cosa misma la Colonizacion y la Secularizacion? no; pero el Supremo gobierno le manda que ocupe todos los bienes pertenecientes a las misiones: ¿con que caracter o investidura debe avocarse el conocimiento de estos intereses? yo no lo entiendo: sirvase V. E. meditar este punto y consultarme lo mas justo. = Dios y Libertad. Monterrey 17 de Octubre de 1834. = Jose Figueroa. = Ecsma. Diputacion territorial de la alta California."

„Gobierno politico de la alta California. = Ecsmo. Sr. = Desde que empuñe las riendas del gobierno de este territorio, miraba con placer la marcha constitucional que sin tropiezos ni alborotos seguian estos pacificos habitantes: yo como depositario de la confianza publica he venerado las leyes en que estan consignadas las garantias sociales; pero uno de aquellos azares en que el genio del mal ecstiende su maligna influencia, quiere arrebatarnos la envidiable tranquilidad que solo es dado gozar a los Californios. = Inopinadamente se han enlazado los sucesos que motivan una divergencia de opiniones en el espiritu publico, y a V. E. no le seran desconocidos los resortes que se ponen en juego para afectarnos de las ideas ecsageradas que por desgracia devoran a nuestros hermanos en lo interior de la Republica. = El motivo ostensible de descontento consiste en la Suprema orden que tengo manifestada

a V. E. referente a que no entregue el mando politico al Sr. D. Jose Maria Hijar que habia sido nombrado para ese encargo: V. E. esta impuesto de las comunicaciones habidas en este respecto y sabe que yo no he tenido parte alguna en esta variacion por que ni pretendo ni deseo continuar con tal encargo. Lo he desempeñado y seguiria entre tanto el Supremo gobierno y los moradores de este suelo me honren con su confianza; pero si mi permanencia en el mando ha de producir discordias y descontento entre la familia de los Californios, con quienes estoy identificado en sentimientos, estoy resuelto a renunciarlo. = En prueba de mi desprendimiento he ofrecido a V. E. que si es conciliable el deber de obedecer con las ecsigencias publicas, me indique los medios de que debo valerme y ninguna otra consideracion me detendra en entregar el mando. Consecuente a esta protesta ofrezco a V. E. hacer una espontanea dimision del mando, si a este precio se conserva la tranquilidad de los Californios cuya suerte me es tan interesante: mi resolucion se apoya en la opinion publica manifestada energicamente por la separacion del mando politico del militar, y que el Gobierno supremo interesado como yo en los progresos de este afortunado pais, aprobara mi conducta y la apreciara como emanada del verdadero patriotismo y de las

circunstancias. = Ningun sacrificio Ecsmo. Señor: ningun sacrificio me es costoso por conservar la libertad y tranquilidad del territorio: yo quiero ser la unica victima que se inmole en las aras sagradas de la concordia: conservense en paz los Californios y vengan sobre mi los resultados y la responsabilidad. La voluntad de este naciente pueblo es mi norte: V. E. es el organo por donde debe ecspresarla: veanse cumplidos mis votos y satisfechos los deseos de mis compatriotas. = Dios y Libertad. Monterrey 17 de Octubre de 1834. = Jose Figueroa. = Ecsma. Diputacion Territorial."

Sabia muy bien que la Direccion de Colonizacion no le daba facultad de disponer ni administrar los intereses de las misiones, pero deseba complacer sus deseos y solo queria establecer garantias que afianzaran en sus manos la seguridad de tales intereses cuya responsabilidad era mia como Gefe politico; mas las sutilezas con que se me quiso sorprender me obligaron a variar de pensamiento y poner la cuestion en su verdadero punto de vista.

Los adictos al Sr. Hijar pretendieron ecstraviar la opinion publica y alarmar a los habitantes de este territorio para lanzarme ignominiosamente y apoderarse furtivamente del gobierno: se propagaron especies subversivas so pretecsto de dividir los mandos

en dos distintas personas, y hacerse independientes de la Republica Mejicana: se invito a los abyectos indigenas: se pusieron en juego intereses y pasiones innobles, y en resumen se me quiso intimar con amagos de revolucion bajo diversos y especiosos pretecstos, tal como el de que el Ecsmo. Sr. Presidente de la Republica habia variado el sistema de Federacion y destruido de mano armada la representacion de la Soberania Nacional: mi conducta en tales circunstancias esta de manifiesto en la protesta que hice a la Ecsma. Diputacion: obedecer al gobierno y no contrariar la voluntad general: he aqui mi decision: se me ordena que no entregue el mando al Sr. Hijar, pero yo estaba pronto a depositarlo en manos del primer vocal que es el que la ley de 6 de Mayo de 1822 llama a gobernar cuando falta el Gefe politico; sin embargo queria apoyar mi resolucion en el voto de los representantes del pueblo.

La Diputacion para emitir su opinion, paso el ecspediente a una comision de su seno y estos fueron los momentos en que mas se apuraron los resortes de la politica, de la amistad y de la intriga para sorprender a aquella corporacion: ella no obstante, obro con la dignidad que corresponde a su investidura y acordo lo siguiente.

„Ecsmo. Sr. = La Comision de Gobierno espone: que los inopinados acontecimientos que tan justamente han llamado la atencion publica, fueron presentados en su verdadero punto de vista, y del ecsamen prolijo que se ha hecho de ellos resulta: que resuelto por el Supremo gobierno la separacion del mando politico del militar nombro al Señor D. Jose Maria Hijar cuyo personage arribo a S. Diego el primero de Septiembre procsimo pasado, conduciendo ademas una Colonia de personas de ambos secsos, con el caracter de Director de ella. El mismo Supremo gobierno por causas que no ecspresa y en uso de sus atribuciones manda, que no se entregue el mando al Sr. Hijar y que el Sr. General D. Jose Figueroa continue desempeñando aquel encargo. Este incidente se ha traslucido al publico de una manera imperfecta: se ha tergiversado el sentido de la orden Suprema, y se ha atribuido a un cambio de sistema intentado por el Presidente de la Republica: tales especies y otras invectivas se han hecho valer en publico para ecstraviar la opinion, harto tiempo manifestada en favor de la separacion de los mandos: un suceso de tanta importancia, era preciso que alarmara los animos: se trataba de las libertades patrias y de la suerte de este territorio, y nadie puede ser indiferente al ventilar el ejercicio de sus derechos politicos; mas la razon y la verdad hacen desaparecer, las tinieblas, y asi V. E. debe rectificar la opinion publica presentando a la faz del mundo los sucesos tal como han ocurrido. = No nos ocuparemos en discurrir si se deben o no separar los mandos, por que ni el Supremo gobierno se ha negado ha hacerlo, ni los habitantes de este territorio estan destituidos del derecho de peticion, ni la Diputacion como representante inmediata del pueblo dejara de hacer escuchar su voz ante el Ejecutivo de la Union y aun en el Santuario mismo de las leyes, para reclamar el ejercicio de los derechos politicos de sus comitentes. Tratase unicamente de saber ¿quien ejercera las funciones de Gefe politico? la Suprema orden de 25 del ultimo Julio no deja lugar a interpretaciones: terminantemente previene que no se entregue el mando al Sr. Hijar, y que continue desempeñandola el General Figueroa; luego ¿que causa puede inducirnos a contravenir a este mandato? ¿no se diria que era una rebelion, o una usurpacion de las atribuciones del Poder ejecutivo contra las formulas constitucionales? Se objetara que la Republica se halla envuelta en convulsiones ¿y porque nuestros hemanos se hallan divididos por la fatal discordia, dejaremos nosotros de marchar por la senda constitucional? no Ecsmo. Señor: la libertad subsiste en tanto que son acatadas

las leyes, y desgraciado pueblo aquel que las invade por frivolos pretestos: la anarquia es el resultado y las consecuencias, el aniquilamiento de las fortunas y ecsistencia de los ciudadanos: libremonos del contagio venenoso de la discordia que devora a nuestros hermanos, ya que la naturaleza nos ha librado por medio de un muro inespugnable: si e nemigos de la libertad y del orden los provocan a la lid, nosotros no estamos en ese caso, y si por desgracia alguna vez nos viesemos comprometidos, sabremos hacer valer nuestros derechos. Cumplase pues por ahora la orden Suprema en cuestion y habremos llenado nuestro deber dando un testimonio publico, de nuestro amor al orden y a la justicia. Hagase al mismo tiempo una ecsposicion al Supremo gobierno para que se digne resolver la separacion del mando politico, proponiendole esta Corporacion una o mas personas de las que considere aptas para desempeñar ese destino, y nos atrevemos a pronosticar el mejor resultado. = El Sr. Figueroa impulsado de su patriotismo ofrece espontaneamente dejar el gobierno politico si asi conviene a la tranquilidad del territorio, sometiendose a los resultados y responsabilidad que pueda sobrevenirle; pero la tranquilidad publica esta asegurada bajo el mando de este Señor, y no hay merito para hacer esa variacion. La Diputacion que observa de cerca su conducta y que vela por el bien procomunal, sabe que no ha desmerecido la confianza publica, y apoyada en este concepto debe continuarle el reconocimiento, a reserva de llamarlo al orden si llegare a estraviarse. = Autorizado el Sr. Hijar con la doble investidura de Gefe politico y Director de la Colonia que ha traido en su compañia, vemos que la Superioridad le retira el poder del primer encargo y se desentiende del segundo: la comision pudiera considerarlo como inherente al primero, y destituido de ambos al mismo tiempo por virtud de la precitada Suprema orden; pero atenida al tenor de la letra opina, que puede continuar en la comision especial de Director de la Colonia que ha traido, como ecspresa su nombramiento, para lo cual se le ministraran de las misiones los aucsilios a que pueda estenderse el Gefe politico, sin perjuicio de los indigenas y las demas atenciones anecsas a dichas fundaciones; pues las erogaciones de las Colonias debe sufrirlas, o el fondo piadoso llamado de Californias, segun el decreto de 26 de Noviembre de 1833 que autorizo al Gobierno para ello, o de la Federacion segun el decreto de 6 de Abril de 1830, que pedimos se lea; pero de ninguna manera de los bienes de las misiones que son el fruto esclusivo del improbo trabajo de los neofitos de las misiones, y unico patrimonio que les espera en remuneracion de un siglo de esclavitud. ¿Con que derecho pues se despojara a esos desventurados del fruto de su trabajo y privaciones? ¿No diran, y con justicia, que pertenecen a una sociedad leonina? Esta es Ecsmo. Sr. la ocasion en que sobreponiendose a las bellas teorias y preocupaciones, haga escuchar la imperiosa voz de la justicia ante la autoridad suprema para que en desagravio de la humanidad, haga respetar las propiedades de nuestros infortunados compatriotas. No es Ecsmo. Sr. el Supremo gobierno quien dispone de estos intereses, son los palaciegos que engalanados con la capa del patriotismo, invocando la santa libertad y el bien publico sorprenden la buena fe del primer Magistrado de la Republica y le arrancan providencias, que debiendo hacer en su concepto la felicidad de los hombres, causa su ruina y los envuelbe en la miseria. Descorrase pues el velo, y hagamos ver al Ecsmo. Sr. Presidente con el respeto debido a su alta representacion, que si S. E. cree hacer un bien a nuestros indigenas, las instrucciones conferidas al Sr. Hijar sancionan el despojo de sus intereses para aplicarlos a objetos que si bajo otro respecto son atendibles, debe ser sin detrimento de esa clase desgraciada de nuestros progenitores que gimen aun entre las tinieblas de la ignorancia, · y que a V. E.

como encargado de velar y promover su felicidad, corresponde defender sus derechos, no con teorias ni sofismas, sino apoyado en principios eternos de justicia. Los hombres se han reunido en sociedad para asegurar sus vidas y propiedades, y no se puede despojarlos de la menor parte de sus bienes, sin violar el pacto y el derecho comun de las naciones. Sentados estos incontestables principios, la comision es de sentir, que se suspenda la ejecucion de las instrucciones dadas al Sr. Hijar en la parte que mandan apoderarse de los bienes de las misiones, distribuirlos y realizarlos, y que se represente al Supremo gobierno con insercion de este dictamen, pidiendole que se digne revocar esa providencia: que los bienes de las misiones sean distribuidos a los indios y en objetos de su aprovechamiento por ser los unicos dueños: que en tanto se aucsiliara con parte de dichos bienes a los Colonos, bajo la condicion de que se reintegren a sus dueños del fondo piadoso de California o de la hacienda federal. = De estos antecedentes se deduce, que no se deben poner a disposicion del Sr. Hijar los bienes de las misiones, por que no debiendo reasumir el mando de Gefe politico, tampoco debe entender en la ejecucion de la ley de secularizacion: las instrucciones que presento, ecspresamente dice su encabezado. „Instrucciones a que debe

arreglar su conducta D. José Maria Hijar Gefe politico de la alta California y Director de la Colonizacion de esta y de la baja." El sentido literal de estas prevenciones, no deja duda en que lo autorizaban como Gefe politico y de ninguna manera como Director de Colonizacion, cuyo nombramiento no le da jurisdiccion politica: no tiene atribuciones detalladas por ninguna ley y el Supremo gobierno apoyado en las vigentes sobre Colonizacion, solo le ha delegado la facultad de conducir la Colonia; establecerla y distribuirle terrenos: eso consta en la Suprema orden de 16 de Julio de 1833 y en las instrucciones de que hemos hecho mencion; pero es necesario repetir que dichas instrucciones le fueron dadas como a Gefe politico y en ese sentido se dejaba a su eleccion el lugar donde la Colonia debia establecerse; mas destituido de ese encargo, debe subordinarse al actual Gefe y recabar su deferencia en cuanto al lugar donde deben situarse las familias. En resumen su comision especial es de Director de la Colonia y esta si puede ejercerla poniendose de acuerdo con dicho Gefe politico de quien debe recibir instrucciones y los aucsilios necesarios, en consonancia de las ordenes Supremas relativas a este negocio. = Los Colonos merecen nuestra consideracion, y han marchado bajo la proteccion del Supremo gobierno; seran atendidos y distinguidos

de total conformidad a las promesas de la Superioridad, pues la variacion de la persona que ejerce la autoridad politica, no debe influir en contra de la suerte de estas familias que apoyadas en la fe publica, han venido a vivir con nosotros: les prodigaremos nuestro aprecio y la confraternidad de hermanos al abrigo de la paz, les hara sobrellevar las privaciones de la soledad: los Californios Sr. son hospitalarios, y partiran con gusto su fortuna entre todas las gentes que se acerquen a sus hogares = El publico espera el desenlace de este drama que tanto ha llamado su atencion, y para precaverlo de seducciones de funesta trascendencia opina la Comision, que se instruya de lo acontecido haciendo que se publique este dictamen y la resolucion de la Ecsma. Diputacion, por constar terminantemente en los fundamentos en que apoya su determinacion a fin de evitar siniestras interpretaciones. == Por tanto somete a la deliberacion de V. E. las siguientes proposiciones. = 1.ª Que se obedezca la Suprema orden de 25 de Julio de este año relativa a que no se entregue el mando al Sr. D. Jose Maria Hijar, y que el Sr. D. Jose Figueroa continue desempeñando la Gefatura politica. = 2.ª Que el Sr. D. Jose Maria Hijar, si gusta, desempeñe la comision especial de Director de Colonizacion con sujecion al Gobierno politico del territorio y las bases que para ello acordare la Diputacion. = 3.ª Que el Sr. D. Jose Maria Hijar no tendra ingerencia alguna en la Secularizacion de las misiones, ni se entregaran a su disposicion como solicita los bienes de ellas. = 4.ª Que entre tanto el Supremo gobierno resuelve lo que tubiere por conveniente se lleve a efecto el cumplimiento del reglamento provisional acordado por la Diputacion para la secularizacion de misiones, y se ponga a los indios en posesion de sus bienes y tierras. = 5.ª El Gefe politico, de las ecsistencias de las misiones mandara dar a los colonos las herramientas y demas aucsilios que ecspresan las instrucciones luego que lleguen donde se han de establecer sacando a prorata dichos aucsilios para no perjudicar a una sola mision: por cuenta de la asignacion señalada a cada persona, les ministrara semillas, carnes y lo mas preciso para su manutencion: el Sr. Director de la Colonia estara sujeto al Gefe politico y le dara una relacion circunstanciada del numero de personas que van a colonizar, y un presupuesto de lo que importe el pago que debe hacerseles cada mes, para que a ese respecto arregle proporcionalmente las subministraciones. Los terrenos de las misiones son de los indios y no se establecera en ellos ninguna Colonia. = 6.ª El Gefe politico retendra en su poder las instrucciones dadas

por el Supremo gobierno al Sr. Hijar, a quien le pasara copia autorizada de ellas si las necesitare, devolviendole la Suprema orden de 23 de Abril de este año con que las acompaño. = 7.ª Que se de cuenta al Supremo gobierno con este dictamen y lo que se acordare para su superior aprovacion. Que igualmente se le dirija una ecsposicion pidiendole la revocacion de las instrucciones en la parte que despoja a los indios de sus propiedades, y la aprobacion del Reglamento provisional dado por la Diputacion Que se le dirija una reverente representacion pidiendole la separacion de los mandos politico y militar postulando tres personas de las que se consideren aptas. = 8.ª Que este dictamen y lo que se acordare por la Diputacion se publique y circule para inteligencia del publico, con la oportunidad que sea posible. = Monterrey 21 de Octubre de 1834. = Jose Antonio Carrillo. = Pio Pico. = Jose J. Ortega."

Las antecedentes cuestiones afectaron al publico y todos se ocuparon de su discusion: no pudiendo disimular sus sentimientos varios individuos que se creian ofendidos en sus intereses echaron el resto a su indiscrecion dando publicidad a materias que por su propio honor debieron tener reservadas. Entonces dieron a conocer la avaricia que agitaba sus espiritus, y la desmesurada ambicion que devoraba sus

corazones: entonces se descubrieron los compromisos en que habian empeñado los intereses de las misiones: entonces se hicieron publicas las empresas mercantiles de la Compañia Cosmopolitana que no contaba otros fondos para sus giros mas que los capitales de las misiones, entonces en fin se hace alarde de que el gobierno mismo, esto es, el Sr. Gomez Farias consiente que se grave una de las fincas del fondo piadoso de Californias hipotecandola a responder por el valor de catorce mil pesos en que fue contratado el Bergantin Natalia, y que debian pagarse con sebo de misiones de California: proyecto injusto a la verdad por que ninguna utilidad resultaba a estas comunidades: se dijo con la misma publicidad que la Compañia Cosmopolitana debia abrazar esclusivamente el comercio interior y ecsterior del territorio poniendo una casa en cada mision o pueblo y los buques necesarios en la costa para la importacion de efectos nacionales y estrangeros, y para la ecsportacion de los frutos del pais: he aqui el verdadero objeto de la ecspedicion colonial que tantos sacrificios costo a la Nacion: este era el fin a que se dirigian los esfuerzos del Sr. Padres y que nos encarecio hasta el fastidio como inspirados del mas eminente patriotismo. El pueblo conocio el ataque que se preparaba a las propiedades, la bancarrota que amenazaba a los unicos ca-

pitales que forman la riqueza publica y ruinoso monopolio a que se aspiraba: asi es que chocaron abiertamente las pretensiones de los Sres. Hijar y Padres con la opinion publica y este es el origen de la animadversion que se les demostro posteriormente. Ciegos en sus caprichos erroneos, tocaron otros arbitrios menos decorosos para obtener el resultado que deseaban. El Sr. Hijar ofendido en sumo grado por el acuerdo de la Ecsma. Diputacion me contesto un oficio lleno de imputaciones gratuitas: me lo dirigio acompañado de algunos desprecios que yo atribui a una ecsaltacion de bilis o falta de reflecsion y sin hacer merito de ellos me le apersone a brindarle con mi amistad y suplicarle, que se prestara a una conferencia para discutir los asuntos que nos ocupaban a fin de escusarnos de contestaciones odiosas: le ofreci manifestarle las leyes, ordenes y reglamentos en que apoyo la Diputacion el acuerdo referido, y que si me acreditaba que estaban derogadas esas disposiciones se variaria la resolucion: asi quedo acordado y el 25 y 26 de Octubre nos reunimos los Sres. D. Jose Maria Hijar, D Jose Maria Padres, D. Jose Antonio Carrillo, D. Pio Pico, D. Jose Castro, el Juez de distrito Lic. D. Luis del Castillo Negrete, Lic. D. Rafael Gomez y yo: se abrio la discusion dando lectura al oficio del Sr. Hijar cuyo contenido por abrazar diversos puntos lo insertare dividido en varios trozos que ire refutando por su orden, como que fue el fundamento y objeto primordial de la conferencia para llegar al fin.

„Direccion general de Colonizacion de Californias. = Me he impuesto con detenimiento de la nota de V. S. fecha de ayer. Ella contiene una orden del Gobierno general para que no se me entregue el gobierno político del territorio que me habia confiado: una esposicion que V. S. hizo a la Ecsma. Diputacion territorial sobre los males que podia causar el cumplimiento de la orden de que antes se hace referencia por la tendencia que hay en el pais para que se separen los gobiernos politico y militar y por ultimo, ocho proposiciones aprobadas por la misma Ecsma. Diputacion con las que parece V. S. conforme. = Yo desearia que los asuntos se hubiesen tratado con la debida separacion, pero ya que no se ha tenido a bien hacerlo, contestare las materias por el mismo orden que se ecspresan. = En cuanto a la orden para que no se me entregue el mando politico del territorio nada tengo que objetar supuesto que emana del mismo gobierno que me nombro: yo soy un respetuoso servidor del gobierno y nunca desconocere sus disposiciones si estas se contraen a la orbita de su poder, solo ecstraño que nada se me haya comunicado para saber si mi encargo ha cesado del todo, o si

37

V. S. debe continuar solo por alguna circunstancia; pero esto no es cuestion que nos toca resolver y por consiguiente seria inutil tratarlo en este punto."

La orden Suprema de 25 de Julio para que no entregara yo el gobierno político al Sr. Hijar es muy terminante: las Colonias segun el Reglamento de 4 de Febrero de 834, articulo 9 seran trasportadas bajo la direccion de las personas que el gobierno designare; y segun el articulo 10 „quedaran sometidas al Gefe o gefes politicos que el Gobierno designare;" luego no admite duda que el encargo del Sr. Hijar ceso del todo. La Diputacion no obstante dice que aunque pudiera considerarlo destituido de ambos encargos, esto es, de Gefe politico y Director de Colonizacion, opina que puede continuar en la comision especial de Director de la Colonia con sujecion al gobierno político del territorio. Parece que esto es muy conforme con los deseos del Sr. Hijar a pesar de que el titulo de Director de Colonizacion no es un empleo determinado por ley alguna.

„Nada tengo que decir de la ecsposicion que V. S. hizo a la Ecsma. Diputacion pues debe conocer cual es la situacion del territorio y la opinion de sus habitantes: tampoco añadire nada sobre la primera proposicion que aprobo la Ecsma. Diputacion por estar conforme con los principios que antes he sentado.=

38

La segunda proposicion se contrae a que si me agrada, continue dirijiendo la Colonia sujetandome al gobierno politico y a las bases que para ello acordare la Diputacion. Las dos condiciones con que concluye esta proposicion son ciertamente remarcables: la primera, por inutil supuesto que todo hombre sin fuero privilegiado, debe sujetarse a las autoridades locales; la segunda, es atentatoria contra el gobierno general, contra mi y contra la Colonia: ¿quien ha facultado a la Ecsma. Diputacion para dar bases de Colonizacion? ¿Como es que la Ecsma. Diputacion pretende abrogarse facultades que solo son propias del Congreso de la Union o del Ejecutivo general si se encuentra como en este caso facultado por el lejislativo? ¡Cuantas aberraciones Sr. General y de cuan funestas trasendencias! Si yo continuara dirijiendo la Colonia bajo otras bases que las que me dio el Supremo gobierno, haria traicion a este mismo gobierno que me nombro: faltaria a la confianza con que me honro, y a los deberes de un buen ciudadano reconociendo disposiciones de un poder ilegitimo cual es el de V. S. y la Ecsma. Diputacion para el caso presente. = Si yo me sujeto a las bases que de la Ecsma. Diputacion debe inferirse entonces que no sere Director de Colonizacion. ¿Y quien ha facultado a V. S. ni a la Ecsma. Diputacion para despojarme de una comision especial que me ha

confiado el Supremo Gobierno general? La Colonia que he conducido tampoco puede ni debe dirijirse por otras bases que las que se me dieron por el Supremo gobierno. Este, al arrancar de sus hogares a las trescientas personas que me acompañan, les ofrecio ciertas condiciones que es necesario se cumplan si se tiene interes en conservar el decoro del gobierno. Por otra parte ¿que garantias ofrecerian las bases de la Ecsma. Diputacion si, como dije antes, emanaban de un poder ilegitimo? Considere V. S que soy un Director de Colonizacion, y no solo de la Colonia que ha venido: por consiguiente los naturales del pais y los estrangeros que gusten tienen un derecho a colonizar; mas si las bases se varian, todos se retraeran por falta de seguridad, y los males son para el territorio que tanto necesita de brazos utiles."

La Diputacion nunca tuvo la vana presuncion de atribuir a sus determinaciones el caracter de ley y por lo mismo que reconoce los limites de su autoridad quiso que el Director de Colonizacion tubiera la dependencia necesaria del gobierno: la Diputacion y yo no hemos pretendido dictar bases generales de Colonizacion pero si creiamos deber dar algunas reglas para la que se iba a establecer en este territorio por que las leyes nos han conferido facultad bastante paro hacerlo: registrense si se duda, la constitucion española que es la que rige en este territorio, y la ley de 33 de Junio de 1813 titulo 2.$^{\circ}$ y 3°: yo no me detendre en copiar sus articulos por no ser tan prolijo, por que el Sr. Hijar esta convencido de que „todo hombre sin fuero privilegiado debe sujetarse a las autoridades locales,'' y por que la Diputacion que nunca se propuso contrariar las leyes y disposiciones del gobierno, hizo una ecsplicacion de su concepto redactando la proposicion en los terminos siguientes.

„Que el Sr. D. Jose Maria Hijar si gusta, desempeñe la comision especial de Director de Colonizacion con sujecion al gobierno politico del territorio y a las leyes y reglamentos dados sobre la materia.''

Ya vera el Sr. Hijar que la proposicion que ha combatido no es como dice, atentatoria contra el gobierno general, contra su persona y contra la Colonia; y que aunque pudimos legalmente dar bases para el establecimiento de la Colonia, desistimos de ello por evitar una contienda puramente nominal supuesto que el Sr. Hijar se somete al gobierno territorial, y no es como supone, ilegitimo el poder que ejerce, por que es emanado de las leyes que han marcado el modo de trasmitirlo a los ciudadanos que ejercen algun cargo publico.

Y ¿cuales son las atribuciones del Director de Colonizacion? lo ignoro, pero creo

que no tiene atribuciones por que no es un empleo: el titulo debe su origen a un proyecto de ley iniciado en la Camara de Diputados del Congreso general y de alli se tomo para darlo al Sr. Hijar; mas como el Reglamento de 4 de Febrero de 834 somete las Colonias que se establezcan a los Gefes politicos que nombre el Gobierno y el Sr. Hijar dejo de ser Gefe politico claro es, que la investidura de Director de Colonizacion no le confiere jurisdiccion politica y estó no obstante la Diputacion lo respeta como un comisionado del Supremo gobierno en prueba de que no he intentado despojarlo de tal encargo como falsamente asienta dicho Sr. Hijar.

Cierto es que la Colonia debe establecerse arreglada a las bases dadas por el Supremo gobierno, pero esto no le quita que este subordinada al gobierno territorial, ni esta sujecion puede impedir el cumplimiento de las condiciones que le estan ofrecidas. Por consiguiente se conserva el decoro del gobierno, y queda intacto el derecho de los estrangeros y nacionales para colonizar; pues nadie ha tratado de embarazarlo.

„La tercera proposicion dispone que no tenga ingerencia alguna en la secularizacion de misiones, ni se entreguen a mi disposicion los bienes de ellas: esta resolucion es escandalosa y como la anterior atentatoria contra el gobierno general y subversiva. Yo nun-

ca he pretendido ingerirme en la secularizacion de misiones y por consiguiente no se a que viene la primera parte. = El Supremó gobierno de la Union facultado por el decreto de 26 de Noviembre de 1833 dispuso que yo ocupase los bienes de las misiones para darles la inversion que le parecio conveniente, y en la proposicion de que se trata se desobedece absolutamente aquella resolucion. Es ciertamente un escandalo que el que las personas encargadas de cumplir y hacer cumplir las leyes y disposiciones gubernativas sean las primeras en dar el ejemplo de desobediencia, ejemplo funestisimo que tiende a trastornar todo el orden social. ¿Donde iriamos a parar si cada uno fuese desobedeciendo las leyes a su antojo?: al estado natural en que el mas fuerte es el señor del debil. Considere V. S. que en el mismo hecho de aprobar esta resolucion ha autorizado el derecho de insurreccion. Si V. S. y la Ecsma. Diputacion creen tener un derecho para atacar las leyes, de ese mismo derecho podra usar cualquiera otro y entonces el pacto termino. Aun hay mas: un ciudadano puede hacer todo aquello que no le prohiben las leyes, pero V. S. y la Ecsma. Diputacion no pueden hacer sino aquello que ellas previenen; y siendo su principal deber el cumplirlas y el hacerlas cumplir es tanto mas remarcable su infraccion tanto mas escandalosa

su desobediencia como que comete un doble crimen pues ataca la ley que desconoce y aquellas que le imponen la obligacion de hacer cumplir las demas. ¿Como podra V. S. reprender a un soldado por la infraccion de una ley, si V. S. mismo y las primeras autoridades le han dado el escandaloso ejemplo? Concluire por esta parte afirmando, que la proposicion es subversiva por que induce directamente a subvertir el orden social segun he manifestado: es escandalosa por que da un ejemplo funesto a los subditos, y es atentatoria contra el Supremo gobierno por las mismas razones que manifeste en las anteriores. Ni el Sr. Gefe politico ni la Ecsma. Diputacion territorial pueden ni deben sobreponerse a las disposiciones del gobierno. Obedecer y representar si se pulsan males: he aqui la conducta de un magistrado integro, de un buen ciudadano; pero la desobediencia sera siempre funestisima a los pueblos.''

El Sr. Hijar en sus oficios de 16 y 17 de Octubre que constan a fojas 14 y 16 de este escrito, me pide que ordene a los comisionados que he nombrado para la secularizacion de misiones, que obren segun sus prevenciones; pide que se le entreguen los intereses de dichas misiones, y en suma quiere abrogarse la administracion de temporalidades y esto, ¿no es pretender ingerirse en la secularizacion de las misiones?: si no es asi

¿bajo que respecto pretende el gobierno de estas, o con que titulo quiere apodrarse de sus intereses? veanse sus oficios citados y digase si la administracion de temporalidades es o no es anecsa a la secularszacion de misiones. Por eso consulte a la Ecsma. Diputacion si el Sr Hijar era Director de Colonizacion y de Secularizacion o solo del primero, y por eso mismo la Diputacion en la parte ecspositiva de su dictamen que corre a fojas 24 de este escrito desde el parrafo 4 ° al 6.° emitio con mucha propiedad los fundamentos que la indujeron a consultar la tercera proposicion que tan fuertes sensaciones causo al Sr. Hijar. Se infiere de lo espuesto que hubo un robusto motivo para decir en la primera parte de dicha proposicion „que „el Sr. D. Jose Maria Hijar no tendra inge-„rencia alguna en la secularizacion de misio-„nes."

El Sr. Hijar multiplicando el catalogo de dicterios y diatribas con que me obsequia asegura, que el Supremo gobierno se halla facultado para disponer de los bienes de las misiones por el decreto de 26 de Noviembre de 1833 y que nosotros hemos desobedecido sus providencias: para contestar a este cargo ecsaminaremos previamente el decreto citado, el dice asi. „Se faculta al Gobierno „para que tome todas las providencias que „aseguren la Colonizacion, y hagan efectiva

„la secularizacion de las misiones de la Alta „y Baja California, pudiendo al efecto usar „de la manera mas conveniente de las fincas „de obras pias de dichos territorios, a fin „de facilitar los recursos a la comision y fa-„milias que se hallan en esta Capital con „destino a ellos."

Yo no entiendo de logica, pero me parece que en el mismo caso se halla el Sr. Hijar, por que solo su Señoria ha entendido que ese decreto autoriza al Supremo gobierno para disponer de los bienes de las misiones: las personas que lo han meditado entienden que lo faculta, para que haga efectiva la Secularizacion de misiones, y el despojar a los neofitos de sus intereses no es lo que la efectua: secularizacion dice el diccionario castellano, „es el acto o efecto de secularizar." „Secularizacion: es hacer secular lo que era „eclesiastico:" „sacar del estado regular alguna „persona o cosa &a." Ademas la ley de 17 de Agosto de 833 ha determinado la forma en que se ha de hacer la secularizacion y en ninguno de sus articulos manda que el gobierno ocupe los intereses de los neofitos, antes bien los ecsime de gravamenes, disponiendo que la dotacion de parrocos que deben sustituir a los religiosos misioneros y los gastos del culto, sean satisfechos de los productos de las fincas, capitales y rentas del fondo piadoso de las misiones de California. La

consecuencia que se deduce de todo lo dicho es muy clara, y por mas tormentos que se den al decreto de 26 de Noviembre no aparece la autorizacion que el Sr. Hijar supone en el Supremo gobierno para disponer de los bienes de las misiones, pues la unica facultad que le confiere es, para que pueda disponer de las fincas de obras pias para habilitar en Mejico a la comision y familias destinadas a estos territorios, mas los intereses de los neofitos, ni estan en Mejico, ni son fincas de obras pias. Por lo espuesto queda probado que lejos de desobedecer las leyes hemos obligado al Sr. Hijar a que las respete y cumpla.

Cierto es que el Supremo gobierno en las instrucciones insertas a fojas 11 manda ocupar y distribuir todos los bienes de las misiones; ¿a quien le confiere su ejecucion? al Gefe politico, y como el Sr. Hijar fue destituido de ese encargo a virtud de la Suprema orden de 25 de Julio que consta a fojas 7 no comprendo como se aventura a reclamar el ejercicio de una facultad que bajo ningun titulo le corresponde.

La administracion de temporalidades mientras permanescan proindiviso solo puede pertenecer al gobierno territorial y de ninguna manera al Director de Colonizacion: asi lo persuaden las mismas instrucciones en que pretende apoyar sus pretenciones el Sr. Hijar y asi lo determinan espresamente las leyes cu-

yo contenido se aparenta ignorar.

Probado suficientemente que el Supremo gobierno no esta facultado para disponer de los bienes de los neofitos queda desmentida la imputacion de que hemos desobedecido la ley: tampoco desobedecemos la orden del Supremo gobierno por que el representar no es desobedecer. El Supremo gobierno manda que el Gefe politico se apodere de los bienes de las misiones, que distribuya una parte entre los colonos y que realice otra: estamos seguros de que el gobierno no calculo los daños que iba a causar, por que no habria dictado tal providencia y este error que embuelve una infraccion de la ley fundametal, se oculto al gobierno con apariencias de beneficencia. Facil es conocer la falsa idea que se procuro inspirar al gobierno cuando consiente y manda ejecutar el despojo de intereses pertenecientes a mas de veinte mil personas. El gobierno territorial estrechado entre el deber de obedecer una orden suprema y el de conservar las propiedades de la clase mas abatida de sus conciudadanos, busco un medio que conciliara ambos estremos y adopto la medida de suspender la ocupacion de las temporalidades, tomando de ellas lo muy preciso, con calidad de reintegro, para sostener la Colonia y representar a la Superioridad pidiendo la revocacion de tan injusta como anticonstitucional providencia. De esta manera creimos respetar y cumplir las disposiciones del Supremo gobierno, cubrir su responsabilidad y la nuestra ante las leyes, afianzar la observancia de estas, y garantizar las propiedades de nuestros infortunados compatriotas. Pocos o ningunos perjuicios se seguian de esta medida y al contrario, seria muy dificil y quiza imposible restituir los bienes a los neofitos si se llegara a verificar el despojo: bien sabiamos que tal disposicion no debia cuadrar a los intereses del Sr. Hijar, pero tampoco debiamos posponer la suerte de mas veinte mil personas a las pretenciones de un particular, ni el respeto debido al Supremo gobierno nos obligara a consumar la ruina de tantas familias, sin representarlo a la Superioridad que tal vez lo ignoraba. He aqui el objeto de la siguiente nota.

„Gobierno politico de la alta California.= N.° 38.= Ecsmo. Sr. = Desde que se recibio la ley de 17 de Agosto del año procsimo pasado por la cual quedo sancionada la Secularizacion de misiones de este territorio, esperabamos con ansia que el Supremo gobierno espeditara su cumplimiento por medio de un Reglamento prolijo que determinara no solo lo relativo a la administracion espiritual, sino que abrazara la distribucion de los intereses ecsistentes en cada una de las comunidades. Despues de esperar un año las instrucciones de la Superioridad, y no pudiendo

demorar por mas tiempo los efectos de una ley tan benefica y tan deseada y tan solicitada por los mismos neofitos y por todos los hombres sensatos, la Diputacion territorial en uso de sus facultades, con la solemnidad debida formo el Reglamento provisional que con fecha 9 de Agosto ultimo diriji a V. E. solicitando la superior aprobacion del Gobierno. = Entonces y en todo tiempo ha reputado propietarios de los bienes de las misiones a los neofitos de ellas, por que todos son adquiridos con su personal trabajo en comunidad, bajo la direccion de los religiosos misioneros que como unos tutores, han administrado y economizado los bienes ecsistentes despues de mantener, vestir y cubrir las necesidades de los indigenas reducidos como unos menores cuya educacion les fue encomendada por el Gobierno. = Asi es que las fincas, los templos, los bienes raices y semobientes, y cuanto ecsiste en las misiones ha sido adquirido por el constante trabajo y privaciones de los indios. = El erario publico nunca se ha invertido en el fomento directo ni indirecto de estos bienes: al principio se hicieron las primeras fundaciones a costa de los mismos misioneros: despues fueron aucsiliadas por la piedad de algunos particulares, que donaron varios capitales con que se crio el „fondo piadoso de las misiones de Cali„fornia." = De este fondo se daba de limosna

cuatrocientos pesos anuales a cada religioso, con los cuales quedaban satisfechas todas sus necesidades; y un mil pesos por una sola vez en clase de avio temporal para mision y labranza, a cada fundacion: las mas antiguas aucsiliaban con pocas cosas a las nuevas y este fue el unico fomento que recibieron en su origen: todo lo demas fue adquirido por el constante trabajo de los indios. = Asi lo atestigua el Reglamento de 1781 en el titulo 15 articulo 2.°; y asi opino la Junta de fomento de Californias en la esposicion que dirijio al Supremo gobierno el 6 de Abril de 1825 al proponerle un plan para el arreglo de estas misiones. = Por esto y por que es incuestionable el derecho de propiedad que los indios tienen a los bienes que poseen bajo la tutela del gobierno y de la inmediata administracion de los misioneros, no vacilo la Diputacion en determinar que se les adjudicase y distribuyese en pleno dominio y propiedad la mitad de ello, reservando la otra mitad a disposicion del Supremo gobierno para la inversion que tuviere a bien mandarles dar en beneficio de los mismos indios, tanto para el pago de preceptores que los eduquen, como para fondos de propios de sus pueblos, pago de los parrocos que los administren, gastos del culto y otros que se han de ofrecer. = Esto es muy conforme con la justicia y arreglado a las prevenciones que

el Supremo gobierno hizo a los Sres. Echeandia, Victoria y a mi en las instrucciones que se nos dieron al confiarnos el encargo de Gefes politicos. = Apoyada la Diputacion en tan robustos fundamentos, y por que considero al Sr Hijar sin facultad para disponer de los bienes de las misiones con perjuicio de mas de veinte mil indios que son los unicos dueños, se opuso a la entrega, de la manera que observara V. E. en el acuerdo de 22 de Octubre procsimo pasado que le dirijo con esta fecha en copia bajo el num. 5 por el cual determino lo siguiente. = „Que „entre tanto el Supremo gobierno resuelve lo „que tuviere por conveniente, se lleve a efec„to el cumplimiento del Reglamento provisio„nal acordado por la Diputacion para la se„cularizacion de misiones y se ponga a los „indios en posecion de los bienes y tierras. „= Que se de cuenta al Supremo gobierno „con este dictamen y lo que se acordare pa„ra su superior aprobacion. Que igualmente „se le dirija una esposicion pidiendole la re„vocacion de las instrucciones en la parte „que despoja a los Indios de sus propiedades, „y la aprobacion del Reglamento provisional „dado por la Diputacion." = Y tengo el honor de insertarlo a V. E. acompañandole copia de las instrucciones por las cuales se manda ocupar los bienes de las misiones, dar de ellos una parte a los Colonos, realizar una

52

mitad sin objeto ni reglas que garantizen la seguridad de sus productos, y reservar otra mitad para pago de parrocos, preceptores, gastos del culto &a. Ninguna mencion se hace de los indios, siendo los dueños de estos intereses y a la verdad, que este es un despojo violento. = Creemos que sera por olvido padecido en la Secretaria, pero nunca por intension deliberada del gobierno para privar a mas de veinte mil personas indigentes del fruto de sus afanes, unica herencia que recibieron de sus antepasados. = El Sr. Hijar en su oficio 23 de Octubre sostiene, que ni los indios sos propietarios de sus mismos bienes, ni la Diputacion ha debido mandar que se les distribuyan: opina que los indios deben continuar en la misma servidumbre sin mas diferencia que pagarles en lo sucesivo sus jornales: a la verdad Sr. Ecsmo. que en este caso, valiera mas que no cambiaran de situacion por que es empeorar sus males: dice el Sr. Hijar que se les mandaran recojer los intereses que ahora se les distribuyan y que eso sera mas sensible: tal procedimiento creemos que solo ha ecsistido en la cabeza del Sr. Hijar. = De tan erroneos principios se resiente la justicia, la politica y la humanidad: todo el mundo sabe que los indios por su industria y trabajo han adquirido y conservado los bienes de las misiones, de ellos han subsistido y los poseen desde que de

53

grado o por fuerza se hicieron cristianos: luego ¿quien podra privarlos de ellos sin atacar las garantias sociales? La Constitucion federal en el art. 112 restriccion 3ᵃ dice lo siguiente. „El Presidente no podra ocupar la propidad „de ningun particular ni corporacion, ni tur„barle en la posesion, uso o aprovechamiento „de ella; y si en algun caso fuere necesario „para un objeto de conocida utilidad general „tomar la propiedad de un particular o corpo„racion, no lo podra hacer sin previa aproba„cion del Senado, y en sus recesos, del Con„sejo de gobierno, indemnizando siempre a la „parte interesada a juicio de hombres buenos „elejidos por ella y el gobierno." = He aqui Ecsmo. Sr. como el Supremo gobierno no ha podido (hablo con el debido respeto) disponer de la menor parte de los bienes en cuestion: si lo hace como previene la Constitucion „para un objeto de conocida utilidad general" debio preceder tambien la aprobacion del Senado o del Consejo de gobierno: faltando este requisito, es un deber de las autoridades subalternas representar la anticonstitucionalidad de la prvidencia: este es el caso forzoso en que la Diputacion y yo nos encontramos y por lo que reverentemente manifestamos a V. E. que a mas de ser anticonstitucional la providencia es infundada, por que manda realizar una parte de los intereses sin causa justa, sin determinar su inversion, ni mandar que

54

ingresen al Erario federal. = Es verdad que una parte debe invertirse en pago de los Colonos pero no el todo; y lo es tambien, que esta erogacion debe sufrirla las Rentas federales para lo cual, esta autorizado el Gobierno por las leyes de 6 de Abril de 1830 y 21 de Noviembre de 1833; mas ninguna autoriza el despojo de las propiedades de los indios para invertirlas en las colonias. = El Sr. Hijar dice, que el Gobierno esta autorizado para hacerlo por la ley de 26 de Noviembre de 1833, pero este es un equivoco por que la ley dice a letra lo siguiente. = „Se faculta al „Gobierno para que tome todas las providen„cias que aseguren la Colonizacion, y hagan „efectiva la secularizacion de las misiones de „la Alta y Baja California, pudiendo al efecto „usar de la manera mas conveniente de las „fincas de obras pias de dichos territorios, a „fin de facilitar los recursos a la comision y „familias que se hallan en esta Capital con „destino a ellos." = ¿Podra inferirse que por esta ley pueda el Gobierno disponer a su arbitrio de las propiedades de los indios? ¿el despojo de los bienes es para hacer efectiva la secularizacion?: la Diputacion, no le ha dado esa inteligencia, ni cree que el Supremo gobierno la interprete del modo que lo hace el Sr. Hijar. La Diputacion deduce de todo que las referidas instrucciones fueron dadas o con demasiada premura o con sorpresa; y concluye

55

pidiendo a V. E. se digne meditar detenidamente sobre esta dilatada esposicion, y recabar del Ecsmo. Sr. Presidente la debida aprobacion del Reglamento provisional en que se mando dar a los indios, posecion de su libertad, intereses y terrenos: que declare nulos y de ningun valor los articulos 1, 11, 12, 13 y 14 de las instrucciones dadas al Sr. D. Jose Maria Hijar en 23 de Abril ultimo, tanto por ser notoriamente injustas, como por que destituido del mando politico tampoco puede ejercer las funciones respectivas. = Por ultimo Ecsmo. Sr, la Diputacion y yo somos sumisamente obedientes a las leyes y a las autoridades constituidas pero por lo mismo, deseamos acertar, ya por nuestra misma responsabilidad, ya por honor del Supremo gobierno: esto es lo que nos ha inducido a discurrir sobre materia tan delicada: si erramos sera por falta de entendimiento y en tal caso, imploramos la indulgencia de la Superioridad. Rogamos por lo mismo a V. E. que asegure a S. E. el General Presidente nuestro respeto y subordinacion, y que en todo tiempo cumpliremos con gusto sus mandatos. = Dios y Libertad. Monterrey 9 de Noviembre de 1834. = Jose Figueroa. = Ecsmo. Sr. Secretario del Despacho de Relaciones interiores y esteriores."

Creo haber probado suficientemente que no hemos desobedecido las leyes ni al Supremo gobierno como falsamente nos imputa el Sr.

56

Hijar: esto supuesto ¿cual es el mal ejemplo que hemos dado? ¿cual el trastorno del orden social? ¿cual la desobediencia? ¿cual la insurreccion que yo autorizo, y cual en fin, esa multitud de desaciertos con que pretende el Sr. Hijar difamar mi conducta? ¿donde estan esas infracciones que tanto escandalizan a mi detractor? demuestrese una sola pero con hechos positivos, no con esa algarabia de voces que nada significa. Es subversiva la proposicion asegura el Sr. Hijar por que induce directamente a suvertir el orden social, y ¿en que se funda esta impostura? en que no consenti que se usurparan las propiedades de una multitud de ciudadanos: este es mi delito.

Yo dejo este negocio a la calificacion de los hombres sensatos y del Supremo gobierno; mas entre tanto seame permitido interpelar al Sr. Hijar ¿con que derecho me increpa? ¿que facultad tiene para reprenderme? ¿son estos los deberes de un ciudadano? ¿es esta la manera que determinan las leyes para ecsijir la responsabilidad de los funsionarios publicos? ¿el Sr. Hijar puede desobedecerme impunemente? ¿quien lo autorizo para desconocer mi autoridad y declararme infractor? Es preciso convenir, en que mas escandalosa es la resistencia del Sr. Hijar a las prevenciones del gobierno territorial, que la de este con respecto a la entrega de los intereses de las misiones: el Sr. Hijar de hecho, insulta y

desobedece a las autoridades legitimamente constituidas y este si es un delito que debiera castigarse: nosotros evitamos que el Sr Hijar a nombre del gobierno, cometiera el atentado de arrebatar las propiedades de los ciudadanos con infraccion de la Constitucion federal y de las garantias sociales, y esta es una virtud en sentir de las gentes honradas; pero estaba reservado al Sr. Hijar acriminarme por que no tolere sus depredaciones y engaños.

Hagamos un ligero analisis de la inversion que debia darse a etos intereses que pelea el Sr. Hijar: una parte debia invertirse en la mantencion y establecimiento de la Colonia: otra parte debia realizarse y ¿para que? solo el Sr. Hijar lo sabe por que las instrucciones no lo espresan: otra parte debe servir para gastos del culto, de las escuelas, y congrua de los ministros. Y ¿en que ley se encuentra autorizado el despojo de las propiedades de unos ciudadanos para favorecer a otros? en ninguna: ¿que dicen las leyes sobre fundacion de Colonias? la de 18 de Agosto de 1824 establecio las bases generales de colonizacion: la de 6 de Abril de 1830 faculta al gobierno para que pueda colonizar los terrenos que le parescan convenientes, contratandolos y pagandolos a los Estados a que pertenecieren; y para que gaste hasta quinientos mil pesos en el fomento de la colonización: le designa la misma ley un ramo que esclu-

sivamente debe invertirse en la colonizacion, y le da en fin otras atribuciones que seria muy dilatado el referirlas.

La ley de 21 de Noviembre de 1833 autorizo tambien al Supremo gobierno para gastar las cantidades necesarias en colonizar los territorios y demas puntos baldios en que tenga facultad de hacerlo.

La de 26 de Noviembre de 1833 faculto al Supremo gobierno para que tome medidas que aseguren la colonizacion.

El Vice Presidente de la Republica en ejercio del Supremo poder ejecutivo usando de la facultad que le concede la ley de 6 de Abril de 1830 formo en 4 de Febrero de 1834 el Reglamento a que deben sugetarse las Colonias que se establecieren; pero ninguna ley faculta al Supremo gobierno para invertir en colonizar los bienes de las misiones de Californias.

Nada dire del enagenamiento de intereses, que se mandaba ejecutar por que eso, es un misterio insondable de que se puede inferir mucho, y no probarse nada.

En cuanto al pago de la congrua de los ministros, de los gastos del culto y de escuelas nadie descenoce lo util y provechoso que es a los mismos interesados y esa providencia esta en practica por necesidad, pero vease que la ley de 17 de Agosto de 1833 manda que los sueldos señalados a los parrocos

se satisfagan del fondo piadoso de Californias: luego ¿con que derecho hemos de grabar los intereses de la clase de ciudadanos mas menesterosa? yo no encuentro una disposicion legal que justifique el hecho.

,,En la cuarta proposicion se insiste en llevar adelante el Reglamento provisional. Cada vez se aglomeran mas las infracciones y no puede concebirse como una corporacion tan respetable se obstina de tal manera, no solo para desobedecer si no para contrariar las disposiciones del Gobierno general ¿Con que derecho V. S. y la Ecsma. Diputacion han podido disponer de unos bienes que por ningun titulo se han sometido a su inspeccion? ninguna ley, ninguna disposicion les ha autorizado para dar inversion a unos fondos que no les pertenecen, y de que no han podido disponer sin una Suprema resolucion: ¿como respondera V. S. y la Ecsma. Diputacion a los cargos que se hagan por esa arbitrariedad? ¿Que garantias podran tener los poseedores a que hayan de pasar los bienes de las misiones si ni V. S. ni la Ecsma. Diputacion estan facultados para trasmitirlos a ninguna corporacion o persona? Si el Reglamento de que se trata no fuere aprobado como se solicita ¡cuantos trastornos van a causarse! seria necesario estraer los bienes de las manos de los poseedores, y entonces la esperanza burlada haria mil descontentos y acarrearia por consiguiente un cumulo de males que pondrian en consternacion al territorio. == Se insiste en llevar adelante un Reglamento que si se ejecuta, causara ciertamente la ruina del territorio: prescindo Sr. General de las contradicciones que envuelve y de la servidumbre a que quedan sujetos los indigenas: la gran dificultad en politica consiste en encontrar el medio de sacar a los indios de la esclavitud y estado naciente en que se hallan, a un estado de civilidad y libertad. == Ni V. S. ni la Ecsma. Diputacion se han encargado de esta dificultad Con una facilidad que espanta se ha decretado la formacion de pueblos e institucion de Ayuntamientos de la misma manera que se lejislaria para pueblos civilizados y con todos los elementos necesarios al efecto. ¿Que sucedera pues con mudanza tan desconocida y repentina para los nuevos pueblos? Lo que ha sucedido en todos los paises y en todas las naciones donde se ha obrado del mismo modo, perderse, y apelo a la historia. Siempre que un pueblo se saca con violencia de un estado de servidumbre al de libertad, no puede de ninguna manera seguir el vuelo de sus conductores, los pierde de vista y se estravia. Tal es la suerte que han preparado al territorio sus mandatarios. == Siento infinito haber tenido que tocar una cuestion que no me pertenecia, pero al ver que se insiste en llevar adelante un Reglamento que infaliblemente de-

be con el tiempo producir males, crei de mi deber hacer sobre el, estas ligeras reflecciones"

Varios son los cargos y reconvenciones que hace el Sr. Hijar al Gobierno territorial, pero todos carecen de fundamento, como voy a demostrar. El primer cargo es, por que se insiste en llevar a delante el Reglamento provisional de lo cual deduce el Sr. Hijar, que se aglomeran mas las infracciones y que la Diputacion, se obstina en desobedecer y contrariar las disposiciones del Gobierno general. El Reglamento provisional de que se trata es el que formo la Diputacion territorial para espeditar el cumplimiento de la ley de 17 de Agosto de 1833 sobre secularizacion de misiones: en el se determina la forma en que deben distribuirse a los neofitos de cada mision los terrenos que poseen y una parte de los bienes de que tambien estan en posesion, por que son los legitimos dueños de todo. La Diputacion no ha hecho otra cosa, mas que obedecer la ley, y proponer al Ejecutivo el modo de llevarla al cabo: este acto es muy propio de sus atribuciones y ha podido legalmente formar el Reglamento para presentarlo a la aprobacion del Supremo gobierno tanto por que se necesitan conocimientos locales que nadie los posee con mas propiedad que esta Corporacion como por que la ley de 23 de Junio de 1813 y la constitucion española que rige en este territorio, le imponen la obliga-

cion de hacerlo: aquella, la autoriza bajo diversos aspectos y por el articulo 14 del capitulo 2º le manda que presente al Gobierno los planes y proyectos que le parescan mas oportunos, para fomentar la agricultura, la industria las artes y el comercio: esta por el articulo 335 atribucion decima le faculta, para velar sobre la economia, orden y progresos de las misiones.

Si no bastare esta, puede verse la Recopilacion de Indias en cuyas paginas resplandece la sabiduria y caridad con que se dicto aquel codigo en favor de estos mismos indios, que bajo el gobierno libre del Sr. Farias se ha pretendido privarlos aun de los bienes que han adquirido con su trabajo personal. El gobierno territorial no ignora, como el Sr. Hijar, los privilegios que los indios han gozado bajo la ferula del gobierno español: ha tenido presente las leyes 9.ª del tit. 3º lib. 6: la 14ª del tit. 4º lib. 6 y 5ª, 7ª y 9ª del tit. 12 lib. 6 de la Recopilacion de Indias: por ellas esta mandado que no se quite a los indios las tierras donde viven, ni se les moleste: que se les conserven como propias y se les distribuyan: que sus intereses no se inviertan en otros objetos que no sean para su bien y en los objetos para que fueron fundados los pueblos: se hacen otras varias advertencias y prevenciones pero todas en favor de los indios bajo graves penas a los infractores. Tuvo presente

las leyes de 13 de Marzo de 811, 9 de Noviembre de 812, 4 de Enero y 13 de Setiembre de 813, que todas han prevenido se les reparta a los indios sus terrenos.

Convenia, dira mi antagonista, dar importancia politica al Director de Colonizacion y a este fin no se debe perdonar diligencia: por eso quiso rivalizar sus facultades con las del gobierno y despues del grande aparato con que llamaron la atencion publica resulto....... el parto de los Montes.

Las leyes que arreglaron estos establecimientos desde su fundacion sometieron al gobierno territorial y nadie mas que el Sr. Hijar ha desconocido su autoridad en este respecto.

Ignora o no entiende el contenido de las leyes que he citado y solo eso puede servir de disculpa a la audacia con que impropera al gobierno territorial desconociendo sus atribuciones: sepa pues el Sr. Hijar que el gobierno ha prestado sus garantias protectoras para conservar y adjudicar esos intereses a sus propios dueños: que estos aun no salen del estado abyecto en que los coloco naturaleza y que siendo unos niños en la carrera de civilizacion, que no hacen uso de su razon, ni conocen sus verdaderos intereses, debe el gobierno desempeñar las funciones de padre comun y dispensarles todo genero de proteccion: esta es la obligacion de un gobierno justo. ¿Y podra vituperarsele por que de miseros pupilos los convierte en propietarios libres distribuyendoles sus propios intereses? ¿Por ventura la ley de 17 de Agosto de 833 no es contraida a este unico objeto? ¿No es para sacarlos del estado eclesiastico a que estaban sometidos para redimirlos del pupilaje servil en que han vivido? Todos estamos convencidos de estas verdades.

Supuesto que los neofitos son separados del gobierno economico de los religiosos misioneros, quedan indudablemente sometidos al gobierno politico y este tiene obligacion por la ley de 23 de Junio de 813 de establecer sus autoridades locales con arreglo a las leyes de la materia: debe asi mismo distribuirles los intereses que han adquirido en comunidad por que deja de ecsistir esa, y ellos entran en el goce de los derechos de ciudadano. Estos son los fundamentos que tuvo la Diputacion territorial para proyectar el Reglamento en cuestion, y presentarlo a la aprovacion del Gobierno general: operacion que nada tiene de arbitraria, ni comete ninguna infraccion, ni desobediencia, ni contraria orden alguna del Supremo gobierno, operacion en fin, digna del zelo acrisolado de esta Corporacion por el bien estar de sus comitentes; mas a pesar de la justicia con que la emprendio, sufrio la oposicion del Gefe politico que por delicadeza, y por que esperaba que su sucesor trajese la ley reglamentada, contradijo la opinion de la Dipu-

tacion y detubo por mas de seis meses la formacion del Reglamento citado. Sabia yo que debia llegar a relevarme el Sr. D. Jose Maria Hijar, y no queria prevenir su juicio en cuanto al modo de llevar adelante la secularizacion: tampoco queria emprenderla, por que conoci lo delicado y dificil de su ejecucion, y los resultados sensibles que debia producir llevada al cabo simultaneamente y con precipitacion: mi oposicion por estas razones y otras fue publica y notoria, pero como el mal estaba causado, y yo constituido en el deber de obedecer las leyes y cuidar de su cumplimiento, tube que someterme al imperio de las circunstancias contra mi propio convencimiento. No hago merito de este incidente por vindicarme, si no para que se califique si he procedido o no con integridad y franqueza.

Creo que con lo espuesto no le quedara duda al Sr. Hijar de que los intereses de las misiones estan sometidos a nuestra inspeccion y que hemos debido reglamentar el modo de distribuirse entre sus mismos dueños: queda demostrado el error de que ninguna ley nos autoriza para dar inversion a esos fondos. De esta manera respondemos a los cargos que por algun evento se nos hicieran, por la supuesta arbitrariedad de que nos acusa.

Otro de los cargos es contraido a que ninguna garantia tendran los poseedores a que hayan de pasar los bienes de las misiones por

que ni la Ecsma. Diputacion ni yo tenemos facultades de trasmitirlas a ninguna corporacion o persona. Sepa el Sr. Hijar si lo ignora que trasmitir es „ceder 'o traspasar lo que se posee a otro": es asi que nosotros solo reglamentamos el modo de distribuir los intereses entre los mismos poseedores, resulta por consecuencia forzosa, que no hemos cedido ni traspasado cosa alguna de un dueño a otro y que los poseedores de los referidos intereses tienen suficientes garantias para disfrutarlos, por que nadie mas que el Sr. Hijar, les ha disputado el derecho de propiedad y posecion de que han gozado sin interrupcion bajo la proteccion del Gobierno desde la fundacion de las misiones. Y ¿quien sino el Sr. Hijar podra dudar que el Supremo gobierno apruebe el Reglamento de secularizacion? convengamos en que su Señoria vaticina infundadamente que se estraeran los bienes del poder de los poseedores y que esta injusticia, solo pudiera cometerse bajo sus auspicios, pero de ninguna manera bajo el amparo del Gobierno supremo que siempre ha respetado las propiedades de sus subditos y con mas razon, las de esa clase de ciudadanos que reputa como menores, y viven bajo su tutela. ¿En que consiste que el Reglamento causara la ruina del territorio como asegura el Sr. Hijar? ¿Sera acaso por que su Señoria no disfruta a su arbitrio de las fortunas de los neofitos? Solo ellos tienen derecho

a disfrutar el fruto de su trabajo y esto es cabalmente lo que disgusta al Sr. Hijar.

Misteriosamente dice el Sr. Hijar que prescinde de las contradicciones que embuelve el Reglamento y de la servidumbre a que quedan sujetos los indigenas: yo apreciaria que demostrara las contradicciones y la servidumbre de los indigenas que censura para satisfacer a sus objeciones, pero suponer sin datos ni constancias arguye impostura o mala fe.

Ni la Diputacion ni yo, dice, que nos encargamos de ecsaminar los medios de sacar a los indigenas de la esclavitud al estado de civilidad y libertad: que con una facilidad que espanta se ha decretado la formacion de pueblos e institucion de Ayuntamientos como si se legislara para pueblos civilizados: esto a mi juicio acredita una contradiccion inconcebible por que se supone y se murmura la servidumbre de los neofitos, y se objeta al mismo tiempo la ecsesiva libertad que les esta acordada; pero prescindiendo de multitud de redundancias que no vienen al caso me contraere a manifestar que la Diputacion solo ha cuidado de mantener a los indigenas en la depencia precisa e indispensable para conservar entre ellos el buen orden y subordinacion a fin de evitar sus demasias y estravios a que propenden por su estupida ignorancia: ha cuidado asi mismo de no atacar su libertad ni violar las garantias sociales. Estos hechos acreditan la prevision con que hemos procurado sacarlos de la servidumbre al estado de libertad sin desconocer las dificultades que ofrece el cambio: demasiados obstaculos hemos tenido que vencer y con mucha anterioridad a la ley de secularizacion representamos sus inconvenientes no para que se suspendiera, sino para que se determinara mas parcialmente y pausada por ser asi mas adecuado al caracter y circunstancias de los indigenas; pero como no se ha querido escuchar la opinion de las autoridades locales, y entonces el mismo Sr Hijar que ahora nos censura y el Ayudante Inspector Don Jose Maria Padres agitaban en Mejico la sancion de la ley que debia enriquecerlos, no se tubo a bien meditar sobre lo que represento el Gefe politico. Se dio la citada ley y no es ciertamente el gobierno territorial quien la sanciono: esto supuesto tampoco debe ser responsable de los malos resultados, por que no ha hecho otra cosa que obedecer y hacer cumplir las leyes evitando cuanto cabe en sus facultades el estravio de unos hombres sacados repentinamente de la servidumbre a la libertad. Estraña el Sr. Hijar que se formen pueblos cuando el gobierno territorial no les ha dado mas que el nombre puesto que ellos estan formados hace muchos años bajo el titulo de misiones; pero ¿acaso por esto han dejado de ser pueblos no ciertamente: veasc la definicion de esta palabra y se confesara que siem-

pre han sido pueblos. De la misma manera se estraña la institucion de Ayuntamientos siendo una de las principales obligaciones del gobierno territorial el cuidar que se establezcan donde no los haya: asi lo previene espresamente la ley de 23 de Junio de 1813 capitulo 2 articulo 1.º y la constitucion en el articulo 335. Sepa igualmente el Sr. Hijar que si las leyes que arreglan el gobierno de los pueblos no son analogas a los de los indigenas, la culpa no es del gobierno territorial por que no tiene poder para variarlas ni reformarlas y debe hacer la aplicacion de ellas sin restriccion. Vaticina asi mismo el Sr. Hijar que los indigenas no podran seguir el vuelo de sus conductores por que son arrancados con violencia del estado servil al de libertad: que deben perderse lo mismo que ha sucedido en todas las Naciones donde se ha obrado del mismo modo; tales hechos atestigua con la historia y acaba su discurso pronosticando el estravio de los indigenas debido a sus mandatarios, esto es, al gobierno territorial. No me ocupare de probar que son panicos los temores del Sr. Hijar por que en su concepto los neofitos no deben salir del pupilage en que los han mantenido, ni se les deben dar propiedades de ningun genero por que no son dignos de poseerlas, ni se les podra entonces obligar a cultibar los campos de sus feudatarios: tales son las ideas filantropicas de su Señoria; bajo tales bases pro-

yectaba sistemar el gobierno politico de los neofitos de las misiones y a los que mucho favor les hiciera, los contemplaria como Colonos para darles un pedazo de tierra: me permitira el Sr. Hijar que le recuerde estas especies emitidas en varias conferencias que tubimos y que le refute contradiciendo absolutamente su opinion. Tendra muy presente que defendi con las mismas leyes, el derecho que los neofitos tienen a ser nivelados en sus goces al comun de los ciudadanos, y el preferente que les asiste para que se les adjudique los terrenos y bienes que poseen adquiridos con su personal trabajo y el de sus ascendientes: tampoco pude convenir en que se les considerase como Colonos, por que son unos propietarios establecidos en los mismos terrenos donde nacieron y por otras razones que seria dilatado referir. Sea norabuena, que no todos ellos sean capaces de seguir el vuelo de sus conductores por el estado de inepcia en que se encuentran, mas no por esto deben omitirse las medidas beneficas que se han dictado en su favor: se estraviaran algunos, pero se lograran muchos y el resultado, siempre es un bien para la sociedad, y un adelanto en la civilizacion: tratase, no solo de convertirlos de pupilos en propietarios, sino de educarlos y hacrlos industriosos y si esto no se emprende una vez, jamas saldran de la esfera miserable de esclavos: preciso es otorgarles ese transito peligroso, para que lleguen al fin

y esto, no es ciertamente arrancarlos con violencia del estado servil al de libertad como falsamente asienta el Sr. Hijar, por que no quedan abandonados a si mismos sino que permanecen bajo la proteccion y amparo del gobierno, sujetos a leyes y reglamentos peculiares: el Sr. Hijar no se a que naciones o a que hictoria los compara y por lo mismo no puedo contestar a su argumento. Culpa como tiene de costumbre al gobierno territorial por los malos resultados que pronostica sin mas datos que su dicho, apoyado en un juego de voces que nada significa en sustancia.

Confiesa por ultimo, que estas cuestiones no le pertenecen, pero que al ver que se insiste en llevar adelante el Reglamento que con el tiempo debe causar males, se creyo obligado a hacer esas ligeras reflecsiones. Mas honroso le hubiera sido no tomar parte en dichas cuestiones supuesto que no le pertenecen como francamente confiesa: de hecho, ¿con que facultad objeta las providencias del gobierno territorial cuando ha cesado su encargo de Gefe politico? ¿para que tanta acrimonia contra el gobierno territorial por que solicita la distribucion de intereses a sus legitimos dueños y no se entregan a las manos muertas del Sr. Hijar? Es preciso repetir que poco o nada le importa a su Señoria la suerte de los indigenas, y que el unico motivo de su indigesto discurso lo ocaciona el ver que se le escapan los cuantiosos capitales en que pretendia ejercitar su esclusivo agiotage bajo el pretesto ostensible de la Colonizacion, y con detrimento notorio de los acomuladores de esos bienes. En esto estaban cifrados los grandiosos proyectos de felicidad que tanto preconizaron el Sr. Hijar y sus adictos hasta engolfarse en la arrogante presuncion, de titularse los redentores de los Californios. Si como confiesa que no le corresponde tratar estas cuestiones se hubiese abstenido de ingerirse en ellas, me hubiera escusado la necesidad de publicar sus ambiciosas pretensiones.

"La quinta proposicion se contrae a reglamentar algunos procedimientos de V. S. y mios y a declarar con la firmeza de un legislador que no se situe ninguna Colonia en terrenos de las misiones por pertenecer a los indigenas. Por lo que hace relacion a mi, nada tengo que decir supuesto que estoy resuelto a no observar otras instrucciones que las que se me dieron por el Supremo Gobierno general como unicas legitimas que ecsisten hasta hoy: me haria ciertamente despreciable ante los hombres e indigno hijo de Jalisco si tubiera la debilidad de sujetarme a reconocer disposiciones dadas por una autoridad estraviada que saliendose de la orbita de sus atribuciones pretende usurpar las cometidas a los altos poderes de la union. No es V. S. ni la Ecsma. Diputacion quien hade reglamentar mis procedimientos con res-

pecto a mi comision: a mi me rigen las leyes y no los caprichos ni las arbitrariedades. = Si se cree que los terrenos de las misiones son de los indios ¿como es que por el Reglamento de V. S solo se les manda dar en su macsimun un pequeño cuadrado de cuatrocientas varas por lado y esta pequeña porcion para abrevadero en comun? ¡Cuantas contradicciones Sr. General! Parece que solo se trata de alucinar a los miserables indigenas abusando de su candor. No es este el lugar ni a mi me corresponde investigar el derecho de propiedad sobre los terrenos que se procura inculcar a los indigenas con total esclusion del derecho eminente del Gobierno, pero si me sera permitido decir que algun dia sera funesta la inculcacion a los mismos que la han proclamado y perjudicial a la prosperidad del territorio."

Para contestar a los diversos cargos que hace el Sr. Hijar al Gobierno territorial, sera preciso repetir el contenido de la quinta proposicion que ha combatido: ella dice lo siguiente. = "El Gefe politico de las ecsistencias de "las misiones mandara dar a los Colonos las "herramientas y demas aucsilios que espresan las "instrucciones, luego que lleguen donde se han "de establecer, sacando a prorata dichos auc-"silios para no perjudicar a una sola mision: "por cuenta de la asignacion señalada a cada "persona les ministrara semillas, carne y lo mas "preciso para su manutencion: el Sr. Director

"de la Colonia estara sujeto al Gefe politico "y le dara una relacion circunstanciada del nu-"mero de personas que van a colonizar, y un "presupuesto de lo que importe el pago que "debe hacerseles cada mes, para que a ese "respecto arregle proporcionalmente las submi-"nistraciones. Los terrenos de las misiones son "de los indios y no se establecera en ellos "ninguna Colonia." Yo apelo al juicio de los hombres sensatos para que califiquen si estas providencias son del resorte del Godierno territorial y si estan conforme al espiritu de las leyes; mas para alejar las equivocaciones, contestare brevemente a las objeciones del Señor Hijar.

Dice este Sr. que esta resuelto a no observar otras instrucciones que las que recibio del Supremo gobierno, y que se haria despreciable, si tubiera la debilidad de sujetarse a disposiciones dadas por una autoridad estraviada, que ha usurpado los poderes del Gobierno de la Union. Ya he demostrado, y el mismo Sr. Hijar confiesa, que ha cesado su encargo de Gefe politico y con el, todas las facultades que le son inherentes inclusas las que le daban las instrucciones que recibio del Supremo gobierno; pero le es muy sensible desprenderse del poder que tanto alagaba sus esperanzas, y no teme contradecirse con tal de vulnerar los respetos que debe a la autoridad: ha dicho, que todo hombre sin fuero privilegiado

debe estar sujeto a las autoridades locales y que era inutil hacer esa prevencion y en seguida replica, que ni la Ecsma. Diputacion ni yo, debemos reglamentar sus procedimientos. Tengo asi mismo demostrado que por el reglamento de 4 de Febrero de 1834, estan sometidas las Colonias a los Gefes politicos que el Gobierno nombrare y lo estan tambien por derecho civil: he probado que la Diputacion y yo, estamos facultados por las leyes para reglamentar los procedimientos del Sr Hijar como Director de la Colonia por mas que a su Señoria le disguste: de la misma manera he probado, la legitimidad de la jurisdiccion que ejercemos, por que es emanada legalmente del Poder supremo que nos la ha confiado con las formalidades que prescriben las leyes: asi es, que no sabemos en lo que el Sr. Hijar hace consistir la ilegitimidad. y la usurpacion; pero mal que le pese, debe estar sujeto al gobierno territorial, y obedecer sus mandatos sin reprenderlos por que carece de derecho para ello; y aun en la hipotesis de que nosotros ecsedieramos nuestras atribuciones, solo tendria derecho a demandarnos, ecsigiendonos la responsabilidad conforme lo determinan las leyes, pero nunca para desobedecernos: por lo mismo repetire esta pregunta. ¿Quien es el Sr. Hijar para desconocer mi autoridad y declararme infractor? ¿es acaso algun jurisconsulto sin tacha en el caso presente? no es ciertamente mas que subdito, y subdito sin jurisdiccion independien-te del gobierno politico como pretende.

Ironicamente dice el Sr. Hijar, que con la firmeza de un legislador, declaramos que no se situe la Colonia en terrenos de las misiones, por pertenecer a los indigenas. Antes de pa-sar adelante le probare, que no es una dispo-sicion del gobierno territorial, sino una preven-cion terminante de la ley de 18 de Agosto de 1824, cuyo articulo segundo dice lo siguien-te. ,,Son objeto de esta ley aquellos terrenos ,,de la Nacion, que no siendo de propiedad ,,particular, ni pertenecientes a corporacion al-,,guna o pueblo, pueden ser colonizados." El Supremo gobierno reglamento aquella ley en 21 de Noviembre de 1828 y en el articulo 17 previene lo siguiente. ,,En los territorios en ,,que haya misiones, los terrenos que estas o-,,cupan no podran colonizarse por ahora y has-,,ta que se resuelva si deben considerarse co-,,mo propiedad de las reducciones de los neo-,,fitos catecumenos y pobladores mejicanos." Bastara lo dicho para convencer, que no es una petulancia del gobierno territorial la que le obligo a dictar aquella providencia, sino una disposicion terminante de ley que ni esta de-rogada, ni se puede interpretar.

Todas las leyes que he citado dan a los neofitos el derecho de propiedad a los terre-nos que se reconocen por de las misiones, de-recho que respeto el gobierno español durante

su dominacion y que nadie hasta ahora les ha in-terrumpido: pero aunque asi no fuera ¿no es cier-to que les favorece la posesion civil y natural que nadie puede poner en duda? ¿les negara el Sr. Hijar que nacieron en la tierra en que es-tan domiciliados y que la estan cultivando ba-jo la tutela del gobierno mas ha de cincuen-ta años? ¿dejaran ellos a pesar de su inercia, de conocer y creer, que son dueños de la tie-rra que cultivan, y de los intereses que ad-quieren con su trabajo? esto es muy cierto por mas que se trate de obscurecerlo. Pregunta el Sr. Hijar que si el terreno de las misiones es de los indios ,,¿como es que por el Reglamen-,,to de V. S. solo se les manda dar en su ,,macsimun un pequeño cuadrado de cuatro-,,cientas varas por lado y otra pequeña porcion ,,para abrevadero en comun?" El Reglamento no es mio sino formado por el gobierno terri-torial y viene muy mal la satira del Sr. Hijar: a los neofitos se les señalo por primera vez ese pequeño cuadrado, por que no se conside-ran capaces de cultivar mayor cantidad, y por que se procura distribuir la superficie del te-rreno en proporcion al numero de individuos que se consideran con derecho, dejando la puer-ta abierta para aplicarlo a los industriosos que se dediquen con mas empeño a cultivarlo. Es falso, que el terreno señalado para abrevadero comun de los ganados de los neofitos sea tan pequeño como asegura el Sr. Hijar, y la prue-

ba es, que ni aun se determino cantidad fija, sino que se dejo al arbitrio de los comisiona-dos para que pudieran estenderlo o acortarlo, en proporcion del mayor o menor numero de ganados, y de la estension de terreno perte-neciente a cada mision. A mas del terreno que debe darse a cada individuo en pleno dominio y propiedad, se propuso que se señalen egidos, y se asigne a cada pueblo alguna estension de terrenos bajo el titulo de propios, a fin de em-plear sus productos en beneficio comun de ca-da pueblo; pero el Sr. Hijar; no fijo su con-sideracion sobre estos puntos, ni su critica tie-ne otro fundamento que el desahogo injusto de su resentimiento: sus esclamaciones vagas, carecen absolutamente de apoyo y sus im-putaciones, son otras tantas calumnias. Parece (dice) que solo se trata de alucinar a los mi-serables indigenas abusando de su candor. ¿Y de que manera probara el Sr. Hijar su aser-cion? Con el silencio, por que no tiene datos que presentar, como tiene ligereza en inventar imposturas gratuitas. Sepa pues el Sr. Hijar, que el gobierno territorial, a creido de buena fe que hace un bien positivo a los indigenas en cuantas providencias ha dictado a su favor y de hecho ¿como puede ser un alucinamiento el darles una propiedad territorial y libertad para adquirir y gozar cuantos bienes de fortu-na les proporcione su industria? y aun cuan-do no consiguieran esas ventajas positivas que

nada tienen de ilusorias, desconoce el Sr. Hi-jar que los gobiernos, como dice el sabio Bentham, tienen que elejir de los males el me-nor? Confiesa el Sr. Hijar mal de su grado, que no le corresponde investigar el derecho de propiedad sobre los terrenos que se incul-ca a los indigenas con total esclusion del de-recho eminente del gobierno; pero que esa in-culcacion sera funesta a los que la proclaman y perjudicial al territorio. ¿Si no le toca inves-tigar sobre este asunto, con que derecho in-crepa al gobierno territorial? luego ese estilo chocarrero, es una demasia irrespetuosa, si no es criminal. No le toca investigar, y tiene el arrojo de negar abiertamente a los neofitos, no solo el derecho de propiedad a los terrenos que se les ha mandado adjudicar, sino aun de los bienes que han adquirido con su personal trabajo: asi consta en todo su discurso y mas espresamente lo refirio en las diversas confe-rencias que tubo conmigo sobre el particular: si el Sr. Hijar se precia de caballero no podra negar esta verdad. ¿Y cual es el derecho emi-nente del gobierno? yo lo ignoro y he proba-do con la Constitucion que el gobierno no puede tomar la propiedad de ningun particular ni corporacion. El Sr. Hijar tampoco espresa en que consiste ese derecho eminente. Nos tiene muy a mal que inculquemos a los indi-genas sus derechos, y poco antes nos acusa de que los sujetamos a una servidumbre ignominiosa, que ni la Diputacion ni yo nos encargamos de la dificultad de sacarlos del estado de servidumbre al de libertad, que los arrancamos con violencia de aquel y que los precipitamos a este para que se pierdan; a renglon seguido, que solo tratamos de alucinarlos abusando de su candor &a. &a: he aqui una serie prolongada de inconsecuencias que ni el mismo autor podra comentar, si hace un lugar a la razon. Y ¿por que razon nos sera funesto inculcar a los neofitos sus derechos? ¡dejemos a los egoistas que lamenten los progresos de nuestros infortunados indigenas, nosotros respetamos los derechos del hombre sea cual fuera su origen! Se perjudicara por esto el territorio en sentir del Sr. Hijar, pero ¿de donde deduce tales resultados? lo ignoro; pretende que se le crea bajo su palabra, y esta no es una prueba.

„La seesta proposicion, se contrae a mandar retener las instrucciones que me dio el Supremo gobierno. Esta resolucion me ha sorprendido sobre manera: nunca crei que se abusara hasta tal punto de la buena fe con que me preste a obsequiar los deseos de la Ecsma. Diputacion mandandole originales las instrucciones que solicito con el mayor comedimiento hasta proponerme que las manifestase si no encontraba inconveniente. ¿Con que derecho se me despoja de un documento que me pertenece en propiedad mientras el Supremo gobier-

no no me releve de la Direccion de Colonizacion? Estoy abismado Sr. General y nunca crei que una corporacion tan respetable me atacara de una manera que ofende su decoro y delicadeza: ¿con que fin se me recojen las instrucciones? yo no lo alcanzo a la verdad. Si es para representar contra ellas, yo habria dado una copia siempre que se me hubiese pedido: si es para que no tengan efecto bastaria que al calce de la orden hubiera puesto el Sr. Gefe politico „No se cumple en este Territo-„rio." No habiendo pues facultad para recogerme un documento que me pertenece y teniendo que cumplir mi comision en otros puntos fuera del territorio del mando de V S. espero se servira devolverme mis instrucciones para los efectos consiguientes."

Las instrucciones se recogieron, por que fueron cometidas al Gefe politico de la alta California, y no precisamente a D. Jose Maria Hijar: es un documento oficial, que solo pertenece al mismo gobierno, y no al Sr. Hijar como impropiamente pretende: debe ecsistir en el archivo del gobierno que es la oficina de la Nacion: debe en fin, permanecer en poder del Gefe politico, unico encargado por la Constitucion y leyes del cumplimiento de estas, y los decretos del Gobierno supremo. Sin detenerme en relatar todo lo que esta prevenido sobre la materia citare unicamente los articulos 1. ° y 17 capitulo 3. ° de la ley de 23 de Junio de

1813 que dicen asi. „1. ° Estando el gobier-„no politico de cada provincia, segun el arti-„culo 324 de la constitucion, a cargo del ge-„fe superior politico nombrado por el rey en „cada una de ellas, reside en el la superior „autoridad dentro de la provincia para cuidar „de la tranquilidad publica, del buen orden, de „la seguridad de las personas y bienes de sus „habitantes, de la ejecucion de las leyes y or-„denes del gobierno, y en general de todo lo „que pertenece al orden publico y prosperidad „de la provincia; y asi como sera responsable „de los abusos de su autoridad, debera ser tam-„bien puntualmente respetado y obedecido de „todos. No solo podra ejecutar gubernativamen-„te las penas impuestas por las leyes de po-„licia y bandos de buen gobierno, sino que ten-„dra facultad para imponer y ecsigir multas a „los que le desobedezcan o le falten al respe-„to, y a los que turben el orden o el sosiego „publico. 17. Solo el gefe politico circulara por „toda la provincia todas las leyes y decretos „que se espidieren por el gobierno, haciendo se „publiquen en la capital de la provincia, y se „entere de ellas la diputacion provincial, y cui-„dando de remitir las leyes y decretos a los „gefes politicos subalternos, si los hubiere, para „que los hagan circular en su territorio, o a „los alcaldes primeros de las cabezas de par-„tido para el mismo efecto. Siendo de la res-„ponsabilidad del gefe politico la circulacion

„de las leyes y decretos, ecsigira recibos de a-„quellas autoridades a quienes los comunicare."

Esto supuesto, ¿podra el gobierno territorial hacer cumplir las disposiciones del Supremo gobierno sin tener conocimiento y constancia de ellas? ¿o el Sr. Hijar por si y ante si las hara cumplir con independencia del gefe politico? ¿que clase de autoridad es la que ejerce? ¿en que se funda para decir que las instrucciones es una propiedad que le pertenece? Si de la misma manera pretendieran los empleados publicos hacerse dueños de las leyes, ordenes y documentos que reciben, no ecsistirian los archivos y todo seria un barullo. A mas de los motivos espuestos, desconfiaba el gobierno territorial que se hiciera mal uso de las instrucciones como en efecto se verificaron posteriormente sus temores, y por eso las mando recoger, no con otro objeto, que el de procurar su cumplimiento en lo posible, y evitar los abusos del Director de Colonizacion. El gobierno territorial tenia la necesidad de obrar de esa manera, por que tampoco habia recibido otras ordenes que pusieran a cubierto su responsabilidad, en razon de que solo se habia comunicado al Sr. Hijar durante su encargo de Gefe politico; pero que habiendo cesado sus funciones, ninguna jurisdiccion le quedo como Director de la Colonia, a quien el Gefe politico debia comunicar para su cumplimiento las prevenciones del Supremo gobierno comprendidas en las citadas instrucciones referentes a tal encargo. De otra manera ¿como pudiera cumplir el Sr. Hijar esas supremas disposiciones? ¿obraria con total independencia del gobierno territorial? demuestre pues de donde son emanadas esas atribuciones que quiere ejercer; pero su silencio confiirma mi opinion y esta, me vindica de los improperios que se me prodigan. Apesar de lo dicho, se le devolvieron las instrucciones para acreditarle nuestra deferencia a lo que es compatible con el deber y ¿de que le han servido? de nada, por que precisamente ha ocurrido al Gefe politico para apoyar en su autoridad y ordenes el cumplimiento de ellas: este es un hecho que no podra negar el Sr. Hijar.

,,La septima proposicion, se contrae a varias peticiones que la Ecsma. Diputacion cree conveniente dirigir al Supremo gobierno y nada tendria que decir sobre ellas; mas como aparece que se pida la revocacion de las instucciones en la parte que despoja a los indios de sus propiedades, creo de mi deber manifestar que esta idea solo puede nacer de alguna equivocacion o por el diferente concepto que hemos formado de los bienes de las misiones. El Gobierno lejos de quitar a los indigenas, me manda a hacerlos propietarios, y darles poseciones que hasta ahora no han tenido: ellos iban a disfrutar de un bien real y verdadero, en el momento que yo estubiese en aptitud de

desempeñar mi comision; pero V. S. y la Ecsma. Diputacion no lo juzgaron conveniente; por consiguiente no vendra sobre mi la responsabilidad."

¡Esto si es un alucinamiento, Sr. Hijar! ¿tan pronto ha olvidado que solo pretende apoderarse de los bienes de las misiones para repartir algunos a los colonos, y realizar otros? ¿no es cierto que ni una sola palabra se dice por las instrucciones en favor de los neofitos? ¿no es cierto que el articulo primero de las citadas instrucciones previene que se ocupen todos los bienes pertenecientes a las misiones aucsiliandose de la fuerza militar para la espresada ocupacion? ¿no es cierto que por este articulo se les arrebata a los neofitos los bienes que han adquirido con su trabajo personal y que disfrutan en pacifica posesion? ¿no es cierto que se les infiere en este hecho un despojo violento? ¿negara el Sr. Hijar que en las diferentes ocasiones que discutimos este negocio me sostubo que para hacer la felicidad de los neofitos bastaria dejarlos en libertad, y pagar en lo succesivo sus jornales, a los que se ocuparen en los trabajos de las mismas misiones? ¿no es cierto que para desembarazarse de las observaciones que le hice en favor de las propiedades de los neofitos me contesto que cuando mas, debieran considerarse como Colonos a los que pretendieran terrenos para cultivar? ¿y se tiene valor de asegurar con enfasis, que los ba

ha hacer propietarios, cuando pretende despojarlos de los bienes y tierras que poseen? ¿y no es esto abusar hasta del verdadero sentido de las palabras?: tales inconsecuencias son hijas de la acalorada fantasia del Sr. Director de Colonizacion.

,,La octava proposicion se reduce a que se publique el acuerdo de la Diputacion. Publiquese en hora buena, aunque me es sensible que algunos hechos se hayan desfigurado, y lo que es mas sensible, en descredito del Gobierno general, que ambos debiamos sostener. Algun dia, vera la luz publica el conjunto de este suceso: los hombres todos se impondran de las razones de una y otra parte; formaran un juicio comparativo, y fallaran."

Hoy ha llegado el dia que pronostico el Sr, Hijar: el publico va a instruirse de estas ruidosas ocurrencias, y fallara en favor del que tubiere la justicia. Si el representar al Supremo gobierno contra una de sus providencias que ataca la constitucion con violacion de las garantias sociales, es un descredito para el mismo Gobierno, la culpa no es de las autoridades subalternas que tienen la obligacion de manifestarlo, o se hacen complices de la infraccion si la ejecutan sin ecsamen. Ningun deshonor puede resultar al Secretario que firmo la providencia, por rebocarla si se convence de que es anti-constitucional, por que no es infalible, y pudo muy bien equivocarse.

,,Desearia saber por que incidente vino á mezclarse ante la Ecsma. Diputacion la decision sobre entrega del Gobierno politico con la comision especial de Colonizacion; pero V. S. no ha creido conveniente comunicarmelo: yo lo habria apreciado para deshacer equivocaciones en que puede haberse incurrido, por que de otra manera no encuentro como hayan podido dictarse medidas tan anarquicas, estrepitosas y trascendentales al orden social."

¿Que entendera el Sr Hijar por anarquia?: el diccionario castellano dice que es ,,el estado ,,que no tiene cabeza que lo gobierne" está definicion es muy mal aplicada por el Sr. Hijar en el caso presente; pues las medidas que el Sr. Hijar llama anarquicas son dictadas por el gobierno constitucional del territorio, cuya autoridad es legitima como tengo probado: la facultad que ejercio al dictar las espresadas medidas es propia de sus atribuciones y tienen por objeto, llamar al orden al Sr. Hijar que pretende estraviarse en contravencion a las leyes. A esto llama el Sr. Hijar medidas anarquicas y estrepitosas, que solo tienen de esto, el ruido que causo al publico la novedad de pretensiones tan estrañas.

,,En vista pues de todo lo espuesto suplico a V. S. que escuchando la voz de su conciencia y la razon, se sirva mudar de dictamen por ecsigirlo asi el deber y las leyes y espero tendra a bien devolverme mis instrucciones sin necesidad de nuevas reclamaciones por ser a todas luces justa esta devolucion."

Ya he manifestado que las instrucciones a pesar de pertenecer al archivo del gobierno territorial, se le devolvieron al Sr. Hijar, pero en ninguna otra cosa se vario de dictamen; por que lejos de desvanecer las esclamaciones vagas provocaron un ecsamen prolijo de las leyes por las cuales, rectifico el gobierno territorial sus operaciones y las llevo adelante.

„Concluyo pues suplicando a V. S. se sirva manifestarme su ultima resolucion para arreglar mis ulteriores procedimientos y espero se servira disimular el lenguage austero de un republicano que reclama el cumplimiento de las leyes."

No es por reclamar el cumplimiento de las leyes el lenguage que ha usado el Sr. Hijar por que le he provado lo contrario: el publico calificara si los republicanos tienen derecho a contravenir los principios sociales y desobedecer a las autoridades.

„Al concluir esta comunicacion he oido publicar el acuerdo de la Ecsma. Diputacion y segun percivi en la parte espositiva del dictamen de la comision, todo su apoyo para que no se cumplan las disposiciones del Gobierno general consiste en considerar anecsas a la Gefatura politica las instrucciones que nos ocupan. Me permitira V. S. que por moderacion, no manifieste la idea que he formado de equi-

vocacion tan remarcable. El oficio con que aquellas se me acompañaron y que V. S. me devolvio dice a la letra „Acompaño a V. S. „de orden del Ecsmo Sr. Vice Presidente las „instrucciones a que debe arreglarse en el de-„sempeño de su comision relativa a la Colo-„nizacion de California y le participo al mismo „tiempo que por la Secretaria de Hacienda se „da la orden al Comisario general de Jalisco „para que ponga a disposicion de V. S. cuan-„to dinero haya recibido del Sr. General D. „Joaquin Parres, con el fin de que pueda V. S. „llenar las prevenciones que se hacen en las „referidas instrucciones." Que se pregunte a los niños de la escuela si estas instrucciones se dirigian a otro que al Director de Colonizacion. Mi comision se estiende igualmente a la baja California segun las ordenes que tengo, y para aquel territorio no traia ningun caracter politico; parece pues fuera de toda duda que la comision se me cometio como a Director y no como a Gefe politico. = Tengo el honor de reiterar a V. S. las protestas de mi aprecio y distinguida consideracion. = Dios y Libertad. Monterrey Octubre 23 de 1834. = Jose Maria de Hijar. = Sr. Gefe politico General D. Jose Figueroa."

Despues que nos ha llenado de diatribas y dicterios pretende ostentar modestia y moderacion. Usando de esta dice, que se le permita no manifestar la idea que formo de equivo-

cacion tan remarcable. Si tal es su intencion, ¿a que fin nos dirije el sarcasmo de preguntar a los niños de la escuela si las instrucciones fueron dadas al Gefe politico o al Director de Colonizacion? Yo por la inversa, apelo al juicio de los hombres sensatos para que califiquen la persona a quien se dirijen las instrucciones cuyo principio dice lo siguiente „Ins-„trucciones a que debera arreglar su conducta „D. Jose Maria Hijar Gefe politico de la alta „California y Director de la Colonizacion de „esta y de la Baja."

Nada tiene de particular, que en el oficio con que le remitieron las referidas instrucciones se le ordene, que arregle a ellas el desempeño de su comision de Colonizacion por que esta, como he probado, es inherente a la de Gefe politico de que tambien estaba investido y en el hecho de destituirlo de este encargo, quedo ecsonerado del otro: por eso la Diputacion, al consultarme que pueda seguir dirijiendo la Colonia, establece la condicion, de que hade ser sujeto al gobierno territorial; pero a las miras posteriores del Sr Hijar convenia el artificio de sustentar alguna autoridad, para dar un aparente valor a las especiosas pretensiones de sus partidarios Tal es la politica previsora del Director de Colonizacion.

He combatido con las armas de la razon al libelo del Sr. Hijar, y por mas que le invite a que me presentara la derogacion de las

leyes, ordenes y reglamentos en que el gobierno territorial apoyo sus resoluciones no consegui la contestacion satisfactoria que buscaba: de esta verdad dan testimonio todas las personas que concurrieron a la conferencia. Interpelados los Sres. Licenciados D. Luis del Castillo Negrete y D. Rafael Gomez para que espusiesen su dictamen, corroboraron ambos el concepto que yo habia esplicado y añadieron argumentos, doctrinas, y leyes de mucho peso que coincidiendo en todo con lo dispuesto por el gobierno territorial no tubieron los Sres. Hijar y Padres con que destruir verdades tan demostradas. Entonces, aparentando estar sorprendidos, o por que realmente lo estaban, pidieron treguas para meditar y contestar satisfactoriamente o darse por convencidos y de todos modos, poner termino a las contestaciones acaloradas y violentas. Como nuestro objeto al solicitar las conferencias no era otro que el de evitar el escandalo publico y las animosidades, protestamos deferir a cuanto fuese compasible con nuestro honor y obligaciones, y convenimos en que al dia siguiente, nos reuniriamos a continuar la conferencia.

Asi sucedio, pero antes de reunirnos recibi del Sr. Hijar este villete.

„S. C. Octubre 26 de 834. = Mi General y amigo: creo importante que tengamos una entrevista secreta antes de la junta; vea V. si puede dar un paseo a esta luego que pase

el almuerzo o señaleme punto. = Su afmo. a-
migo = Hijar."

Mi contestacion fue presentarme ante el
Sr. Hijar en la casa de D. Jose Joaquin Gomez donde, apesar de mis ruegos y suplicas,
se habia alojado dos dias antes en desprecio
a mi amistad y habitacion en que lo habia hos-
pedado· pero no haciendo mencion de tales a-
contecimientos me le ofreci a servirlo en cuanto me contemplara util. Entonces..... ¡o momento fatal como te borrara yo del tiempo! me
propuso, que como le entregara yo los bienes
de las misiones protegeria mis intereses privados con los mismos bienes de las misiones, con
efectos que contaba en Mejico y Guadalajara,
y con su credito y relaciones que aplicaria en
mi favor de la manera que mejor conviniera
a mis negocios y por ultimo, que pondria a
mi disposicion una memoria de veinte mil o
mas pesos que pediria a Mejico o Jalisco si
asi lo queria yo con tal de que las misiones
se le entregaran: que esto era hecho querien-
do yo ejecutarlo por que la Ecsma. Diputacion
seguiria sin replica mi consejo; que el motivo
de su oposicion consistia en mi persona por
que aquella corporacion solo haria mi voluntad:
que en mi arbitrio estaba hacer la fortuna de
todos. Como interpuso la amistad y la reserva
para proponerme ese acomodamiento me vali
de la misma confianza para ecsigirle que me
convenciera con la justicia y que esa solo me

haria desistir de la resolucion que habia formado, por que el interes no es arbitrio legal
y decente ni lo que me obligara a cometer la
bajeza de vender los intereses de unos inocen-
tes que me creia obligado a defender, y que
solo entregaria a su disposicion por espresa orden del Supremo gobierno despues que le re-
presentara el agravio que se inferia a los neofitos. Discutimos largamente sobre el derecho
de propiedad de estos y el Sr. Hijar rectifico
su opinion sosteniendo que ningun derecho tienen los neofitos a los bienes y tierras de las
misiones y que el Gobierno podia libremente
disponer de todo como mejor le pareciera conveniente; pero todo esto lo funda en su dicho
y nada mas. Sostube la contraria lo mejor que
pude y aun me atrevo a asegurar que conven-
ci al Sr. Hijar pero que empeñado y altamente comprometido, se dejo preocupar de los qui-
mericos proyectos que le sugeria el Sr. Padres,
que no cuido ni aun de su reputacion y por
ultimo recurso me propuso que le entregara los
bienes de las misiones bajo la garantia de no
proceder a realizar ninguna parte de ellos hasta que el Supremo gobierno resolviera a la con-
sulta que sobre el particular se le dirijiera: que
se obligaria formalmente a cumplir esta oferta
si se accedia a su propuesta. Despues de una
discusion bastante dilatada ofreci a dicho Sr.
Hijar, que si la Diputacion accedia a su ultima proposicion yo en obsequio de su honor

no me opondria con tal de que no se enage-
naran los bienes de los neofitos, pero que tampoco apoyaria sus pretensiones por que tendria que incurrir en inconsecuncias muy nota-
bles. Asi dimos fin a nuestra conferencia secreta
de que tubo conocimiento el Sr. Padres aunque no tomo parte en ella; y en seguida nos
reunimos a seguir la que dejamos pendiente el
dia anterior.

El Sr. Hijar comenzo por hacer la proposicion que dejo sentada pero los Sres. Vocales
de la Diputacion y los Licenciados espusieron
en contra razones convincentes que no dejaron
campo a su consecucion: entones tanto el Sr.
Hijar como el Ayudante Inspector D. Jose Maria Padres demostraron su convencimiento manifestando que la Diputacion, habia obrado en
la orbita de sus atribuciones con total arreglo
a las leyes y resoluciones del Supremo gobierno; que las instrucciones en que unicamente
se consideraba autorizado el Sr. Hijar ni estaban tan espresas como se necesitaban para re-
mover toda duda, ni tenian la validez que en
tal caso se requiere por estar contradichas por
la Suprema orden de 25 de Julio que lo des-
tituyo del mando politico, y en contradiccion
con varias determinaciones del Gobierno. Que
por lo mismo no insistia en sus pretensiones
pero que estaba resuelto a llevar la Colonia a
la antigua California donde consideraba mas facilmente establecerla respecto a que alli que-

daba subsistente su comision de Director de
Colonizacion sin la contradiccion que en este
territorio habia sufrido. El Sr. Padres sostubo
la misma resolucion añadiendo, que las instrucciones era cierto que estaban diminutas y en
un estilo que forzosamente daban lugar a varias dudas; pero que esto provino de la ecsesiva confianza que merecieron del Ecsmo. Sr.
Vice Presidente de la Republica quien verbal-
mente les dio las demas ordenes e instrucciones de grande interes que debian poner en practica.

La cuestion quedo terminada, y nos ocu-
pamos de persuadir al Sr. Hijar para que permaneciera en este territorio dirigiendo la Colonia: le demostramos la dificultad que se presentaba para trasladarla a la antigua California,
por falta de recursos para sostenrla durante el
viage retrogrado que debian emprender: la trascendencia que en politica debia tener el mal
ecsito de la empresa dirigida primeramente a
este pais: que tampoco tendria en la antigua
California, ni terrenos donde establecerla por
la natural aridez de aquel suelo, ni arbitrios
para sostenerla por que alli no tienen las misiones mas que muy pocos bienes semovientes
que no producen ni aun lo preciso para los
ministros encargados del culto· le hicimos ver
que su resolucion no haria otra cosa que empeorar la suerte de los Colonos bastante com-
prometida por no tener fondos con que soste-

nerlos: que llenarian aquel pais de calamida-
des por el ingreso repentino de tantas gentes
cuya manutencion no sufriria sin detrimento de
aquellos habitantes que apenas pueden subsistir a costa de grandes afanes y vigilias: que
tanto por la esterilidad del suelo como por la
falta de brazos utiles, se carece alli hasta de
los articulos de primera necesidad para la vida,
articulos que se adquieren a mucho costo de
los estados de Sonora y Sinaloa y nunca se
logra un surtido tan abundante como se necesita: que la hacienda nacional tiene alli menos recursos que en este territorio para cubrir sus atenciones y en suma, que no podia,
ni aun moverse de este punto por la falta de
fondos y buques para aprestar la espedicion.
Le suplicamos que depusiera su resentimiento
y permaneciera con nosotros en buena armonia:
que estableciera la Colonia que habia traido
bajo su cuidado y que disfrutaria los mismos
cuatro mil pesos que le habia asignado el Supremo gobierno a quien se le consultaria y re-
comendaria para obtener su aprobacion: que le
aucsiliariamos eficazmente para que llevase al
cabo la empresa y que en su obsequio haria-
mos cuanto fuese compatible con nuestro deber.
Convencido de que era impracticable su
pensamiento de trasladarse con la Colonia a la
antigua California convino con cuanto le pro-
pusimos y acto continuo tratamos de los medios que debiamos adoptar.

Consecuente a lo que acordamos en las
conferencias pase a la Diputacion la nota siguiente
"Gobierno politico de la alta California.=
Ecsmo. Sr. = Comunique al Sr. D. Jose Maria Hijar las ocho proposiciones acordadas por
V. E. en 22 del presente, y no habiendose con-
formado contesto lo que consta en su nota de
23 que original tengo el honor de acompañar.
La ecsageracion de principios con que pretende ridiculizar las atribuciones del gobierno territorial pudieran ser combatidos por la pluma
victoriosamente, pero deseoso de conservar una
buena armonia y conciliar los intereses publicos con los particulares, crei mas prudente ter-
minar la cuestion por medio de conferencias
a fin de evitar toda animosidad y escandalo
publico. = En consecuencia concurrio el Sr.
D. Jose Maria Hijar, y despues de conferen-
ciar detenidamente sobre los diversos puntos
que abraza su nota de 23, convencido hasta la
evidencia de los justos fundamentos en que el
gobierno territorial apoyo sus determinaciones,
convenimos en lo siguiente. = 1 ° Que el Sr.
D. Jose Maria Hijar desempeñara la comision
especial de Director de Colonizacion con sujecion
al gobierno politico del territorio, y a las leyes
y reglamentos dados sobre la materia: que este sea el verdadero concepto de la segunda
proposicion aprobada por la Ecsma. Diputacion
por que esta es la inteligencia que tubo al es-

presar "las bases que para ello acordaré" y por
lo mismo otorga esta esplicacion. = 2. ° Que
se le devuelvan al Sr. Hijar las instrucciones
dadas por el Supremo gobierno que se manda-
ron recoger, quedando solo copia de ellas en
el archivo del gobierno politico. = Que estando conforme con todo lo demas contenido en
en las ocho proposiciones citadas, se somete y
protesta desempeñar su comision especial hasta
que el Supremo gobierno de la Union resuelva lo que tubiere por conveniente. = El repe-
tido Sr. Hijar recomienda a la consideracion
de V. E. a los individuos venidos en su compañia con destino de Preceptores sobre cuyo
particular espone que recibio del Supremo gobierno orden verbal para su colocacion. = Dignese V. E. resolver sobre todo lo espuesto lo
que tubiere por conveniente y sea mas justo. =
Dios y Libertad. Monterrey 29 de Octubre de
1834. = Jose Figueroa. = Ecsma. Diputacion
de este Territorio."
La Diputacion despues de haber oido a
una comision de su seno aprobo en sesion de
3 de Noviembre el dictamen y proposiciones
que constan en la comunicacion siguiente.
"Gobierno politico de la alta Califosnia. =
La Ecsma Diputacion territorial con fecha de
ayer se sirvio aprobar el dictamen de la comision de gobierno y acordar las proposiciones siguientes. = Ecsmo. Sr. = La comision de gobierno ha ecsaminado el oficio de 23 del pre-

sente suscrito por D. Jose Maria Hijar en contestacion al que le dirigio el Gefe politico con
fecha 22 del mismo comunicandole las ocho
proposiciones acordadas por V. E. en aquel dia.
Su contenido es un conjunto de conceptos e-
quivocados, imputaciones infundadas e increpa-
ciones gratuitas al gobierno territorial. La comision para vindicar el honor de V. E. altamente ofendido, pudiera formar un analisis prolijo para deshacer equivocaciones y desmentir
las calumnias con que se combaten sus justos
procedimientos; pero resuelta a repetir pruebas
de moderacion, politica y urbanidad, se desentiende de la acrimonia en que abunda ese documento, y descansa en el testimonio de su
conciencia y honor: V. E. al consultar las medidas refutadas por el Sr. Hijar, tubo a la vista las leyes y reglamentos que rigen sobre la
materia: nada importa que se pretenda tergi-
versar el sentido genuino de ellas, es preciso
observarlas: los que se ofendan de ello que
usen de su derecho, y la autoridad a quien
toque decidira en favor del que tenga justicia:
V. E. como autoridad cumple con su deber
llevando adelante sus providencias y esplicando
las que ofrezcan duda. El Sr. Hijar aunque
pretendio desconocer la autoridad de V. E. ha
protestado obedecerla, despues que en las conferencias privadas con el Gefe politico conocio su
equivoco: esta es una confesion tacita de su
error, y prueba su convencimiento. Terminadas

de ésta manera las cuestiones que tanto nos han ocupado debemos hacer cesar todo escandalo publico, y sepultar en el silencio todo resentimiento personal. La Superioridad hara la debida aclaracion, y los resultados justificaran nuestros procedimientos. Los individuos que forman esta Corporacion son tan republicanos como el Sr. Hijar, usan como su Señoria de un lenguaje austero pero se abstienen de injurias y diatrivas: pudieran usar de esta justa represalia, pero profesan principios de libertad, moderacion y tolerancia: la unica regla de sus operaciones deben ser las leyes y las ordenes de las autoridades legitimamente constituidas. Esta satisfecha de que no ha traspasado los limites de sus facultades, ni ha usurpado poderes que no le confieren las leyes: Esto supuesto la comision presenta a la deliberacion de V. E. las siguientes proposiciones. = 1.ᵃ Para esplicar la verdadera inteligencia de la segunda proposicion aprobada en 22 del presente a las palabras „y las bases que para ello acordare la Di-„putacion" se substituiran las siguientes „y a „las leyes y reglamentos dados sobre la mate-„ria." = 2.ᵃ Que se devuelvan al Sr. Hijar las instrucciones dadas por el Supremo gobierno, quedando una copia de ellas en poder del Gefe politico. = 3.ᵃ Que supuesta la conformidad del Sr. Hijar a todo lo demas acordado por la Diputacion en 22 del presente, se le inserte este dictamen y las anteriores proposi-

ciones para que esprese por escrito si esta o no conforme con todo lo resuelto por el gobierno territorial. En el primer caso mandara el Gefe politico le abonen el sueldo de cuatro mil pesos, y dara cuenta al Supremo gobierno para recabar su aprobacion. = 4.ᵃ Se autoriza al Gefe politico para que cualquiera dudas referentes a este acuerdo y al de 22 de Octubre, la resuelva conforme a las leyes en los casos que por derecho corresponda intervenir a la Diputacion. = Y tengo el honor de trascribirlo a V. S. con el objeto indicado y por contestacion a su nota de 23 de Octubre procsimo pasado acompañandole las instrucciones dadas por el Supremo gobierno. = Estimare a V. S. que si se ofreciese alguna duda o reclamacion que hacer, se tome la molestia de que conferenciemos antes sobre el particular para acordar los medios mas prudentes de que deba valerse o las medidas que por mi parte deban tomarse. Si no resultare otra diferencia en nuestros conceptos dignese V. S. manifestarmelo en contestacion para disfrutar ese placer. = Con tal motivo le reitero las seguridades de mi mas justo aprecio y consideracion. = Dios y Libertad. Monterrey 4 de Noviembre de 1834. = Jose Figueroa. = Sr. D. Jose Maria Hijar Director de Colonizacion."

El Sr. Hijar contesto con el siguiente oficio.

„Quedo impuesto de la nota de V. S. fe-

cha 4 del presente en que me inserta el acuerdo de la Ecsma. Diputacion territorial sobre mi comunicacion del 23 ultimo; y considero inutil toda disension sobre los puntos que hemos tratado supuesto que no estamos conformes en el modo de ver las cosas. = Solo me permitira V. S. que deshaga una equivocacion. Se asienta en la parte espositiva del dictamen que se me inserta que yo pretendi desconocer la autoridad de la Ecsma. Diputacion. Nunca he tenido tal pretension; lo que he hecho es negarle la facultad de sobreponerse a las leyes; pero, esto no es desconocer su autoridad. Yo conservo el mayor respeto a las legitimas autoridades, y se como debo conducirme cuando estas se estravian. Creo, pues no haber padecido equivoco ninguno como se asienta. = En las conferencias de que se hace merito, solo se alegaron razones de utilidad, de conveniencia, de filantropia y de humanidad acia los indigenas pero no una facultad espresa para obrar del modo que se dispuso. No hay ley, y por consiguiente tampoco derecho para que V. V. S. S. hubiesen deliberado como lo hicieron: esta es mi opinion; pues, si se citaron algunas leyes españolas, estas se encuentran derogadas por las nuestras, por pugnar con el sistema de gobierno. = En la tercera proposicion que se me inserta, se ecsige que diga por escrito si estoy o no conforme con lo resuelto por el gobierno territorial y que en el

primer caso, se me señalen cuatro mil pesos de sueldo. Me ha sido muy sensible que la Ecsma. Diputacion se haya formado un tan bajo concepto de mi, y que quiza creyese que el interes me haria prestar deferencia a todo lo resuelto: no Señor, no solo no estoy conforme, si no que protesto contra lo dispuesto por V. V. S. S. en todo aquello en que se atacan las leyes y disposiciones del gobierno general segun he manifestado en mi comunicacion de 23. = Terminadas como estan las cuestiones que nos han ocupado, solo me resta manifestar a V. S. que estoy resuelto a continuar con la Colonia hasta establecerla en el punto que el gobierno desea, por las consideraciones siguientes. = 1.ᵃ Las afecciones particulares de las familias que componen la Colonia, las tenian decididas a correr mi suerte, y seguirme; por consiguiente, si yo hubiese querido abandonarlas, se habria estraviado la Colonia con grabe perjuicio de las personas. 2.ᵃ Si la Colonia se hubiese desgraciado, seria un descredito para el Gobierno, por que se creeria que no es capaz de empresas de esta naturaleza: que habia arrancado a estas familias de su pais para venirlas a tirar a otro remoto, y por ultimo, jamas volveria a conseguir que ningun hombre abandonase sus hogares y saliese a colonizar. 3.ᵃ Se quedarian sin llenar los deseos del Gobierno, y la importante frontera del norte, amagada por Rusos y Anglo Americanos quedaria sin cubrirse y perdidos los crecidos gastos que se han erogado en la Colonia. Todas estas consideraciones, Sr. General, me han decidido a posponer todos mis resentimientos y amor propio ultrajado por conservar el interes y decoro nacional y por asegurar el bienestar de las familias que se me encomendaron. Yo no he podido resistir a las lagrimas de gratitud que varias veces han vertido, en mi presencia, mis compañeros de viage: me resolvi y estoy decidido a sacrificarlo todo aunque no me recompense el ingrato Gobierno que tan sin motivo me ha ultrajado. Voy pues ha establecer la Colonia, y a tomar la azada si fuere necesario para subsistir; pero me quedara el placer de haber cumplido con los deberes de un buen ciudadano, sosteniendo el decoro nacional y procurando la felicidad de las familias que se me encomendaron. = Concluyo pues esperando que V. S. cumplira, como ha ofrecido, que no falte nada de cuanto el Supremo gobierno ofrecio a los Colonos, y descanso en su probidad para que todo se haga con la puntualidad y oportunidad que es conveniente para que ningun Colono tenga motivo de quejarse. = Son en mi poder las instrucciones que me devolvio con su nota referida a que tengo el honor de contestar con las protestas de mi aprecio y distinguida consideracion. = Dios y Libertad. Monterrey Noviembre 6 de 1834 = Jose Maria de Hijar. = Sr. Gefe politico Ge-

neral D. Jose Figueroa."

Insiste el Sr. Hijar en varios errores que tengo demostrados y combatidos: omito por lo mismo contestar prolijamente sus opiniones emitidas en este ultimo oficio por el cual se vera que dicho Sr. entiende siempre los negocios de diverso modo que los demas hombres: dice que sabe como se hade conducir con las autoridades cuando se estravian, y es inutil advertirle las faltas en que abundan sus escritos: dejemos al tiempo su desengaño y sigamos el curso de los sucesos. Notese la importancia que pretende dar a su persona aun contra el Supremo gobierno por haberlo suspendido del empleo de Gefe politico que le habia confiado: no puede ocultar su resentimiento, a pesar de esas solemnes protestas de sacrificarse en obsequio de la Colonia, y del decoro nacional: ¡ojala que sus hechos hubieran correspondido a sus palabras!

El gobierno territorial complacido por haber arreglado amigablemente estos negocios, demostro publicamente su congratulacion e hizo al Sr. Hijar obsequios dignos de la amistad. Animado de los mejores sentimientos, acordo varias medidas y aucsilios para que el Sr. Hijar estableciera la Colonia. La mitad de esta estaba en S. Gabriel y S. Luis rey doscientas diez leguas distante de S. Francisco Solano que es el punto mas aprocsimado al que debia ocupar: se emprendio trasportarla ven-

ciendo muchos obstaculos y haciendo crecidos gastos a la nacion por haberla desembarcado en S. Diego; pero al fin iban a tener cumplimiento las disposiciones del Supremo gobierno y a este fin se empeñaban los desvelos del gobierno territorial

Cuando con mas entusiasmo se ocupaba de estos objetos, recibio la noticia de que el primer Teniente de la armada nacional D. Buenaventura Araujo habia convocado una reunion de salvages gentiles (los Cahuillas) que invadieron el rancho de S. Bernardino, perteneciente a la mision de S. Gabriel, y cometieron varios robos y otros eccesos. Con tal motivo se destaco una partida de veinte hombres armados para observarlos y someterlos al orden en caso necesario; mas la insolencia que les habian inspirado a esos desgraciados les dio atrevimiento para atacar dicha partida y fue necesario batirlos. D. Francisco Berdusco, uno de los Colonos, al mismo tiempo quiso comprometer a los neofitos de S. Luis rey para sorprender un corto destacamento establecido alli, se descubrio su proyecto y quedo frustrado. Los Cahuillas repitieron su invasion al mismo rancho de S. Bernardino donde cometieron varios asesinatos y robos de consideracion: salio una partida de cincuenta hombres en su alcance y castigo su insolencia con la muerte de algunos que hicieron frente. D. Romualdo Lara, otro Colono que acompaño al Sr. Hijar en su viage de San

Diego a Monterrey, trato en varias misiones por donde transito de seducir a los neofitos para adherirlos a su partido: asi consta del diario que escribio el mismo y llego a mis manos por una casualidad. Todas estas tentativas inspiraron al gobierno la desconfianza natural que debia tener de sus autores, pero se conformo con dictar algunas medidas de precaucion para evitar un trastorno, sin siquiera proceder contra los promovedores creyendolos capaces de escuchar la voz de la razon y desistir. Sucedio todo lo contrario: trabajaron privadamente para colocar por la fuerza al Sr. Hijar a la cabeza del Gobierno politico y disponer bajo sus auspicios de los intereses de las misiones.

Yo miraba a lo lejos la borrasca que debia descargar sobre mi cabeza y no podia conjurarla sin esponerme a la mordaz censura de mis antagonistas, que solo se escudan de las leyes para insultar impunemente a las autoridades.

D. Jose Maria Padres que al momento de desembarcarse queria que le entregara yo el mando militar a virtud de la Suprema orden de 12 de Julio de 1833; que habiendome negado a tal pretension me protesto que no desempeñaria su empleo de Ayudante Inspector por que no queria depender del gobierno militar, y por que era incompatible con su comision de Sub-Director de la Colonia, pretendio a pocos dias que lo hiciera yo Comandante militar de la Frontera del norte; esta versatilidad de pensamientos tan inconsecuentes, me indujo a desconfiar de su persona y le negue sus pretensions: este oficial insubordinado desde antes de llegar al territorio se jactaba de venir segun decia a la cabeza de un pueblo armado: todo el mundo sabia que traia doscientos rifles y un repuesto considerable de municiones de guerra, y lejos de cumplir con la obligacion que tiene de darme noticia de ese armamento, bien sea como a Comandante general o como a Gefe politico, trato de ocultarmelo: mando a los Colonos que nadie se me presentara ni tratara cosa alguna con mi persona por que solo con el debian entenderse: habia yo notado, que tenia una influencia superior en el animo del Sr. Hijar y que lo inclinaba a cuanto queria. Todo esto, la propension que ya le habia conocido al desorden, el interes que de antemano tenia en devorar los bienes de las misiones, las maniobras e intrigas que practico para que la Diputacion desobedeciera la orden del Supremo gobierno y otras consideraciones que seria muy difuso en referir me decidieron de creer que Padres era el movil de todas las conspiraciones y que debia observar con mas cuidado su conducta. La orden que alega Padres para que le entregara la Comandancia general la insertare a continuacion para que el publico se entere de que

no es una orden tan terminante como se necesita, para llenar los deseos de dicho Padres.

„Secretaria de Guerra y Marina. = Seccion 9.ᵃ = Con esta fecha digo al Ayudante Inspector D. Jose Maria Padres lo siguiente. = El Ecsmo. Sr. Vice Presidente en ejercicio del Supremo Poder Ejecutivo, se ha servido disponer que marche V. al Territorio de la Alta California a fin de que se encargue del mando de aquella Comandancia general en el caso que el Sr. General D. Jose Figueroa continuase enfermo y quisiese retirarse. Digolo a V. de la misma Superior orden para su cumplimiento y fines consiguientes. = Tengo el honor de transladarlo a V. S. con igual objeto; en el concepto de que si por sus males le conviniere transladarse a esta Capital, puede V. S. verificarlo. = Dios y Libertad. Mejico Julio 12 de 1833. = Herrera. = Sr. Comandante general de la Alta California General D. Jose Figueroa."

Sin embargo de lo acontecido hasta entonces, tome el mayor empeño en reunir y establecer la Colonia a costa de grandes sacrificios y penalidades por haberla dividido en dos partes sus Directores; mas tanto cuanto yo me esforzaba en su beneficio, los agiotistas se empeñaban en promover el desorden y preparar una revolucion que debia separarme del Gobierno politico y colocar en mi lugar al Sr. Hijar.

A este fin se dirigian todas las maniobras de D. Jose Maria Padres, D. Francisco Berdusco, D. Francisco Torres y D. Romualdo Lara, cuyos personages representaban en la eccena el papel principal: ya se deja entender que cada uno tenia sus satelites y que todos conspiraban a un mismo objeto. Asi es que de varios puntos recibi avisos de que la Colonia intentaba conspirar contra el gobierno segun se espresaban varios de sus individuos. Con fecha 18 de Enero y 12 de Febrero de este año, dos distintas personas dignas de credito me comunican desde la mision de S. Antonio como cierto el proyecto de conspiracion: varios individuos de la misma Colonia me descubrieron secretamente los desordenes a que querian precipitarlos: otros pretendieron separarse de la Colonia aparentando varios pretestos. La sedicion se intentaba de diversos modos en varios puntos del territorio y en la misma Capital donde se hacian las combinaciones mas importantes. En estas circunstancias el Sr. Hijar manifestaba una conducta pasiva y una indiferencia disimulada que lo alejaba de sospechas; pero los principales agentes de la revolucion le hacian la corte, solo con ellos conferenciaba sus asuntos, solo ellos le merecieron la mas alta confianza, y es como imposible que ignorara los proyectos que debian ejecutar bajo sus auspicios y en su nombre.

Cuando ya no debia yo dudar de la re-

solucion que habian tomado, se presentaban diariamente motivos de sospechas vehementes que coincidian con los planes sediciosos. Entonces la estacion del invierno que embaraza toda ocupacion, conspiro contra los desgraciados Colonos que acostumbrados a una temperatura mas benigna, apenas podian soportar el rigor de la estacion; y en estas circunstancias se les obliga a caminar grandes distancias y duplicar sus padecimientos sin mas objeto que el de reunirlos para subvertir el orden social, despues que sacrificaron los intereses de la nacion en gastos inutiles. Estos resultados fueron ocasionados por la impericia o depravacion de los Directores de la Colonia, por que nunca consultaron ni la comodidad de esta, ni la conveniencia nacional, ni el ecsito de una empresa digna de mejores resultados. Todo lo dirigian sin mas prevision ni calculo que los fantasticos delirios de D. Jose Maria Padres y su desenfrenada avaricia por apoderarse de los bienes de las misiones; pero es tal la ceguedad de las pasiones, que parece que todos se dejaban guiar de sus inspiraciones y este hombre infatuado por su arrogante presuncion quiso desempeñar las funciones de Minerva. ¡He aqui el Mentor de la Colonia cuyo voto subordinaba a todos los demas!

Los Colonos habian llegado unos a San Francisco Solano, y otros en marcha ocupaban distintos puntos: un pueblo que se va a fundar requiere brazos robustos, y laboriosos: hombres acostumbrados a los trabajos del campo, y a una vida frugal y sencilla: la Colonia dirigida por los Sres. Hijar y Padres es compuesta en su mayoria de personas delicadas y dignas de mejor suerte: son familias arrancadas repentinamente de la corte donde nacieron y se educaron en medio de los placeres y de la opulencia: por escasa que fuera su fortuna en Mejico, tenian establecido un sistema de vida acomodado a sus fuerzas, a su caracter, a sus iuclinaciones, a sus costumbres, a su genio y a su gusto: a proporcion de su industria y relaciones gozaban de comodidad y placeres que dificilmente podran alcanzar en otra parte: muchos profesan algun arte mecanico o liberal que en Mejico les produciria alguna renta, pero en California les es inutil: diganlo sino, los hojalateros, los plateros, los pasamaneros, los bordadores, los pintores, &a: comparese la diferencia que hay en manejar los instrumentos de las artes a empuñar la mancera, el azadon, la hacha y demas instrumentos con que se cultivan los campos: la diferencia de trabajar dentro de su casa al abrigo del sol, de los vientos y del agua, a trabajar en el campo espuestos a la intemperie y a los azares de una vida llena de privaciones e incomodidades y peligros: ¿seria posible que las niñas, señoras y jovenes delicados que los caminos por donde transitaron, son los campos que por primera vez

se presentaron a su vista; seria posible repito que estos individuos pudieran superar las fatigas, las dificultades, las privaciones, las necesidades, y el cumulo de afliccones y accidentes a que se sujetan las empresas de nuevas fundaciones? respondan por mi los mismos interesados, y los hombres imparciales justificaran las medidas del gobierno territorial al impedir los padecimientos de los Colonos y librarlos del duro compromiso a que los conducian sus Directores para hacer mas desventurada su suerte.

No hay duda en que la Colonia reclutada por el Sr. Padres carece de las cualidades que constituyen una buena Colonia, no por defecto de sus individuos sino por la ignorancia y malicia de los Directores, que solo buscaron en la empresa un pretesto para enriquecerse con detrimento de los neofitos de las misiones de California, y de los infortunados Colonos que se dejaron engañar de los falsos prometimientos y fantasticas pinturas de prosperidad con que los alucinaron para decidirlos a marchar a este pais. Varios individuos llegaron en la creencia de que podian disponer libremente de los caballos y ganado vacuno que necesitaran sin mas requisito que temarlos en el campo donde los bienes era comunes: otros solicitaban ansiosos las playas donde creian poder matar a garrotazos cuantas nutrias quisieran: otros buscaban el placer de perlas para

llenar su bolsillo: otros en fin se creian dueños de las fincas y edificios mas importantes de las misiones que se les habia ofrecido: estos fueron los arbitrios rastreros de que se valio el Sr. Padres para enganchar a las familias que debian escudar sus inicuas miras. Acaban de pasar estos sucesos: hablo delante de los mismos actores: ellos me desmentiran si no digo verdad.

Supuesto pues que la Colonia por su natural incapacidad no podia fundar un pueblo nuevo, que fue la mira politica que el Gobierno supremo se propuso para cubrir la Frontera del norte de las agresiones estrangeras: que la creencia politica de sus Directores estaba en choque abierto con los principios sanos de toda sociedad arreglada: que sus proyectos de subversion debian causar un mal positivo al comun de los habitantes: que al Gefe politico se culpaba de las necesidades, privaciones y trabajos que padecian los Colonos: que estos ni aun podian sufrir con resignacion por que diariamente se les eccitaba a vengar supuestos agravios para indemnizar sus padecimientos: que para eccitar su colera se les leia diariamente en S. Francisco Solano el disparatado oficio que me contesto el Sr. Hijar en 23 de Octubre sobre cuyo contenido se hacian largos comentarios por el Mentor de la Colonia, que por lo comun terminaba vomitando injurias contra mi persona, e invectivas dignas de

su altanera prosopopeya Todos estos elementos eran otros tantos combustibles que se preparaban para el incendio general: yo los tenia por evidentes y veia con serenidad aprocsimarse el dia de la esplosion: nadie creera que en tales circunstancias solo me mantube a la defensiva y asi permaneci desde el mes de Septiembre que llego la espedicion al territorio hasta el mes de Marzo que se quitaron la mascara y me estrecharon a tomar la ofensiva.

Como se aprocsimaba el verano, tiempo en que debian consumar la obra de regeneracion que habian proyectado, fingieron ocuparse de negocios totalmente contrarios. Don Francisco Torres aparento marchar a Mejico en comision del Sr. Hijar quien no se digno comunicarme como debia el objeto de su viage puesto que ningun Colono debe separarse sin el espreso conocimiento del Gefe politico. Esto no obstante, le concedi pasaporte sin hacer objecion alguna sabiendo que el verdadero objeto de su viage era, por trasladarse al Pueblo de los Angeles a pretesto de solicitar pasage en algun buque, para promover alli la revolucion. La casualidad le presento al español D. Antonio Apalategui hombre naturalmente inquieto que nada tiene que perder, adicto a todo genero de revoluciones, que le habia yo negado un destino que pretendio y que buscaba la buena ventura: asi es que facilmente se adhirio a los pretendidos proyectos de Torres y marcharon juntos de esta Capital.

El Sr. Hijar dispuso marchar para S. Francisco Solano en compañia de Berdusco, Lara y Araujo para incorporarse a Padres y la Colonia, que aun estaba diseminada por varios obstaculos que se habian opuesto a su marcha. El verdadero objeto de esta reunion debia ser la revolucion; pero el Sr. Hijar aparentaba ignorarlo. Yo le hice algunas indicaciones para inclinarlo a evitar el trastorno y las consecuencias que trae consigo toda revolucion; pero no se dio por entendido y antes bien me declaro que estaba resuelto a regresar a Mejico y que tan luego como arreglara con Padres los asuntos y cuentas de la Colonia emprenderia su viage. Bajo tal pretesto se dirigio para S. Francisco Solano a fines de Febrero: yo marche hasia el mismo rumbo sin otro objeto que el de observar su conducta y descubrir sus planes: nos reunimos en S. Francisco de Asis donde tubimos una conferencia en que le demostre que sus adictos y amigos querian comprometerlo para burlarse del gobierno y muy particularmente de mi: que sabia yo por varios conductos los proyectos que los ocupaban; que pronto debia estallar la revolucion: que yo tenia la necesidad de defenderme y que tal vez tendria que tomar providencias que le fueran sensibles: le declare quienes eran los principales motores: le hice ver

los males que iban a causar al territorio, que estaba en su arbitrio evitarlo si queria en obsequio de la tranquilidad y de su misma reputacion: le asegure que todo quedaria en silencio si se mantenian pacificos por que ni los perseguia ni los temia. Pero fuese por que creia seguro el triunfo, o por despreciar mis ofrecimientos me mostro la misma frialdad e indiferencia con que acostumbra mirar los negocios mas importantes. Entonces me vi precisado a evitar que reuniera la Colonia por sustraerla de la revolucion a que la convocaban, por que varios individuos asi lo habian pretendido para impedir su ruina que era inevitable sometiendolos al capricho de los Directores que pretendian hasta monopolizar su trabajo personal bajo el pretesto de la Compañia consmopolitana: por que nada habian hecho de provecho, ni podian hacer por su incapacidad fisica segun tengo demostrado; y sobre todo, por que no tenia fondos disponibles para pagar sus diarios como pretedia el Sr. Hijar. Adopte la medida de dejarlos en libertad de establecerse en el lugar que mejor les acomodara para emprender algun giro de que subsistir: asi consta de las contestaciones que mediaron y son las que siguen.

„Estoy para pasar a S. Solano con objeto de fijar el punto en que debe situarse la Colonia; mas habiendome V. S. manifestado en varias conferencias particulares que es imposible

cumplir a los Colonos lo que les ofrecio el Supremo gobierno al contratarlos en su pais para que viniesen al territorio, estimare a V. S. se sirva decirme definitivamente si el Gobierno puede o no cumplir su compromiso, a fin de que yo pueda reglar mis procedimientos y hacer pasar a todos los Colonos al punto en que deben fijarse si V. S. proporcionare los recursos ofrecidos, o en caso que esto no pueda ser, manifestarselos, para que resuelvan lo que les parezca, supuesto que el Gobierno falte a las condiciones del contrato que celebro con las familias que se me encomendaron y que tengo el sentimiento de ver sumergidas en la miseria. = Creo inutil manifestar a V. S. los males que se seguiran de la disolucion de la Colonia, que tantos gastos y afanes ha costado al Supremo gobierno; los resultados en politica que esto debe ofrecer y en que se interesa de una manera inequivoca el decoro del Gobierno general: V. S. conoce tan bien como yo las consecuencias de este paso y espero de su prudencia lo resolvera del mejor modo posible, sin perder de vista su influencia politica, el decoro del Supremo gobierno, el interes individual de los Colonos y el interes publico del territorio. = Dios y Libertad. S. Francisco de Asis Marzo 1.° de 1835. = Jose Maria de Hijar. = Sr. Gefe politico General D. Jose Figueroa.''

„Gobierno politico de la alta California. =

El Supremo gobierno federal nada me ha prevenido con respecto a la Colonia. Las instrucciones conferidas a V. S. cuando fue nombrado Gefe politico, es el unico documento oficial que acredita las providencias dictadas sobre la materia; dicho documento ecsiste en poder de V. S: verdad es que contiene la orden de tomar los intereses de las misiones para invertirlos en la Colonia, pero en esta providencia se ataca la propiedad de los indios, y segun he manifestado a V. S. en varias conferencias es anti-constitucional: asi lo he representado a la Superioridad, y mas propiamente puede verse en el articulo 112, restriccion 3.ª de la Constitucion federal que dice asi. = „El Presidente no podra ocupar la propiedad de ningun particular ni corporacion, „ni turbarle en la posesion, uso o aprovecha„miento de ella: y si en algun caso fuere ne„cesario para un objeto de conocida utilidad „general tomar la propiedad de un particular „o corporacion, no lo podra hacer sin previa a„probacion del Senado, y en sus recesos del Con„sejo de gobierno, indemnizando siempre a la „parte interesada a juicio de hombres buenos „elegidos por ella y el gobierno.'' = Este es el fundamento en que el gobierno territorial ha apoyado la defensa de los bienes de las misiones que siempre ha reconocido como propiedad de los neofitos de ellas; mas arrostrando tan graves inconvenientes, y bajo la so-

lemne protesta de reclamar la debida indem-
nizacion, acordo ministrar a la Colonia todos
los auxsilios necesarios para su establecimiento
y manutencion, pues nunca creyó justo aban-
donar a su propia suerte tantas personas dignas de su aprecio y respeto, ni ha visto con
indiferencia sus padecimientos. = A V. S. le
consta que de conformidad con lo acordado por
la Ecsma. Diputacion territorial en 22 de Octubre ultimo, mande que se pusieran a su disposicion todos los articulos que V. S. mismo
presupuesto para su establecimiento y manutencion: le consta a V. S. que solo se han
entregado algunos y que falta la mayor parte:
que tanto la estacion como la escases de recursos de todo genero, entorpece o paraliza
la empresa: que me veo rodeado de dificultades, y que con motivo de la secularizacion de
misiones y otras complicadas atenciones se frus-
tran a cada paso mis providencias, con respecto a la Colonia: que los gravamenes nuevamente impuestos a los intereses de las misiones, y los quebrantos que estas sufren por consecuencia de las innovaciones que se ponen en
practica, son otros tantos obstaculos que diariamente obstruyen los recursos con que cuento. He manifestado a V, S. las comunicaciones que he recibido de los encargados de las
misiones relativas a los auxsilios que deben dar
a la Colonia, y en ellas se espresan varias
faltas insubsanables. = Todos estos embarazos

estoy resuelto a vencerlos de la manera que
me sea posible, y con tal objeto, he ofrecido
a V. S. no omitir trabajo ni diligencia; pero
se multiplican las erogaciones, a un grado que
no es posible soportarlo sin perjuicios tracsen-
dentales al publico; por que la notoria decadencia en que se hallan las misiones, los grandes creditos que tienen contraidos y deben cubrirse con sus ecsistencias, la emancipacion de
las familias indigenas que pasan de veinte mil
personas a quienes debe darseles bienes para
su establecimiento y manutencion: los crecidos
gravamenes nuevamente impuestos por la congrua de los Ministros, sueldos de Preceptores,
Mayordomos y otros empleados que antes no
ecsistian: pagos de jornales a los trabajadores
que se emplean en la conservacion de la fincas: todo, todo gravita sobre las propidades de
los indigenas, y conspira a su destruccion en
pocos dias sin poder llenar cumplidamente todas las atenciones. = Apesar de cuanto llevo
espuesto repito a V. S, que hare cuantos esfuerzos sean necesarios para ministrar a la Colonia los aucsilios precisos para su subsistencia; mas no puedo comprometerme a pagarle
con puntualidad sus diarios por que no hay numerario, ni es facil adquirirlo: ni tampoco se
puede cubrir en poco tiempo con ningunos o-
tros articulos, la suma de treinta y cinco mil
y mas pesos que importan los diarios, si no es
poniendo en bancarrota las misiones. = Por to-

do lo dicho, por que varios individuos de la
Colonia me han representado de palabra y por
escrito para que les permita establecerse en el
punto que les acomode: por que es notorio que
la mayoria de los individuos que forman la Colonia aunque muy recomendables y utiles en
varias ocupaciones, no lo son para los trabajos del campo en que nunca se han ejercita-
do: por que se han pasado seis meses y no se
ha establecido, ni emprendido algun trabajo provechoso: por que el Sr. D. Jose Maria Padres sin conocimiento de V. S. ni de este gobierno esta reuniendo a la Colonia algunas familias e individuos de los ya radicados en el
pais de que solo resulta el aumento de gastos:
por que el trasporte de los ganados y demas
bienes hasta el otro lado de la bahia de S.
Francisco debe ser muy dispendioso y pausa-
do, a mas de las perdidas que en ello deben
sufrirse: por que es muy dificultoso reconcen-
trar a un solo punto todos los intereses de la
Colonia: por que ecsiste entre los Colonos un
disgusto general que pudiera degenerar en desorden si se apura su sufrimiento, y sobre todo por que V. S. me ha manifastado su resolucion sobre separarse de la Direccion de la
Colonia con cuyo objeto ha representado al
Supremo gobierno y piensa retirarse a la baja
California a esperar sus ordenes. Todo esto me
inclino a meditar una medida conciliadora y
propuse a V. S. que en mi opinion conviene

dejar a los Colonos que se establezcan en el
lugar que mas les acomode para que ayudados de su industria y oficios unidos a los aucsilios que les da el gobierno, puedan propor-
cionarse una vida mas comoda adquiriendo los
mas laboriosos, ventajas que de otro modo no
pueden conseguir. = En esto no solo consulto
la comodidad y gusto de las familias, sino los
ahorros de la Hacienda publica, la tranquilidad general del territorio, la mayor facilidad
en franquear a los Colonos los aucsilios; y el
dejarlos en libertad para que puedan emplear-
se utilmente en sus giros; pues de este unico modo puedo contribuir a minorar sus padecimientos, cumpliendo al mismo tiempo lo que
el Supremo gobierno les tiene ofrecido: ellos
en mi concepto pueden tambien de este modo, ser mas utiles y beneficos a la sociedad,
ya que no pueden conseguirlo en los duros
trabajos del campo. Esto no obstante si alguno de los Colonos o todos conformes y gusto-
sos quieren establecerse en la Frontera, puede
V. S. elegir el lugar que le acomode y alli
le aucsiliare con todos los recursos que esten
a mi alcance. = El honor Nacional, el decoro
del Gobierno y la conveniencia publica quedan
a cubierto con la medida indicada: los Colonos seran satisfechos de sus haberes proporcionalmente y quiza con menos demora, con menos gravamen del erario y mas a contento de
ellos. = Mucho he meditado sobre este negocio

y diariamente me convence la esperiencia de que no hay otro remedio mas adecuado a nuestras circunstancias ni que mejor concilie los intereses privados con los del comun. Esta es mi opinion y apreciaria que los Colonos se impusieran de ella para que elijan lo que les convenga; bajo la protesta de que en su obsequio empleare gustoso mi cuidado y eficacia para proporcionarles, como lo tengo acreditado hasta la fecha, cuantos socorros dependan de mi arbitrio, pues las escaseces que algunos hayan padecido son debidas o a la incomodidad del tiempo, a lo ecsausto del erario, o algunos otros accidentes; pero V. S. y el Sr. Padres estan satisfechos de la franqueza y equidad con que se han distribuido los intereses nacionales entre todos, y de la buena voluntad con que he mandado enterar todos los pedidos que me han hecho desde el momento que desembarcaron. = Consecuente a mis ofrecimientos y a la solicitud de V. S, le dirijo con esta misma fecha las ordenes respectivas para que perciba y distribuya a la Colonia la cantidad de dos mil pesos en los efectos que le sean necesarios por no haber numerario. = Todo lo que tengo el honor de manifestar a V. S. en contestacion a su nota fecha de ayer que trata de la materia. = Dios y Libertad. S. Francisco de Asis. Marzo 2 de 1835. = Jose Figueroa. = Señor Director de Colonizacion D. Jose Maria Hijar."

„El medio que V. S. me propone de dejar a la voluntad de los Colonos el que se establezcan donde mejor les parezca no salva mi responsabilidad; y si el Supremo gobierno puede cumplir el compromiso que celebro con ellos, deben pasar al punto que el mismo Gobierno los destinaba para llenar el objeto que se propuso; por que para dejar cuatro o seis personas mas en cada uno de los puntos poblados del territorio no se habrian emprendido los crecidos gastos que se han hecho. V. S. debe estar convencido que una mira politica, que tiende, entre otras cosas, a conservar la integridad del territorio de la Repubica, fue la que inclino al Gobierno a hacer sacrificios estraordinarios en medio de las mas apuradas circunstancias. = Si el Supremo gobierno puede llenar su compromiso, los Colonos no deben quejarse de que se les haga pasar a un despoblado, por que se contrataron para llevarlos al punto que fuese conveniente. = En esta virtud y la de pender actualmente la suerte de la Colonia, solo de las disposiciones de V. S, le suplico me diga terminantemente si el Supremo gobierno se halla en el caso de cumplir su contrato, o si como varias veces me ha manifestado V. S, le es imposible llenar su compromiso; con esta respuesta terminante creo salvada mi responsabilidad, y entonces quedaran los Colonos donde les acomode o percibir sus diarios cuando buenamente

se pueda. = V. S. sabe muy bien que el prorateo que se hizo a las misiones sobre mi pedido para la Colonia no se ha verificado sino en una corta cantidad; y esto sera dificil colectarlo por los obstaculos que se ponen. Aunque V. S. ha dictado sus providencias para aucsiliar a la Colonia, es un hecho que ellas no se han obsequiado sino en muy pequeña parte: por todas partes se presentan dificultades y embarazos que han impedido el establecimiento de la Colonia; dificultades que obligaron a V. S. a disponer que los Colonos invernasen diseminados en las misiones, donde como transeuntes aun no han podido emprender ninguna clase de trabajos. = Todo esta indicando Sr. General, que es necesario tomar una medida definitiva; y yo desearia que V. S. me dijese terminantemente dejase a los Colonos donde mejor les acomodase, para que cada uno se aplicase a lo que le pareciera, contando solo con los aucsilios que buenamente se les puedan ministrar, segun ofrece V. S. y no con lo que por contrato se les debe: con esto saldrian los Colonos de una fatigosa incertidumbre y yo salvaria mi responsabilidad. Si despues de algunos dias, se ha de decir que no hay con que llenar el compromiso, vale mas hacerlo desde ahora y se causaran menos males a los desgraciados que me acompañaron. Sera conveniente sepa V. S. que los Colonos no pueden ecsijir precisamente nume-

rario, por que desde Mejico se les dijo que aqui era muy escaso; pero que se les compensaria con valores equivalentes. = Concluire diciendo a V. S, que si el Sr. Padres ha recibido como Colonos a algunos individuos residentes en el pais, esto no grava los fondos publicos, por que solo se les daran tierras, y ninguna otra cosa de las que se ofrecieron a los contratados en el interior. Tambien añadire que aunque yo me separe de la Colonia, como he solicitado del Supremo gobierno, esto no debe influir de ninguna manera sobre la futura suerte de la Colonia; ni mucho menos sobre las miras que el Gobierno se propuso al remitirla. = Todo lo que he creido conveniente decir a V. S. en contestacion de su nota de ayer, sin mezclarme en la cuestion sobre propiedad de los fondos con que debe aucsiliarse la Colonia por no ser cosa que me pertenece. = Dios y Libertad. S. Francisco de Asis Marzo 3 de 1835. = Jose Maria de Hijar. = Sr. Gefe politico General D. Jose Figueroa."

„Gobierno politico de la alta California. = Repetidas ocasiones he manifestado a V. S. lo dificil que es cubrir en su totalidad los gastos que deben erogarse en el establecimiento de la Colonia, por falta de fondos, y por que se multiplican diariamente los gastos, al mismo tiempo que se disminuyen notablemente los recursos por motivos que no esta en mi arbitrio evitar. Esto supuesto, he creido necesario dejar a los Colonos en libertad de establecerse donde mejor les acomode con el fin de que, ayudados de su industria y de lo que buenamente pueda ministrarseles por cuenta de sus diarios, puedan subsistir sin miseria. = V. S. ha palpado los inconvenientes y esta convencido de que no es posible llevar al cabo la empresa, mas como para cubrir su responsabilidad me ecsije en su nota de ayer una resolucion terminante le manifiesto: que no es posible ecsibir cumplidamente todo lo ofrecido por el Supremo gobierno a la Colonia por que los intereses puestos a mi disposicion no alcanzan. En consecuencia, dispongo, que los Colonos, quedan en libertad para establecerse dentro de los limites del territorio en el lugar que a cada uno le agrade, donde seran aucsiliados en proporcion a los recursos con que cuento. = Y tengo el honor de decirlo a V. S. por contestacion a su citada nota suplicandole, se digne comunicarme lo que disponga para mis posteriores providencias. = Dios y Libertad. San Francisco de Asis 4 de Marzo de 1835. = Jose Figueroa. = Sr. Director de Colonizacion D. Jose Maria Hijar."

A pesar de la felonia con que se me trataba quise apurar mi sufrimiento y aucsiliar a la Colonia de cuantos modos era posible: asi es que a nadie moleste ni le hice cargo de sus crimenes, con la esperanza de que retrocedie-

ran de sus estravagantes pretensiones. Con esta resolucion me retire despues que puse a disposicion del Sr. Hijar dos mil pesos para que socorriera a la Colonia. En las misiones de Sta. Clara y S. Juan Bautista me detuve pocos dias en la practica de diligencias para acabar de descubrir los cabecillas de la revolucion. Tenia bastante adelantado hasta el 13 de Marzo que recibi por estraordinario la noticia de que en el Pueblo de los Angeles hubo el 7 del mismo mes un pronunciamiento revolucionario capitaneado por Juan Gallardo a la cabeza de cincuenta aventureros del Estado de Sonora: que estos fueron seducidos y comprometidos por D. Francisco Torres y D. Antonio Apalategui bajo diferentes pretestos y embustes; pero que habiendo tratado de ecsimirse dieron a entender la depravacion y cautela con que habian obrado y los mismos pronunciados los entregaron a disposicion del Alcalde para que los juzgara conforme a derecho, protestando todos que estaban obedientes al gobierno en cuyo nombre se les habia convocado por Torres y Apalategui, que por lo mismo los presentaban a la autoridad ante quien ofrecian deponer las armas que habian tomado incautamente, y no volver a perturbar bajo ningun pretesto el orden publico. El Ayuntamiento de dicho Pueblo de los Angeles me dirigio el parte y plan cuyo tenor es el siguiente.

„Secretaria del Ilustre Ayuntamiento del Pueblo de los Angeles. = Una reunion acefala de Sonorenses se han pronunciado la madrugada de este dia por el plan que en copia tengo el honor de acompañar a V. S; el considerado en su esencia y puesto en verdadero punto de vista no contiene otra cosa mas que miras particulares, que a la vez no han sido agenas de la consideracion de este Ilustre Ayuntamiento; prudentemente determino reunirse en junta estraordinaria de cuya sesion tambien acompaño a V. S. una copia. = Ha sido muy estraño en la generalidad de este Pueblo que una multitud de Sonorenses por miras particulares traten de innovar las disposiciones establecidas en este territorio; es verdad que el plan referido en cuestion en su articulo 6.° se ve que los pronunciados prestan su docilidad y obediencia a la justicia, empero se contradicen en el mismo diciendo que no dejaran las armas de la mano hasta no ver realizadas sus intenciones; se reputan protectores de las leyes, y son los primeros que las han iufringido; proclaman el orden y han usado hasta de la violencia de sorprender a un Regidor que tenia la llave del juzgado para sacar los aucsilios y pertrechos que en el habia. En medio de los criticos estremos de repeler aquella fuerza sin tener con que competirla o ceder al intento de los pronunciados preciso era tomar un medio y fue el que se advierte en el a-

cuerdo que tubo la Corporacion en la segunda junta. = En conclusion los pronunciados permanecieron con las armas hasta las tres de la tarde y el mismo que aparece como agente de la faccion D. Juan Gallardo condujo presos al juzgado a las personas del español Don Antonio Apalategui y a D. Francisco Torres y presento D Felipe Castillo la representacion que en copia acompeño: se pusieron en segura prision a los mencionados Apalategui y Torres y se les esta formando la correspondiente causa. = Tengo el honor de protestar a V. S. a nombre de esta Ilustre Corporacion las consideraciones de mi aprecio y respetos. = Dios y Libertad. Pueblo de los Angeles y Marzo 7 de 1835. = Francisco J. Alvarado. = Manuel Arzaga. Secretario. = Sor. Gefe superior politico de la alta California."

„En el Pueblo de Nuestra Señora de los Angeles a los siete dias del mes de Marzo de mil ochocientos treinta y cinco: reunidos una multitud de ciudadanos con el fin de acordar las medidas mas convenientes para salvar al territorio de la alta California de los males que ha sufrido y sufre por la administracion del General D. Jose Figueroa y considerando. Primero, que este Gefe no ha cumplido con diversas ordenes que le ha dirigido el Supremo gobierno de la Union para mejorar la suerte de los habitantes de este pais: que abusando de su docilidad ha eccedidose de la orbita de las facultades que le conceden las leyes reasumiendo indebidamente los mandos Político y Militar contra el sistema de federacion y contra leyes espresas que prohiben esta reunion de poderes: que con la ley de secularizacion de misiones ha hecho un monopolio escandaloso reduciendo sus productos ó esquilmos a un comercio esclusivo, sorprendiendo la buena fe de la Ecsma. Diputacion territorial para que reglamentase a su capricho una ley general: que infringiendo el reglamento de Comisarias dispone del haber del soldado a su antojo sin el respectivo conocimiento del Gefe de hacienda, y sin las formalidades que establecen para iguales casos diversas leyes y reglamentos. == Segundo, que no teniendo la Diputacion territorial facultades para reglamentar o adicionar una ley general como lo ha hecho con la de secularizacion de misiones. == Tercero, que caminando estas como caminan a su total ruina á pasos agigantados por las medidas estrepitosas que se han dictado para reclusion de indigenas y la respectiva distribucion de sus intereses. == Y cuarto, que algunos Comisionados ya por su crasa ignorancia para el manejo de esta clase de negociaciones, o por su maliciosa conducta se han propuesto progresar en sus intereses particulares, arruinando los correspondientes a las misiones con notable injuria de los indigenas que con su trabajo personal los han adquirido: han venido en acordar y han acordado

lo siguiente. == Articulo 1.° Se declara indigno de la confianza publica el General D. Jose Figueroa. En consecuencia el Alcalde primero constitucional de la Capital se encargara provisionalmente del mando politico del territorio, y el Capitan D. Pablo de la Portilla como oficial mas antiguo y de mas graduacion del militar conforme a la ordenaza general del ejercito. == 2.° Se declaran nulos, irritos y sin ningun valor ni efecto los acuerdos de la Diputacion territorial con respecto a los reglamentos que ha dictado para la administracion de misiones. == 3.° Los MM. RR. PP. Misioneros se encargaran esclusivamente de las temporalidades de las respectivas misiones, como hasta aqui lo han hecho, y los Comisionados entregaran los documentos relativos a su administracion a los mismos religiosos, quienes haran las convenientes observaciones. == 4.° Por el articulo anterior no se embarazan las facultades del Director de Colonizacion para que obre con arreglo a las instrucciones que le dio el Supremo gobierno. == 5.° El presente Plan se sujeta en todo a la aprobacion del Gobierno general. == 6.° Las fuerzas pronunciadas no dejaran las armas de la mano hasta ver realizados los articulos anteriores y se constituyen protectoras de la recta administracion de justicia, y de las respectivas autoridades. == Aqui las firmas. == Es copia. Angeles Marzo 7 de 1835. == Juan Gallardo. == Es copia. Angeles

Marzo 7 de 1835. == Manuel Arzaga. Secretario "

Este libelo infamatorio no tiene mas fundamento que la calumnia. Si Torres y Apalategui no fueran tan bajos y cobardes que niegan ser autores del plan, los hubiera demandado de injurias por falsos calumniadores, obrando por separado del juicio criminal que se les sigue por conspiradores, perturbadores del orden publico y sediciosos. Pero ya que no puedo usar de este recurso que me permite la ley para castigar la insolencia de esos entes miserables, los denunciare ante el Tribunal inecsorable de la opinion publica, desmintiendo con el lenguage de la verdad, el catalogo de mentiras que estamparon en su farrago despreciable. Primeramente asientan que una multitud de ciudadanos se reunieron con el fin de acordar medidas para salvar al territorio de los males que sufre bajo mi administracion. Esta es la primera blasfemia politica de esos idiotas: los ciudadanos que dicen se reunieron son unos aventureros que acavaban de llegar al pais procedentes del Estado de Sonora a buscar fortuna por que no trahian destino alguno: lo mismo eran Torres y Apalategui: acaban de llegar al territorio y no saben ni entienden como esta gobernado ¡necios! ¿ni siquiera pudieron conocer que los Californios me obedecen mas bien por amor y con gusto, que por la autoridad que ejerzo? ¿no conocen el desprecio y

odio general que a ellos se les tiene? ¿no les consta que ningun Californio tomo parte en su asonada apesar de haberlos seducido por el espacio de siete meses contados desde Setiembre a Marzo? ¿no les consta que sin necesidad de emplear la fuerza volvieron al orden los mismos que habian seducido? ¿ellos mismos no han esperimentado la lenidad con que los he tratado apesar de sus crimenes? ¿no saben que habiendo atentado contra mi autoridad militar me competia juzgarlos y he renunciado ese derecho por no verme obligado a fallar aunque legalmente contra mis enemigos declarados? ¿estos seran los males que sufre el territorio bajo mi administracion? ¡mentecatos, si tubieran uu rasgo de integridad no mentirian con tanto descaro! Y ¿cual es el derecho que los ciudadanos tienen para reunirse tumultuariamente, conculcar las leyes que arreglan la sociedad y atacar la autoridad publica? ¿en que publisista ha leido el Sr. Torres esas doctrinas? ¿pretendera aplicar en politica los conocimientos que posee en la farmacia, y los especificos que determina la farmacopea? ¿creia acaso que su plan, seria tan esactamente obedecido como sus recetas en las boticas:? pues se engaño miserablemente, y ojala que este suceso lo haga escarmentar para que vuelva a socorrer la humanidad doliente, engrosando de nuevo el enjambre de los fisicos de cuyas filas ha desertado.

Siguiendo la narracion del celebre plan aseguran sus autores, que no he cumplido diversas ordenes que me ha dirigido el Supremo gobierno para mejorar la suerte de estos habitantes: ¡Embusteros! hablan como los papagayos: si lo hicieran con algun fundamento y espresaran cuales son esas ordenes Supremas que he dejado de cumplir, yo les contestara, pero en el hecho de no demostrar la falta esta probada la calumnia.

La segunda clausula de la primera consideracion de su plan afirma que eccediendo la orbita de las facultades que me conceden las leyes, reasumi indebidamente los mandos politico y militar contra el sistema de federacion. ¡Barbaros! ¿en que he traspasado la orbita de mis facultades? ¿no sabe que la reunion de los mandos politico y militar me fue conferida por el Supremo gobierno de la Union y que ha podido hacerlo sin contravenir ninguna ley por que espresamente lo autoriza la de 23 de Junio de 1813, articulo 5.º titulo 3.º? Y ¿en que se opone esta medida al sistema de federacion? en nada por que en tal caso, tambien se necesitarian dos Presidentes de la Republica, uno militar y otro politico: ¿estos dos mandos, corresponden al resorte de alguno de los tres poderes en que se divide la Soberania de la Nacion? no ciertamente, por que uno y otro corresponden al poder ejecutivo; luego debemos inferir que los autores de tal invectiva

son unos idiotas que no entienden lo que es el sistema de federacion.

La tercera clausula de la primera consideracion del plan es, por que de la ley de secularizacion hice un monopolio escandaloso reduciendo los productos de las misiones a un comercio esclusivo, y que sorprendi a la Diputacion para que reglamentara la ley segun mi capricho ¡Impostores, con que probaran tan atroces calumnias! ¿en que consiste ese monopolio, o que entiende el Sr Torres por monopolio? ¿donde esta ese comercio esclusivo? solo ha ecsistido en el fantastico plan de Torres y si este tubiera algun pudor, no mentiria con tanto descaro a la faz de la Republica. ¿De que manera sorprendi a la Diputacion? ya he manifestado que lejos de pretender la formacion del reglamento de secularizacion, la resisti y contuve publicamente mas de seis meses: mas contra ese testimonio intachable quiso lucir el taco el Farmaceutico, pero no ha querido someterse a dar pruebas de su dicho por que le parecio bastante dar credito a la calumnia con solo escribirla.

La cuarta clausula de la primera consideracion del plan se contrae a asegurar, que infrinjo el reglamento de Comisarias, que dispongo del haber del soldado a mi antojo sin conocimiento del gefe de hacienda, y sin las formalidades que establecen las leyes y reglamentos. ¡Sr. Farmaceutico! ¿en que o por que he

infringido el reglamento de Comisarias? ¿sera por que he cuidado de su esacta observancia y arreglado la Subcomisaria y la Aduana al sistema de cuenta y razon que han determinado las leyes? ¿sera por que no he dejado esas importantes oficinas en la confusion y desorden que tenian desde su fundacion hasta mi ingreso al mando de este territorio? ¿sera en fin, por que intervengo la distribucion de caudales y no consiento que se malversen? digan pues los impostores de que modo se ha infringido por mi parte el reglamento. Diga el gefe de hacienda y los comandantes y habilitados de los cuerpos que militan a mis ordenes si alguna vez he interrumpido sus funciones: digan si antes que yo mandara en este territorio se ha cuidado de ajustar y liquidar las tropas como ahora se verifica: digan si alguna vez antes que yo mandara ha habido tanto orden y metodo en la distribucion equitativa de los caudales: y sobre todo; vease lo que dice el actual Subcomisario.

„Jose Maria Herrera Sub–Comisario de la Alta California. = Certifico, que en el tiempo que llevo de desempeñar dicho encargo desde siete de Octubre del año procsimo pasado hasta hoy dia de la fecha, el manejo y conducta que ha observado con respecto a esta oficina de mi cargo el Sr. General de Brigada D. Jose Figueroa Comandante General y Gefe Politico de este territorio, no han sido otros

que la intervencion prevenida en las leyes y reglamentos de la administracion de la Hacienda publica. Y para que conste y obre los efectos que convenga, doy la presente a pedimento del interesado en Monterrey a treinta de Junio de mil ochocientos treinta y cinco. == Jose Maria Herrera."

Yo desafio a Torres y Apalategui y a todo el que guste para que pruebe, la mas ligera falta que yo haya cometido en el manejo de la Hacienda federal o de los haberes de los cuerpos. Me bastaria responder a tan atroz impostura, que la responsabilidad es del Subcomisario y de los habilitados a cuyo cargo corren los intereses; pero no obstante eso, quiero y es mi voluntad someterme al juicio de responsabilidad siempre que alguno lo intente con datos positivos.

La segunda consideracion del plan se reduce a que la Diputacion no tiene facultad de reglamentar una ley como lo ha hecho con la de secularizacion. Tengo probado que la Diputacion pudo y debio proponer el Reglamento de secularizacion por que es una de sus atribuciones prevenida por la ley de 23 de Junio de 1813 articulos 1, 14 y 16 capitulo 2.

Otra de las causales que motivo el plan es la decadencia de las misiones por la reclusion de los indigenas y por que se les iban a repartir los intereses. Este si es un motivo poderoso, para la revolucion de Torres por que distribuyendose los intereses entre sus mismos dueños no han de permitir que se los arrebaten y entonces la compañia Cosmopolitana quedaria sin fondos de que disponer: por eso el sabio Torres, como principal accionista, quiso asegurar los intereses de las misiones por medio de la revolucion. ¡Ecselente pensamiento, pero vano por que no pegó!

Tambien se asienta como causal, el que los Comisionados por progresar en sus intereses privados arruinan los de las misiones con injuria de los indigenas que los han adquirido con su trabajo. ¿Luego confiesa el Sr. Torres que los indigenas son los dueños de esos intereses? ya veremos como sin embargo trata de despojarlos de ellos. Y ¿como califica los daños que los Comisionados han hecho a las misiones? valiendose de la arma terrible de la calumnia: los Comisionados probaran su conducta por los resultados y aun no es tiempo de analizarlos.

Supuestas las antecedentes causales sancionaron el plan cuyo primer articulo debia ser declararme indigno de la confianza publica, para despojarme del mando politico y militar transmitiendo este al Capitan D. Pablo de la Portilla y aquel al Alcalde primero de Monterrey. Es cierto que los facciosos Torres y Apalategui me declararon indigno de la confianza publica; pero el publico, es decir todos los habitantes de California ecepto muy pocos cosmo-

politas, me honraron con mas confianza de la que merezco. Ridiculo seria yo si me ocupara de impugnar el farrago inmundo de Torres. Hare unicamente un analisis de la distribucion de los mandos. Destinabase el politico al Alcalde que aunque en ningun caso llama la ley, convenia desorganizar el gobierno en su totalidad para abrir paso al Sr. Hijar que debia ser llamado despues del triunfo so pretesto de haber estado nombrado Gefe politico y ser el unico capaz de hacer feliz al rerritorio: el vocal mas antiguo de la Diputacion que a falta del Gefe politico debe desempeñar sus funciones segun la ley de 6 de Mayo de 1822 no convenia a la sabia prevision del Farmaceutico, y por eso lo declaro tacitamente indigno de la confianza publica. El mando militar se depositaba en el Capitan Portilla para engañarlo, entretenerlo y comprometerlo de ese modo, interin se presentaba en la escena el ingeniero Teniente Coronel Ayudante Inspector y Subdirector de la Colonia &a. &a. D. Jose Maria Padres que debia obtar el mando por el orden de sucesion y por que ya debia darse por enfermo y en disposicion de marchar a Mejicó el General Figueroa. ¡No hay duda que ertaba convinado maravillosamente el plan! ¡produccion digna de Torres!

El segundo articulo del plan declara nulos, irritos y de ningun valor los acuerdos de la Diputacion referentes a la administracion

de las misiones. ¡Esto es entenderlo Sr. Doctor! ¿Que dira el Sr. Hijar de este modo de legislar? yo aseguro que no se espantaria, como cuando la Diputacion dictamino los acuerdos que anula el legislador Torres.

El tercer articulo manda restituir a los Religiosos misioneros la administracion de temporalidades ¿Quien creerá que aqui hai una siniestra intencion? pues voi a demostrarla. Si Torres conociera como yo la providad de los Religiosos no les hubiera hecho la injuria de estimularlos con el molesto interes de administrar las temporalidades que repetidas ocasiones han renunciado espontaneamente; no es bastante aliciente para comprometerlos a una revolucion desastrosa, aunque fuese positivo el ofrecimiento; pero a mas de la injuria que hace a la honradez de los Religiosos pretende engañarlos como a los muchachos, constituyendolos en instrumentos pasivos de sus depredaciones. ¡Hipocritas perfidos! no temen insultar la sana razon y por eso aparentan y ofrecen lo que menos piensan ejecutar. ¿Como es que ofrecen restituir la administracion de temporalidades a los Religiosos, cuando por el articulo cuarto que sigue del plan no deben embarazar las facultades del Director de Colonizacion segun las instrucciones que recibio del Supremo gobierno? ¿y esas instrucciones no previenen en su articulo primero la ocupacion de todos los bienes de las misiones? ¡luego que han de admi-

nistrar los Religiosos? ¿y esto no es engañar a cara descubierta? ¿cren esos mentecatos que no entendemos su embrollo? ¿no he probado hasta la evidencia que las instrucciones dadas a Hijar por el Ministro de Relaciones fueron arrancadas por sorpresa para despojar a los indios californios de sus intereses? ¿no he representado al Gobierno supremo sobre la inconstitucionalidad de aquella providencia para que la revoque? ¿no he demostrado con datos y constancias que el verdadero objeto de la espedicion colonial es apoderarse de los bienes de las misiones? ¿se ignora acaso los designios y planes de la Compañia cosmopolitana? ¿no es publica y notoria la ecshibicion a que estan condenadas las misiones para pagar el Bergantin Natalia? ¿no es cierto que las fincas de obras pias de las mismas misiones van a pagar el valor de dicho buque por que asi lo ha querido el Director de Colonizacion y su comparsa? ¿no es cierto que a mas de ese gravamen y el haber usado de los fondos de la nacion para habilitar la espedicion del Natalia, se demanda a la misma Nacion el pasage y flete de los Colonos y equipages que vinieron en el? ¿y las misiones o la federacion han sacado o esperan algun fruto de tantas esacciones? nada . . . nada absolutamente; pero con todo, dirian Torres y Apalategui, nada cuesta sorprender y engañar a los padres si se dejan, ofreciendoles la administracion de temporalidades: ellos contribuiran a derrocar al gobierno y despues caeran ellos. ¡Tal es la estravagancia de sus pretensiones!

Aun pudiera hacer otras observaciones sobre el articulo tercero del plan, pero seria molestar demasiado al publico. Tengase presente que por el citado articulo ofrecen a los Religiosos misioneros la administracion de temporalidades y a continuacion se contradicen del modo siguiente. „4.° Por el articulo anterior „no se embarazan las facultades del Director „de Colonizacion para que obre con arreglo a „las instrucciones que le dio el Supremo go-„bierno." ¡Ah malvados, aqui esta descubierto todo el secreto de vuestra desenfrenada avaricia! ya he dicho que consta en varios lugares de este escrito, que las instrucciones que quieren hacer valer son contrarias a la Constitucion federal, y que so pretesto de cumplirlas a nombre del Supremo gobierno, quieren los cosmopolitas enriquecerse sobre la ruina de mas de veinte mil personas, que son los dueños legitimos de los intereses de las misiones. Este es el resultado forzoso siempre que se pongan en practica por el Sr. Hijar las precitadas instrucciones. Ellas son el unico objeto de la revolucion, por cuyo medio unicamente pudieran haber a las manos los intereses a que aspiran, ya que no han podido adquirirlos por el camino del honor.

Por el quinto articulo someten su plan a

la aprobacion del Gobierno general. Esto es una ficcion para engañar al publico; por que ni los faccionarios han contado con el Gobierno, ni aprobaria en ningun caso los ataques a la autoridad cualquiera que sea el pretesto proclamado por los sediciosos: ¿donde se ha visto un gobierno que apruebe su misma destruccion por un puñado despreciable de freneticos demagogos? ¿quien les ha confiado la suerte y gobierno de los ciudadanos? ¿quien les ha dado poder para juzgar o residenciar a las autoridades constituidas legalmente?

No es menos disparatado el sesto articulo: por el protestan no dejar las armas hasta que se realice su plan, y se constituyen protectores de la administracion de justicia y de las autoridades. ¿Quien entendera esta gerigonza? ¡ni el sapientisimo caballero de la triste figura seria capaz de tanta bravura y destreza politica! Ofrecen no dejar las armas hasta ver realizado su plan, y en los momentos de su pronunciamiento se ocultan de la vista de sus profanos dejando a cargo de sus escuderos la defensa de sus juramentos ¡ya se ve, que los cuitados tenian que hacer sus cabriolas, y no debian esponerse a la espectacion publica! ¿Y como se entinde esto de la proteccion a la justicia y las autoridades, cuando se da un golpe mortal al cuerpo politico cortandole la cabeza que es el gobierno? eso en sentir de los caballeros andantes es la razon

de la sinrazon ¿luego tenemos desfacedores de agravios? no hay duda, de que los hay, los hay: el caso es que ya enfadan, ¡protectores de la justicia, imitad a Sancho en el gobierno de su Insula!

Me he detenido en analizar el plan abortado en el pueblo de los Angeles por que se ataca atrozmente mi honor, y aunque los criminales que lo proclamaron estan a disposicion del Tribunal que debe juzgarlos, deseo que el publico conozca la depravacion de sus autores, quienes tubieron el tragico fin que se advierte por la ecsposicion que sigue.

„Sr. Alcalde constitucional. = Juan Gallardo y Felipe Castillo a nombre de la fuerza armada que el dia de hoy se ha presentado representando derechos del pueblo ante V. con el debido respeto parecen y dicen: que habiendo sido invitados por los ciudadanos Antonio Apalategui y Francisco Torres a que cooperasemos con nuestras fuerzas fisicas al bien y prosperidad del territorio de la alta California como lo acreditan con el plan que al efecto presentaron al Y. Ayuntamiento el que no fue adoptado; y satisfechos que el Y. Cuerpo debe haber premeditado con mas juicio y madurez el asunto; y considerando al mismo tiempo, que el unico y mejor medio que hay para evitar un rompimiento, hemos convenido en presentar como en efecto presentamos a los promotores del hecho, para que si su empresa

es conforme a la razon se justifiquen ante la ley, y deduzcan sus derechos por el orden que designan las leyes. Bien convenido tanto su autoridad como la vindicta publica, que si el paso dado es criminal juzguese la buena intencion con que se hizo, y revalidese el concepto que se merece. = Por lo espuesto unanimes suplicamos a V. se sirva absolvernos decretando la indulgencia, justicia que imploramos, protestando el respeto a las leyes. = Pueblo de los Angeles Marzo 7 de 1835. = Por si y los alarmados. = Felipe Castillo. = Es copia. = Alvarado."

Los documentos que siguen es la contestacion que di al Ayuntamiento del Pueblo de los Angeles y una proclama al publico.

„Gobierno politico de la alta California. = Por el oficio de V. S. de 7 del corriente quedo enterado de las desagradables ocurrencias habidas en ese pueblo y de la audacia de D. Francisco Torres y D. Antonio Apalategui que no contentos con vivir pacificamente bajo la proteccion de las leyes, maquinan constantemente contra la sociedad que los alimenta. He ecsaminado su plan y por mas que han disfrazado sus miras ambiciosas no pueden ocultar el furor con que desean devorar los bienes de los infelices indigenas de las misiones. Por eso, y por que miran en mi persona un obstaculo a sus miras, piden mi separacion del mando politico y militar; por eso anulan los acuerdos de

la Ecsma. Diputacion territorial que impidieron
el robo de los intereses; y por eso en fin en
su articulo cuarto de su plan determinan poner en posesion de ellos al Director de Colonizacion con arreglo a las instrucciones del
Gobierno: he aqui el veneno mortifero con que
quieren sacrificar al territorio esos aventureros.
El verdadero y unico objeto de su plan es el
de apoderarse de los bienes de las misiones
para saciar su avaricia a costa del sudor de
los Californios: yo que resueltamente he defen-
dido esos intereses soy el blanco de sus tiros,
pero no importa: cumplo con mi deber aunque me sacrifiquen con tal de que los Californios no sean defraudados. = Yo defiendo
la justicia, la libertad, seguridad, y propiedades de los ciudadanos: mi causa es la de los
pueblos y las leyes: ellas hablan por mi: yo
sostengo el gobierno que se me ha confiado:
si abuso de mi autoridud o cometo algun crimen, que se me acuse al gobierno mismo, o al
tribunal que deba juzgarme: si he desmerecido la confianza publica, estoy pronto a dejar
el mando, pero en manos de autoridad com-
petente y ante quien las leyes han facultado
para el caso; pero nunca lo hare en manos de
una reunion tumultuaria que solo apellida el
orden para subvertirlo, y las leyes para vulne-
rarlas. = He ofrecido a los Californios y estoy
pronto a cumplirselos, que me separare del mando: lo he renunciado ante el Supremo gobierno

y la Ecsma. Diputacion territorial ha interpuesto su respetable influjo para que se me nombre un sucesor de Gefe politico: pronto vendra
la resolucion y quedaran satisfechos los deseos;
mas entretanto es un deber de todo ciudadano respetar y sostener mi autoridad. = Aunque V. S. ha conocido lo monstruoso del plan
y el objeto a que se dirige, me ha sido preciso hacerle las presentes indicaciones para rectificar su juiciosa opinion y que lo haga entender a los individuos que se comprometieron
en el pronunciamiento manifestandoles: que su
pronto retroceso al orden, me da ha entender
sus sanas intenciones, y que solo fueron sorprendidos y engañados por los perfidos Torres
y Apalategui enemigos de la felicidad de los
pueblos y de todo gobierno: que ellos han dado un testimonio que me asegura de su buen
proceder en lo succesivo entregando en manos de la justicia a los seductores, quienes seran juzgados con arreglo a las leyes: que todos los individuos comprendidos en el pronunciamiento y que desistieron el mismo dia, quedan perdonados a nombre del Supremo gobierno a quien dare cuenta, con tal de que no
vuelvan a mezclarse en revolucion o alvorotos
que alteren la tranquilidad: que se retiren a
vivir en paz a sus casas bajo las garantias de
las leyes y las seguridades que en este se les
ofrecen, y que denuncien a cualesquiera persona que bajo cualesquier pretesto intente al-

terar el orden publico. = Restame tributar a
esa Ilustre Corporacion y honrado vecindario
los debidos homenages de mi gratitud y respeto por su heroico comportamiento, y la noble firmeza con que reuso tomar parte en los
atentados que momentaneamente pudieron al-
terar la tranquilidad publica. Doy pues a V. S.
por tan eminente servicio las mas espresivas
gracias recomendandole, que duplique sus cui-
dados y desvelos por la salud publica, y que
no permita que se altere el orden bajo ningun pretesto de los que inventa la maledicencia. = Los reos Torres y Apalategui recomien-
do a V. S. muy mucho que sean bien ase-
guradas sus personas y sustanciada su causa con
toda la brevedad posible; pues aunque el conocimiento de ella corresponde al ramo militar, supongo que el Alcalde ha prevenido el
juicio y debe sustanciarla hasta ponerla en estado de sentencia. = Si para esto u otros objetos del servicio publico necesitare V. S. aucsilios de fuerza armada, puede pedirla al Teniente Coronel D. Nicolas Gutierrez interin lle-
ga la division que marcha a ese rumbo para
acabar de afianzar la tranquilidad. = Todo lo
que tengo el honor de decir a V. S. en contestacion a su nota de 7 del corriente con que
me acompaña el plan de los pronunciados y
las contestaciones habidas con ese respecto. =
Dios y Libertad. S. Juan Bautista 13 de Marzo de 1835. = Jose Figueroa. = Muy Ilustre

Ayuntamiento del Pueblo de los Angeles."
„El Comandante general y Gefe politco de
la alta California a los habitantes del territorio. = Conciudadanos: el genio del mal ha a-
parecido entre vosotros esparciendo el mortifero veneno de la discordia: los enemigos del orden envidiosos de la felicidad que ha gozado
este pueblo, y no satisfechos de la sangre que
han hecho derramar de sus compatriotas en el
interior de la republica, trageron a los Californios el funesto presente de la anarquia: las repetidas pruebas que han recibido de que los
Californios no sucumben a sus inicuos proyectos, han irritado su presuntuoso orgullo y quieren sacrificarlos a cualesquiera costo. He aqui
la suma de bienes que Hijar, Padres, Torres,
Berdusco y otros trageron a California: a un pais
que progresaba a la sombra de la paz y confianza se le quiere arrancar su reposo para su-
mirlo en los desastres de la guerra civil. Estos
son, Ciudadanos, los grandiosos proyectos que
ocupan la acalorada fantasia de esos hombres.
Desde que pisaron las playas del territorio estan maquinando su ruina ocultamente hasta que
el 7 del corriente descorrieron el velo de su
desmesurada ambicion. En el pueblo de los Angeles, unos cuantos individuos de Sonora seducidos por D. Francisco Torres y el español
D. Antonio Apalategui, proclamaron un plan
de conspiracion contra el gobierno territorial:
ese famoso aborto de la maledicencia, abunda

en artificiosas atroces calumnias y falsedades con que se pretende alucinar al pueblo para inducirlo a la desobediencia, destruir el prestigio de la autoridad, y atentar contra las personas que la ejercen. Tal es el conjunto de acriminaciones con que me obsequian, y que me propongo refutar por medio de un manifiesto luego que me lo permitan las atenciones publicas; mas entre tanto indicare sus pretenciones: piden mi separacion del mando por que me opuse a que dilapidaran los bienes de las misiones, y por que quiere colocarse en mi lugar el Sr. Hijar: se valen del artificio de elegir al Alcalde primero de la capital para Gefe politico sin acordarse que por falta de este magistrado, la ley llama en su lugar al primer vocal de la Diputacion; pero es preciso para ocultar la ambicion del aspirante desorganizar en su totalidad al gobierno para abrirle paso: piden al Capitan Portilla de Comandante general para sustituir despues al Sr. Padres que quiere serlo: anulan los acuerdos de la Ecsma. Diputacion territorial, por que garantizan el goce de las propiedades de los indios que les quieren quitar; suspender la secularizacion de misiones volviendo aparentemente a los religiosos la administracion de temporalidades por que creen engañarlos para interesarlos en la revolucion: y por ultimo, poner al Director de la Colonia, en posesion de los bienes de las misiones para que disponga de

ellos segun las instrucciones que le diera el Supremo gobierno, como si el publico no estubiera informado de que es anticonstitucional esa providencia por que infiere el despojo de las propiedades de mas de veinte mil personas. En suma, todo esto se quiere por la fuerza que es el derecho de los salteadores: en ello se ataca directamente la constitucion y leyes, se violan todas las garantias de la sociedad, se disuelve el pacto dejando la suerte del pueblo al arbitrio del atrevido usurpador que quiere dominar aunque sea contra la voluntad del Supremo gobierno que aparentan respetar, y de los ciudadanos que quieren someter. = He referido en compendio el objeto de la revolucion que afortunadamente termino en su misma cuna: los mismos comprometidos luego que conocieron el crimen que iban a cometer, que el Ilustre Ayuntamiento de los Angeles desaprobo su conducta, y que ningun hijo de California tomaba parte en sus descarrios, desistieron de la empresa, se sometieron al gobierno, entregaron a los seductores, y la justicia calificara su delito para aplicarles las penas que impongan las leyes que han quebrantado. = La tranquilidad que momentaneamente pudo alterarse por estos sucesos, quedo inmediatamente restablecida; pero los abogados de la anarquia, no cesan de predicar la discordia, ni yo perdere de vista sus planes liberticidas. = Esto es conciudadanos todo lo acaecido: en cuanto

a mi persona, el publico calificara mis procedimientos, el Gobierno me ecsigira responsabilidad si acaso la he contraido, y el tribunal a quien compete, me aplicara la ley si he cometido algun delito. El destino de Gefe politico, lo he renunciado, y la Ecsma. Diputacion ha interpuesto sus respetos para que se me nombre un sucesor: pronto vendra la resolucion y me vereis sumiso depositar en sus manos el poder que me delego el Ecsmo. Sr. Presidente de la Republica para gobernar este territorio. Entre tanto conciudadanos, no deis credito a las falaces sugestiones de los enemigos del orden y del gobierno, que ciegos por la ambicion y avaricia, invocan el santo nombre de la justicia para profanarla y prodigar vuestra sangre y vuestros intereses. Seguid unidos y pacificos en el goce de vuestros bienes sociales: esa es la verdadera felicidad, y unico galardon a que se estiende mi ambicion. = Monterrey 16 de Marzo de 1835. = Jose Figueroa.''

Aunque la revolucion aparecio y espiro en un mismo dia en el pueblo de los Angeles, tenia sus ramificaciones a cuya cabeza estaban los principales aspirantes: a pretesto de establecer la Colonia quisieron organizar una fuerza en que apoyar sus pretensiones: al efecto trahian desde Mejico cantidad de rifles y cartuchos que les mando franquear el Gobierno: esto y otros varios preparativos procuraron o-

cultarmelos: yo tenia descubiertos sus designios y solo los toleraba por esperar que descubrieran mas publicamente su crimen o que retrocedieran: esto no lo pude conseguir a pesar de repetidas pruebas de consideracion y sufrimiento; pues cuanto mas me esmeraba en convencerlos para desviarlos de sus tortuosas miras o cuanto mas disimulaba yo sus intentos, tanto mas se insolentaban quiza por que mi moderacion la caracterizaban de debilidad o cobardia. Asi es que animados de esa confianza adelantaban diariamente sus aprestos y aun el mismo Sr. Hijar a pesar de su aparente modestia no podia disimular la parte que tomaba en esos movimientos: por eso se dirigio a S. Francisco Solano en pretensiones de reunir la Colonia cuando siempre la habia visto con la mas alta indiferencia; por eso tambien remitio bajo su firma al mes de Febrero al R. P. Presidente Fr. Narciso Duran una copia del disparatado oficio que me contesto en 23 de Octubre: por eso ocultaba las maniobras de Berdusco y Lara que en su nombre y bajo su inmediata proteccion ecsitaban a la revolucion: por eso el mismo Sr. Hijar sin haber recibido el mando peroraba a los indios en las misiones por donde transito ecsortandolos a defender la libertad que nadie atacaba: por eso se reunia con Torres, Berdusco, Lara y Araujo en conferencias secretas que tubieron en la casa de Bonifacio: por eso en fin miraba con tanto desprecio las proposiciones de paz que le hice varias veces suplicandole que contuviera a sus protejidos para no verme obligado a castigrlos, puesto que ya tenia descubiertos sus planes y suspendia todo procedimiento por consideracion a su persona. Sea pues que el Sr. Hijar proteja decididamente la revolucion, o bien que servia de un instrumento ciego a sus autores, el hecho es que se palpaba su adhesion, y despues que amigablemente y de varios modos reconoci su apego a mis enemigos, ninguna confianza podia inspirarme; por que aun haciendole favor de creerlo inocente de lo que urdian sus criaturas, tiene una alma tan insensible y apatica que le seria indiferente su misma ecsistencia. Esto supuesto, y el estallar la revolucion de un modo ostensible ¿que deberia hacer con el Sr. Hijar? ¿no es el rival que me presentan mis emulos para cubrir sus crimenes y engañar al publico? ¿debia permitir que por mas tiempo se burlara de mi condescendencia? ¿deberia yo esponer mas de lo, que habia espuesto la tranquilidad publica por una imprudente tolerancia? Crei que estaba en mi deber alejar todo motivo de trastorno y esto no podia ser dejando ecsistentes las causas. No estaba yo en el caso de aguardar a que previamente se instruyera un proceso, por que a mas de que en tales ocasiones se dificulta probar esactamente los secretos crimenes de los revoltosos, ellos no esperan mas que la

ocasion favorable para descargar sus golpes: la poca fuerza militar que tengo a mis ordenes, y las diversas atenciones que debe cubrir en la estension de mas de doscientas leguas es otro motivo que me obligo a obrar con mas energia. Por todas estas consideraciones mande arrestar a Lara y Berdusco; a Hijar y Padres los suspendi de la comision de Directores de la Colonia y los hice marchar a Mejico a disposicion del Supremo gobierno, para lo cual le dirigi al primero la nota siguiente.

„Gobierno politico de la alta California. = Se verifico por fin la revolucion que fue a promover D. Francisco Torres segun anuncie a V. S amistosamente manifestandole que sus amigos querian, comprometerlo para burlarse del gobierno. Este hecho que me fue revelado con anterioridad, y otros antecedentes que manifeste a V. S. contraidos todos a conspirar contra el orden publico y contra las leyes, me imponen el deber de dictar providencias que aseguren la tranquilidad publica constantemente amenazada; pues no ha bastado a contener la audacia de sus adictos el prudente comportamiento que he usado con todos, y la conducta franca con que he manifestado a V. S. sus solicitudes erroneas para que los contenga dentro de los limites del deber. A pesar de que ha llegado a mi noticia con anterioridad los proyectos que han tramado para lograr os fines, he guardado silencio para que se asegu[...]

caso se me culpe de violento; pero hoy que se ha descorrido el velo, han recibido muy pronto un desengaño sensible; los incautos a quienes Torres logro seducir por sorpresa reconocieron su error y ellos mismos lo entregaron preso a la justicia lo mismo que a su asociado Apalategui. = En consecuencia de estos acontecimientos he dispuesto que V. S. y el Ayudante Inspector D. Jose Maria Padres queden suspensos de la comision que les confio el Supremo gobierno, entregando el armamento, municiones e intereses y todo lo que tienen a su cargo al Alferez D. Mariano G. Vallejo y que marchen inmediatamente a disposicion de dicho Supremo gobierno ante quien responderan de los cargos que les resulte por la conducta que han observado desde su ingreso a este territorio. Tengo el honor de comunicarlo a V. S para su inteligencia y cumplimiento. = Dios y Libertad. S. Juan Bautista 13 de Marzo de 1835. = Jose Figueroa. = Sr. D. Jose Maria de Hijar."

El Sr. Hijar me contesto con el oficio que sigue.

„Me dice V. S. en su oficio de 13 del presente que al fin estallo la revolucion que fue a promover D. Francisco Torres, segun me habia manifestado en lo particular: que quedan presos los promovedores y que esto lo obliga a tomar providencias que aseguren la tranquilidad; disponiendo al efecto que quedemos sus-

pensos de la comision que nos confio el Supremo gobierno yo y el Ayudante Inspector D. Jose Maria Padres, entregando al Alferez Don Mariano G. Vallejo el armamento, municiones, intereses y todo lo que tengamos a nuestro cargo, concluyendo con que marchemos inmediatamente a disposicion del Supremo gobierno para responder a los cargos que nos resulten por la conduta que hemos observado desde nuestro ingreso al territorio. = En cuanto a lo primero, me permitira V. S. que le diga, que la revolucion de que me habla me parece solamente imaginaria: nunca podre persuadirme que el Sr. Torres, que iba de transeunte conduciendo pliegos importantes para el Supremo gobierno general fuese a empreder una revolucion sin objeto y en un pais donde no tiene relaciones ni conocimientos. Yo no veo en todo esto mas de un misterio que el tiempo descubrira: si el velo se ha descorrido para V. S, para mi aun permanece bastante denso; pero espero que pronto se rasgara, las cosas apareceran como son en realidad y todo quedara tan claro como la misma luz. = Quiero suponer que algunos Colonos escaltados y justamente resentidos hubiesen querido revolucionar: pero no se por que motivo esto pudiera ser trascendental a mi, como si yo los hubiese inducido o tomado parte en la revolucion. Sin embargo, V. S. me manda suspender, dandome con esto el golpe mas terrible e hiriendome en la fibra mas delicada. V. S. ha procurado manchar mi reputacion que estimo mas que toda la ecsistencia; se me quiere hacer aparecer con crimenes o faltas que ciertamente no he cometido, mas yo protesto solemnemente arrastrar a mi perseguidor, cualquiera que sea, hasta los tribunales competentes en donde ecsigire la condigna satisfaccion. = V. S. sabe muy bien que si yo me quede en este territorio fue solo a las repetidas suplicas e instancias de V. S. de una comision de la Ecsma. Diputacion y de otros particulares que V. S. conoce: sabe igualmente que yo iba a dejar el territorio dentro de pocos dias y que por consiguiente no tenia interes en seguir dirigiendo la Colonia. Hago esta pequeña digresion para que V. S. entienda, que el profundo sentimiento que me devora, no nace de que se me haya suspendido de una comision que yo iba a dejar; si no del injurioso modo con que se ha hecho. = Siempre he desempeñado con lustre muchas delicadas e importantes comisiones; y los distintos Gobiernos que se han servido de mi inutilidad, han quedado satisfechos de mi comportamiento, sin haber merecido nunca la menor reconvencion: mi conducta publica, bastante conocida en el interior, no habia recibido una sola tacha, y esto formaba todas mis glorias: pero parece que el cielo habia reservado a V. S. el que me infiriese la injuria mas atroz. Si Sr. General, si no esperara vindicarme, me hubiera

pegado un tiro para no arrastrar una ecsistencia oprobiosa, y para no aparecer como un objeto despreciable ante los ojos de mis semejantes. = Yo no encuentro en V. S. facultades para suspenderme; pero es necesario ceder a la fuerza: por consiguiente seran en todo obsequiadas sus disposiciones y estoy pronto a partir tan luego como V. S. me lo proporcione. (¡Ojala y fuese mañana!) Me presentare al Supremo gobierno con la serenidad que infunde una conciencia tranquila y alli espero confundir a mi acusador = Terminare esta comunicacion manifestando a V. S. que hemos sufrido tropelias inauditas; que se nos ha tratado de una manera escandalosa y cual no se usaria con una cuadrilla de bandidos, atacando bruscamente los imprescriptibles derechos del hombre, que garantiza nuestra carta. Todo se hubiera evitado y yo hubiera hecho se entregasen las armas, municiones y todo lo demas, sin necesidad de atropellar a nadie, si el Sr. Vallejo me hubiera presentado el oficio de V. S; pero de intento se nos ha querido hacer sentir todo el peso de la arbitrariedad, tratandonos mas bien como a foragidos que como Mejicanos: paciencia Sr. General, quiza algun dia imperaran las leyes. = He transcrito al Ayudante Inspector el oficio de V. S. para su conocimiento, con todo lo que creo dejar contestado su citado de 13 del presente. = Dios y Libertad. S. Francisco Solano 17 de

Marzo de 1835. = Jose Maria de Hijar. = Al Sr. Gefe politico General D. Jose Figueroa."

Es tanta la obsecacion del Sr. Hijar que aun los hechos publicos de sus paniaguados pretende oscurecer poniendolos en duda como si yo fuera algun farsante que me habia de ocupar de bagatelas, o en suponer por entretenimiento el suceso que oficialmente le comunico. Adviertase como dice que Torres conducia pliegos importantes para Mejico, prueba nada equivoca de la gran confianza que le merecia este aventurero Esculapio: y asi añade, que nunca podra persuadirse hubiese emprendido este una revolucion sin objeto, y en un pais que le es desconocido; ¡que hipocresia! ya queda probado hasta la evidencia, que Torres fue el agente inmediato de la rebelion; y que esta tenia su determinado objeto. ¿Por que no estallo antes que el mismo Torres llegara a los Angeles? ¿a que fin su amistad intempestiva con Apalategui, con este camarada de los Sonorenses? ¿y por que los mismos Sonorenses arrepentidos de su punible alzamiento señalaron a Torres y a Apalategui como sus seductores, y moviles principales; y presos los entregaron a la autoridad?

Por mas paralogismos y circunloquios que use el Sr. Hijar, nunca podra persuadir a los Californios que no tuvo parte en este suceso, que yo mismo le anuncie con antelacion, por las fidedignas noticias que tenia de sus atrai-

dorados proyectos. Con tirar la piedra y esconder la mano o escudarse con testaferros piensa evadir la severidad de las leyes; mas se engaña: todos sus pasos lo condenan como hemos visto.

Vaticina que me arrastrara ante los tribunales: ya iran a estos todos los antecedentes necesarios: y yo estoy pronto a presentarme y confundir con la razon, la ley y la justicia al que procuro hollar mi autoridad. La providad de los jueces no puede menos de ser favorable al que salvo la integridad de la republica, y sostuvo la paz y la ley en este territorio.

Nunca se le rogo al Sr. Hijar que permaneciera en el pais; solo me interese, como los demas Señores de las conferencias en que no condujera los fatigados Colonos a la baja California, como imprudentemente querian o suponian querer sus Directores.

Si los servicios de que blasona el Sr. Hijar han sido en otra parte provechosos, aqui ha sido perjudicial su reservada apatia y simulado manejo para asaltar por sorpresa el mando politico: y si el espiritu de los Californios no fuera tan perspicaz y yo hubiese reposado en una vana confianza, es indudable el triunfo de los Cosmopolitas; por que sus gefes son diestros en el arte de la intriga y saben aprovecharse de su florida y vana locuacidad; mas su energia y valor franco y leal son tan escasos, que les falta, hasta para la cobarde accion de pegarse un tiro, como el Sr. Hijar, poseido de su anglomania dice, lo hubiera ya hecho si no esperara vindicarse.

Me niega las facultades para suspenderlo, y antes tiene asegurado que vive sumiso al Gobierno politico y reconoce su autoridad.

Las tropelias inauditas de que se queja no fueron otras que las medidas absolutamente necesarias para recojer las armas y municiones que ocultaba el Sr. Padres, y para impedir que este alarmase a los Colonos y fuese necesario hacer uso de la fuerza; asi es, que nadie resulto herido ni aun contuso, mediante el tino y militar prudencia con que desempeño esta comision el Alferez D. Mariano G. Vallejo. Ya se deja ver que el ataque a los imprescriptibles derechos del hombre, no fue otro, que el haber impedido el mal uso de las armas: pero era una frase retumbante que no debia omitirse: dejo la nota.

Recibidos abordo de la fragata sarda la Rosa, que se hallaba en la bahia de S. Francisco, los Sres. Hijar, Padres, Berdusco, Lara y algunos otros fueron conducidos a la rada de S. Pedro; y trasbordados a la goleta angloamericana la Loriot, salieron en Mayo ultimo con los Sres. D. Buenaventura Araujo, D. Francisco Torres y D. Antonio Apalategui para S. Blas a disposicion del Supremo gobierno.

Los Colonos han mejorado de situacion con haberles separado los gefes que los escla-

vizaban y conducian a su total ruina. Establecidos en el dia donde mas les acomoda, aucsiliados en cuanto es posible por este gobierno y acogidos por los Californios no les falta su subsistencia, ni en que ocuparse a los laboriosos; notandose ya los adelantos de algunos de ellos.

La paz se ha consolidado, y con ella sus inestimables beneficios. Inutil parece decir que la compañia Cosmopolitana se deshizo por si misma, y como fundada esencialmente en la triple representacion de los Sres. Hijar y Padres como fundadores y primeros accionistas de ella, como Directores de la Colonia y gefes del territorio: la Colonia y los mandos eran pues la base de la compañia, y el mas poderoso aucsilio para la grandiosa especulacion que idearon, atropellando las leyes que prohiben a los empleados ser comerciantes.

D. Jose Maria Padres ha sido el agente mas solapado y activo de esta empresa: ya he referido que con sus proyectos sobre las misiones, cuya incumbencia no le pertenecia, y su tortuosa conducta altero la tranquilidad del territorio eu 1830, y fue causa de que se desconociera el legitimo gobierno del Teniente coronel D. Manuel Victoria por algunos incautos ciudadanos, por lo que aquel merecio la desaprobacion del Supremo gobierno: mas no obstante, consiguio a fuerza de amaños volver con la Colonia y el destino de Ayudante Ins-

pector a este territorio, de donde habia sido ecspulsado. He tocado esta especie para que se vea, desde que fecha se ocupa en sus miras mercantiles sobre California.

Es de presumir que este mismo oficioso Señor, con la ifluencia que tenia sobre el animo del Sr. Hijar y la que se preciaba de gozar en el del Ecsmo. Sr. Vice Presidente Gomez Farias, seria el que intrigase en Mejico, para que el Gobierno supremo no pidiese informes a esta Ecsma. Diputacion ni a mi, sobre los recursos con que se contaba aqui para la colocacion y sosten de los Colonos, que venian asalariados hasta que pasase el año de su establecimiento definitivo, debiendo suministrarseles, como he dicho, granos, ganados y aperos; para todo lo cual se necesitaba erogar crecidisimos gastos, incapaces de ser soportados por la hacienda publica del territorio; que no cubre ni aun la mitad de sus atenciones ordinarias, y que ni tenia ni tiene aun orden Suprema para tales suministros. Mas como el informe de este gobierno politico no podia ser favorable al objeto, de los que desde Mejico especulaban sobre los bienes de estos indigenas, se omitio el pedirlo, al paso que se formaba un bonito plan de dilapidacion; reducido a secularizar las misiones para quitar a los padres ministros la tutela de los neofitos y dejar a estos indefensos, mientras que posesionados el Director y Subdirector de la Colonia de los

mandos politico y militar disponian a su arbitrio, y a pretesto de aucsiliar y establecer los Colonos de todos los intereses de los indios; pues separados los pastores facil es a los lobos devorar el rebaño.

Mas la Providencia frustro proyectos tan estraviados por una hilacion de sucesos que no eran capaces de preveer los Directores, que desde su salida de Mejico fueron pulsando los inconvenientes de su mal meditada empresa de Colonia y los de su jactanciosa compañia mercantil Cosmopolitana, tan falta de fondos como rica de esperanzas y notable por la pedanteria de su nombre; la que tuvo el pesar de ver estrellado en esta costa a su bergantin Natalia por falta de amarras, e impericia y descuido de sus dueños a los pocos dias de hallarse surto en este puerto.

Hemos visto que el Sr. Hijar a pretesto de su comision y fundado en unas instrucciones anticonstitucionales, impoliticas y tal vez subrepticias quiso apoderarse de las riquezas de las misiones y atacar el incuestionable derecho de propiedad de los indigenas, y que desconocio la autoridad legal de la Diputacion sobre los bienes comunales y la inspeccion y vigilancia que a mi me correspondia como Gefe politico encargado en conservar indemnes las garantias sociales, y en guardar y hacer guardar las leyes: y ya he referido, como pretendio valerse de mi autoridad como Comandante general para envilecer las armas nacionales, haciendolas servir a sus injustas pretensiones para apoyar y autorizar con ellas el inicuo despojo de bienes que se fraguaba contra el desvalido indio.

Admira el ver a los Sres. Directores de Colonizacion tan obstinados en su funesto empeño de usurpar las propiedades agenas, que se ven en el apuro de traer de los cabellos en su aucsilio el que llaman derecho eminente del gobierno, y alegar que las misiones no tienen ningun derecho sobre sus bienes por ser cuerpos morales, y como tales incapaces de adquirir propiedad y menos de retenerla. ¡Que sublime filosofia, y que teorias tan ilusorias tienen los revolucionarios para apoderarse de los bienes agenos! mas cobardes que los bandidos se valen de sofismas y de palabras huecas y altisonantes; y puesta una mascara de patriotismo y religiosidad, cuando ultrajan a su patria y se burlan de su religion, abierta su escuela, hecho su proselitismo de incautos y contando con poder suficiente no hay ya barrera que los detenga, y con formulas legales todo lo atropellan; y solo respetan, solo es sagrado lo que a su bando pertenece. ¿No ven estos Sres. que si los cuerpos morales no pueden adquirir ni retener la propiedad, como ellos dicen, tampoco la puede adquirir ni retener el Gobierno? ¿y no infieren de sus principios que el derecho eminente del Gobierno es nulo en

el caso que aqui nos lo alegan, pues que nadie puede dar lo que no tiene? ¡Cuantas contradicciones trae el prurito de pasar por ilustrados, y el querer ser ricos a fuerza de filosofias!

¿A quien no llamara la atencion el ver que el Sr. Hijar dice en su nota de 6 de Noviembre que las leyes españolas que protejen la propiedad de los indios pugnan con nuestro sistema? Mejor diria que pugnan con el sistema de depredacion que trahian adoptado. Quiso desvirtuar la sabia ley recopilada que ordena se obedezcan pero que no se cumplan las disposiciones soberanas que tiendan a despojar a alguno de su posesion sin ser antes oido y vencido en juicio contradictorio: y no obstante pretendia que el indio, ignorante aun, menesteroso y medio selvatico fuese igual identica y absolutamente en derechos politicos en ejercicio a los demas ciudadanos; acaso para alucinarlo mejor, o para sorprenderlo indefenso con mas facilidad. Segun estos principios, debiamos borrar de nuestros codigos las leyes que norman la patria potestad, las que arreglan la gefatura del hombre en el matrimonio, todas las que hablan de la curatela y tutela de los menores, fatuos, dementes, prodigos y otras varias.

Llevada a tal estremo la igualdad legal se desquiciaria la sociedad. Tal es el fatal empeño de nivelar todo en la apariencia para desi-

gualarlo en el fondo, para destruirlo y para que solo impere el fanatismo de los pretensos filosofos, intolerante y despota. Este es el rumbo de nuestros sofistas y politicastros; de los mismos Sres. que niegan a los indios el derecho de propiedad sobre los bienes de sus misiones: mas el plan era colmarles de derechos y privarles de su hacienda Esta es la filantropia que se iba a aplicar al indio Californio.

Por fortuna, las teorias y pomposas promesas de los Sres. Directores de la Colonia, y su garrulidad y espiritu de proselitismo no han tenido sequito alguno entre los juiciosos Californios, y desesperanzados de poder contar con ellos para sus proyectos de revolucion, apelaron, como he dicho, por medio de sus emisarios a seducir unos cuantos emigrados de Sonora, que venian a buscar fortuna en este territorio y se hallaban en el Pueblo de los Angeles. Y a la verdad, que solo en el animo de unos miserables aventureros pudiera encontrar acojida la mision de les Sres. Torres y Apalategui, que salieron de aqui y de la misma casa del Sr. Hijar con ese especial objeto. Pero su seduccion y pronunciamiento fue momentaneo, y solo sirvio para acarrear a sus autores y promotores la animadversion general, para que los acabase de condenar el espiritu publico, y para que tubieran sus inmediatos corifeos la degradante humillacion de verse presos entregados al brazo inecsorable de la jus-

ticia por los mismos incautos Sonorenses, que al punto conocieron su error, y la perfidia de los que habian abusado de su situacion y comprometido su descuidada confianza.

Han negado los Sres. Directores de la Colonia haber tenido parte en el criminal alzamiento de que hablo, promovido por sus satelites Torres y Apalategui: pero ¿quien ignora en Monterrey que Torres era favorito de Hijar, y uno de los que con Lara, Berdusco y otros componian la plana mayor de la Colonia? ¿quien duda quo este medicastro era de los diarios consejeros de Hijar, y que por su gran cabeza, conocimientos medicopoliticos, su genial taimado, calmoso, y su caracter hipocrita y subterraneo merecia el alto aprecio de sus gefes? Bien lo acredita el mismo Hijar, cuando confiesa en su oficio de 17 de Marzo, que lo habia despachado con pliegos del mayor interes para Mejico. Pero hay mas; en la causa que obra en el juzgado civil de esta capital, y que fue seguida contra el Sonorense D. Miguel Hidalgo por conductor de ciertas cartas dirigidas desde los Angeles por Torres a Berdusco y otros resulta, que en las reuniones preliminares que, para verificar el pronunciamiento contra mi autoridad, se tenian en la casa de D. Antonio Trujillo, se propuso con claridad por el mismo Torres, que el principal objeto de los pronunciados habia de ser el colocar en el mando politico al Sr, Hijar y en el militar al Sr. Padres; y nadie lo ha dudado en el territorio: la opinion publica y unanime lo atestigua: y por esta misma razon a muy pocos dias de haber salido Torres para los Angeles, salió Hijar con sus satelites para reunirse en San Francisco Solano con Padres, y secundar por el norte, con la parte de Colonos que pudieran contar, los movimientos de los Sonorenses que se hallaban por el sur.

Este fue el plan estratejico que juzgaron mas conveniente; pero les fallo, y fueron completamente desconcertados y confundidos por el espiritu publico, por mi vigilancia, y por el celo y energia que desplegaron los beneméritos oficiales que sirven a mis ordenes, especialmente el Alferez Vallejo comandante de San Francisco Solano. Y no es dudable les hará graves cargos el Supremo gobierno, a cuya disposicion los he remitido con los demas fautores de la rebelion.

Como la gran cuestion de que se trata en este manifiesto, no es de un interes topico sino nacional, y que por otra parte es el flanco por donde los especuladores mis antagonistas intentan denigrar una reputacion que he procurado conservar sin mancha, no he podido menos de dilatarme en la narracion de los sucesos y en la ecsposicion y refutacion de las doctrinas antisociales, con que se ha tratado de corromper a la virginal California, para regar con sangre sus campos de paz y fertilidad, destruir

la riqueza de sus misiones, sembrar la anarquia, y sobre las ruinas del territorio alzarse los mogigatos politicos, patriarcas de la revolucion y del desorden, con los bienes cuantiosos de los indios, adquiridos con su personal trabajo, bajo la direccion y evangelica paciencia de sus venerables misioneros.

Mis continuas atenciones y mi muy quebrantada salud me deben disculpar a los ojos del publico, si inadvertidamente he dejado de tocar algun punto de los necesarios para formar una completa opinion: yo creo no haber omitido nada esencial. Hay muchos testigos presenciales e imparciales instruidos en la serie de estos acontecimientos, que pueden deshacer mis equivocaciones, mis inesactitudes, y debatir mis errores y omisiones, si, contra mi voluntad, he incurrido en tales faltas.

Sobre todo, mis declarados rivales los Señores Director y Subdirector de la Colonia, D. Jose Maria Hijar y D. Jose Maria Padres tienen libertad para contestarme, y publicar probadas sus acusaciones contra mi, y sus imputaciones contra el pueblo Californio a quien han vilipendiado ostensiblemente: tenemos libertad de imprenta, ellos pasan por literatos y politicos superfinos; tienen pues instruccion y libertad para impugnar racionalmente mi manifiesto, y hacer valer por medios licitos sus doctrinas y acrisolar su conducta; la que en opinion de muchos, y como lo prueba el relato

de los sucesos y la pintoresca y ridicula creacion de la cumpañia Cosmopolitana tiene mas de torticera, de comerciante y monopolista que de patriota. ¡Que lejos estan algunos languidos republicanos, preciados de austeros, de aquella virtud, de aquel desprendimiento de los Porfumios, de los Cincinatos, de los Papirios y Fabios! Sus palabras son desmentidas por su conducta, y serviles, y despotas y codiciosos, en medio de su pretendido liberalismo, disipan con sus hechos la ilusion de sus promesas, y pierden paulatinamente el prestigio que sus ominosas teorias lograran introducir en la imprevisiva infancia de nuestra patria.

Ya es tiempo de persuadirnos que estos hombres nacieron para ser poetas adocenados, escritores de romances y novelas, y no para directores de un pueblo culto y morigerado. Tales hombres han hecho correr con abundancia la sangre mejicana; sus nombres manchan las paginas de nuestra historia; la anarquia, el desorden, la confusion, las ruinas son el fruto de sus afanes y el resultado de sus teorias, brillantes en la superficie y sobremanera corrompidas en su fondo.

Hombres tinturados en las escenas revolucionarias, y secuaces de las doctrinas anarquicas fueron los que aportaron a este territorio, capitaneando a los desventurados Colonos, y haciendoles sufrir por su despilfarro y torpe manejo mil privaciones e incomodidades

no necesarias, como es notorio.

A su llegada, me encontraba yo al frente de la administracion politica y militar del pais, me parece hice lo que debia en tan criticas circunstancias. Contuve pues sus pretensiones, descorri el velo de sus designios, descubri su impudencia, combati sus doctrinas, confundi su presuncion, desbarate sus proyectos, humille su arrogancia, deshice sus planes, enfrene su audacia, les apague la tea rebolucionaria que habian encendido, y salve las propiedades de los indios y la riqueza de las misiones, salve a los infortunados Colonos del precipicio a que los conducian; y mantuve la paz, y el orden y el bienestar de esta California; de este punto importante de la Republica, que necesita de un particular cuidado y esquisita tutela, para que no lo lancen en la carrera de los desordenes las sugestiones de los muchos aventureros propios y estraños, que, a manera de relampagos en noche tempestuosa, cruzan entre nosotros por todas partes.

Desde mi niñez he servido en las filas de la Independencia desde sus primeros tiempos; con mi escaso talento y menor instruccion, y con todas mis fuerzas, y con mi sangre y con mi salud he contribuido, en cuanto me ha sido dable, a las glorias de la patria. El nombre de mis rivales solo es conocido en los fastos de la guerra fratricida, en las discordias civiles, en la farsa de los anarquistas, en esa secta ominosa y aborrecida en la America y en la Europa, que hace la desgracia de nuestro siglo. Permitaseme hacer este cotejo en desahogo de mi pundonor, tan injusta como calumniosamente ultrajado: algun punto hay en este manifiesto tan desnudo de pruebas inmediatas y concluyentes, que solo la opinion particular, que del Sr. Hijar y de mi tenga cada uno en lo privado, puede hacer inclinar la balanza de la opinion: hablo sobre la secreta conferencia a que dicho Señor me convoco por su billete del dia 26 de Octubre, y queda referida en la pagina 92.

He procurado esplicarme ceñido estrictamente a la verdad, y sin devolver injurias por injurias: si en alguna parte se notare a mi estilo de duro o energico en demasia tengase presente que me defiendo calumniado, y que soy un militar que ha trascurrido su vida en las fatigas de penosas campañas y en oficinas tambien militares; y que por consiguiente no estoy avezado a los piropos y flores retoricas, con que engalanan sus producciones otros escritores de mas merito literario que el que yo pudiera tener.

Pero esta mi iusuficiencia no me acobarda: no soy retorico ni politico; soy un soldado mejicano, y no pretendo pasar por literato. En un estilo marcial y llano, al paso qne ecsacto y razonado y con la claridad que me es posible he procurado escribir, para poner en

todos sus aspetos las artificiosas miras de los Directores de la Colonia, y sus bulliciosos satelites cosmopolitanos.

No me arredra la malevolencia de los refractarios: hablo delante del publico, sobre el teatro de los sucesos, a mis coetaneos, a la faz de todos los testigos presenciales: todo esta a la vista, nada esencial omito, manifiesto todas las contestaciones y refiero con puntualidad los sucesos. Califiquese mi conducta, comparese con la de mis adversarios, y tenganse presentes todas las circunstancias que dejo espuestas. Esto es lo que suplico a los lectores; interin yo descansado en la sanidad de mi intencion, y pureza y legalidad justificada de mis procedimientos, espero que me haga justicia y me favorezca con su incorruptible opinion EL SENSATO PUEBLO MEJICANO.

Puerto de Monterrey 4 de Setiembre de 1835.

Jose Figueroa.

NOTA.

Estandose imprimiendo este Manifiesto falleció el 29 del mismo Setiembre el Sr. Ge-

neral de Brigada D. Jose Figueroa: en consecuencia a este funesto acaecimiento acordo la Ecsma. Diputacion se insertara en este impreso el espediente que sigue.

———————

ESPEDIENTE

Sobre perpetuar la memoria del finado Señor General de Brigada D. JOSE FIGUEROA, Comandante general y Gefe politico de la alta California, promovido en la Ecsma. Diputacion de este Territorio.

Ecsmo. Sr. = Murio nuestro Gefe, murio el protector del Territorio, el Padre de nuestra California, nuestro amigo, nuestro Mentor el General D. Jose Figueroa: los ciudananos rodean su lecho funebre, y clavados los ojos en el yerto cadaver enmudecen y suspiran llorando al grande hombre que la muerte nos arrebata. La triste, la infausta nueva se propaga veloz y a todos sobrecoge la pena y el sentimiento es general.

El eco doliente de las campanas y el lugubre estampido de la artilleria hacen brotar del corazon las mas comprimidas lagrimas: todo es amargura, todo dolor. Los Californios lloran a un benefico padre que ha dado a su prosperidad un incalculable fomento y que con

un esmero sin ejemplo, y con una constante y sin igual laboriosidad ha promovido todos los ramos del bien publico; al que apago la tea de la discordia y evito que fuera regada esta tierra virgen con la sangre de sus hijos; al que planto la oliva de la paz y ha cultivado a su sombra todo genero de virtudes que progresivamente se desenroyan en los leales pechos de estos habitantes; al que debe seguridad y estension nuestra agricultura y proteccion nuestro comercio; al que supo rechazar la anarquia cuando osara abordar a nuestras pacificas playas; al que consolo la viuda, amparo al huerfano, socorrio al soldado; al que protegio el merito y fomento la ilustracion; en una palabra al que trabajo en arreglar nuestro orden social.

Aun los estrageros muestran en su dolor el afecto que le profesaban y el elevado concepto que tenian formado del genio superior que nos presidia: el hijo del desierto, el indio selvatico nos indica aunque con modales rusticos el sentimiento que lo domina por tamaña perdida.

El nombre del General Figueroa se oye por todas partes, se relatan sus meritos, se encarece su tino politico, su celo y eficacia por el bien comun y aquel don de gentes con que sabia captarse las voluntades. Su honradez, su providad las reconoce el publico que le califica de patriota eminente y de hijo benemerito de la patria; todos alaban y reconocen el relevante merito del General Figueroa ¿y la Ecsma. Diputacion del territorio, no espresara cuanto participa de este sentimiento? Veo en los dignos miembros que la componen las inequivocas señales de la pena que les causa la prematura muerte de nuestro Gefe amado: este sentimiento es justo si, es justo, es laudable; sepalo el mundo todo y vease que en la alta California se sabe apreciar el verdadero merito.

Y ya que adorando las inescrutables disposiciones de la Providencia hemos implorado al pie de los altares la clemencia divina para el hombre de que nos priva la diestra del Omnipotente, y ya que se le han tributado todos los honores funebres politicos y militares que le son debidos; demos, benemeritos Diputados un publico y eterno testimonio de nuestra gratitud y de nuestro amor al General Figueroa; colmemos su memoria con nuestra estimacion y hagamos en su obsequio y honor cuanto sea dable; inmortalicemos su gloria y nuestro reconocimiento y con una corona de siemprevivas ciñamos su frente. Si Ecsmo. Señor oiga V. E. y sirvase aprobar las proposiciones siguientes.

1.° El retrato del General D. Jose Figueroa se colocara en el Salon de sesiones de esta Ecsma. Diputacion en prueba del aprecio que la misma ha hecho de su distinguido merito.

2.° Para perpetuar la grata memoria del mismo Sr. y la gratitud de esta Corporacion se levantara un monumento duradero con una inscripcion analoga, en uno de los sitios mas publicos y despejados de esta Capital y para ello se eccsitara, con remision de espediente, al Ilustre Ayuntamiento para que todo se haga bajo su direccion y cuidado, como se debe esperar de su acendrado patriotismo, de sus nobles sentimientos y del amor que ha profesado al hombre que lloramos.

3.° Del espediente se sacaran otras tres copias, una se entregara a los albaceas de nuestro difunto General y Gefe: otra se remitira a su Señora viuda e hijos y la tercera se pasara a la imprenta para que se imprima y publique a continuacion del manifiesto del mismo Sr. que esta en la prensa. = Monterrey 9 de Octubre de 1835. = Juan B. Alvarado.

Monterrey 10 de Octubre de 1835. = En sesion de este dia se dio cuenta a la Ecsma. Diputacion con esta proposicion y se mando pasar a la Comison de gobierno. Castro. Presidente. = Manuel Jimeno. Vocal Secretario.

Ecsmo. Sr. = La Comision de gobierno ha ecsaminado la proposicion del Sr. Alvarado en la que manifiesta la infausta nueva de la muerte del Sr. General y Gefe politico del territorio D. Jose Figueroa, y que esta Ecsma. Diputacion haga en su memoria y en su obsequio cuanto sea dable, pidiendo, primero. Que

el retrato del Sr. General D. Jose Figueroa se coloque en el salon de sesiones de esta Ecsma. Diputacion. Segundo. Que para perpetuar la grata memoria del mismo Sr. se levante un monumento duradero con una inscripcion analoga en uno de los sitios mas publicos y despejados de esta Capital, eccsitando al Ilustre Ayuntamiento para que todo se haga bajo su direccion y cuidado. Tercero. Que del espediente se saquen tres copias para que una se entregue a los albaceas de nuestro difunto General y Gefe, otra se remita a su Señora viuda e hijos y otra se pase a la imprenta para que se estampe y publique a continuacion del manifiesto del mismo Sr. que esta en la prensa. La Comision cree que los motivos alegados por el Sr. Alvarado son de aquellos que por ser publicos y notorios no tienen objecion que hacer, por que el nombre del Sr. General D. Jose Figueroa se relata por todas partes; todos alaban y reconocen su sobresaliente merito y distinguidos y antiguos servicios hechos a la Patria; siempre observo e hizo observar las leyes, y se sacrifico por dar el lleno a sus encargos publicos, fue el que al pisar las playas de estas costas planto la oliva de la paz; fue el que dio seguridad a la agricultura; fue el que velo por el establecimiento de instruccion y escuelas de la juventud; fue el que promovio todos los objetos que interesan al bien general del territorio; fue el que apago la tea de

la discordia; fue ultimamente el que por su ejemplo y laborosidad cultivo todo genero de virtudes mereciendose por estas razones el nombre de Padre de nuestro territorio. Si Ecsmo. Sr, la Comision creeria hacerse indigna a los ojos de los ciudadanos si intentase contrariar unos sentimientos tan naturales como los que demuestra el Sr. Alvarado y por lo mismo concluye la Comision poniendo a la deliberacion de la Ecsma. Diputacion las siguientes proposiciones.

1.° Que se aprueben las tres proposiciones del Sr. Alvarado y se pongan en ejecucion inmediatamente.

2.° Que al pie del retrato del Sr. General D. Jose Figueroa se le de el titulo de Bienhechor del territorio de la alta California. Monterrey 14 de Octubre de 1835. = Manuel Jimeno.

Monterrey 14 de Octubre de 1835. = En sesion de este dia aprobo la Ecsma. Diputacion el dictamen antecedente con sus dos proposiciones. = Jose Castro. Presidente = Manuel Jimeno. Vocal Secretario.

Es copia. Fecha ut supra. = Manuel Jimeno.

Nota. El antecedente espediente ha pasado al I. Ayuntamiento y actualmente se ocupa en su ejecucion, y parece que se trata de poner en el monumento a que se contrae, las siguientes inscripciones.

D. O. M.

DOMINO JOSEPH FIGUEROA.
PRÆFECTO ATQUE MILITARI DUCI
SUPERIORIS CALIFORNIÆ,
PATRIÆ PARENTI,
IN PIGNUS OBSERVANTIÆ
GRATIQUE ANIMI SENSUS,
CŒTUS CURATORUM PROVINCIÆ
HUJUSQUE METROPOLIS MUNICIPIUM
SUMPTIBUS DICARANT PUBLICIS
HOC MONUMENTUM.
OBIIT, MONTERREGIO.
III, CAL. OCT. A. D. MDCCCXXXV,
ÆTATIS SUÆ XLIII.

A. D. O.

A LA ETERNA MEMORIA
DEL GENERAL D. JOSE FIGUEROA
GEFE POLITICO Y MILITAR
DE LA ALTA CALIFORNIA,
PADRE DE LA PATRIA,
DEDICAN ESTE MONUMENTO
LA DIPUTACION PROVINCIAL
Y EL AYUNTAMIENTO DE MONTERREY,
A COSTA PUBLICA
EN SEÑAL DE GRATITUD.
MURIO EN ESTA CAPITAL
EL 29 DE SETIEMBRE DE 1835,
43 DE SU EDAD.

Bibliography

PRIMARY SOURCES

Manuscripts

The following collections of manuscripts at the Bancroft Library, University of California, Berkeley (BL in footnotes) were used for this study: Juan B. Alvarado, "Memoirs"; Manuel Castro, "Relación sobre acontecimientos de la Alta California"; Antonio Franco Coronel, "Cosas de California"; José Fernández, "Cosas de California"; Vicente P. Gómez, "Lo que sabe sobre cosas de California"; Antonio María Osío, "Historia de la California"; José de Jesús Vallejo, "Reminiscencias históricas de California"; Mariano G. Vallejo, "Documentos para la historia de California" vol. 31, and "Historia de California (Recuerdos Históricos)"; the Cowan Collection; Departmental State Papers, C-A40, vol. 1; Legislative Records, vol. 2; State Papers, C-A53, vol. 2; State Papers, Missions and Colonization, vol. 2; Superior Government State Papers, Decrees and Despatches, vol. 8; Departmental State Papers, Benicia Military, vol. 77.

The Beinecke Collection at the Yale University Library, New Haven, Conn., provided "Berdusco Criminal." Material from the Latin American Collection at the University of Texas, Austin, Texas, includes García folders 69 and 70 of the Vicente Guerrero Correspondence.

At the Archivo General de la Nación in Mexico City, the following manuscripts were consulted: legajos (unbound bundles) nos. 209, 1367, and 1991, and an unnumbered expediente, "Guerra," dated 1825, all in the series entitled "Gobernación"; "Californias," vol. 20; "Justicia eclesiástica," bound vol. 41; and "Operaciones de Guerra," bound vols. 911 and 914. At the Archivo Histórico of the Museo Nacional de Antropología, the "Testamentaria Iturbide" was consulted; and the archivo de cancelados in the Archivo Histórico Militar de Mexico, also in Mexico City, contains the service records of Buenaventura Araujo, José Figueroa, and José María Padrés. The diary of Carlos María de Bustamante may be consulted in the original at the Zacatecas State Library, Zacatecas, or on microfilm at the Museo Nacional de Antropología in Mexico City.

Printed Materials

Alamán, Lucas. *Historia de Méjico*, 2nd ed.; 5 vols. Mexico, 1969.

Bustamante, Carlos María de. *Cuadro histórico de la revolución mexicana;* 3 vols. Mexico, 1961.

Calendario de Galván. Mexico, 1831.

Cole, Martin, and Henry Welcome, eds. *Don Pío Pico's Historical Narrative.* Glendale, Calif., 1973.

Colección de los decretos y órdenes del soberano congreso mexicano desde su instalación en 24 de febrero de 1822 hasta 30 de octubre de 1823. Mexico, 1825.

Colección de los principales trabajos en que se ha ocupado la junta nombrada para meditar y proponer al supremo gobierno los medios más necesarios para promover el progreso de la cultura y civilización de los territorios de la alta y de la baja California. Mexico, 1827.

Cuevas, Mariano, ed. *El Libertador: Documentos selectos de Don Agustín de Iturbide*. Mexico, 1947.

Dublán, Manuel, and José María Lozano, eds. *Legislación mexicana;* 52 vols. Mexico, 1876–1910.

Figueroa, José. *Manifiesto a la república mejicana*. Monterey, 1835.

———. *The Manifesto which the General of Brigade, Don José Figueroa, Commandant-General and Political Chief of U. California, makes to the Mexican Republic*. San Francisco, 1855.

———. *The Manifesto to the Mexican Republic*. Foreword by Joseph A. Sullivan. Oakland, Calif., 1952.

González Ramírez, Manuel, ed. *Lorenzo de Zavala, Obras: El Historiador y el representante popular*. Mexico, 1969.

Mateos, Juan A. *Historia parlamentaria de los congresos mexicanos;* 25 vols. Mexico, 1877–1912.

Maza, Francisco de la, ed. *Código de colonización y terrenos baldíos*. Mexico, 1893.

Memoria que el secretario de estado presenta. Mexico, 1823.

Mora, José María Luis. *Obras sueltas;* 2 vols. Paris, 1837.

"Plan de colonización de nacionales," in *Colección de los principales trabajos en que se ha ocupado la junta nombrada para meditar y proponer al supremo gobierno los medios más necesarios para promover el progreso de la cultura y civilización de los territorios de la alta y de la baja California*. Mexico, 1827.

Proceso instruido en contra de don Mariano Matamoros. Morelia, Mexico, 1964.

Reglamento para el gobierno de la provincia de Californias. Mexico, 1784. English translation, *Regulations for Governing the Province of the Californias,* trans. John Everett Johnson. Bibliographical note by Oscar Lewis. San Francisco, 1929.

Reglamento para la Compañía Cosmopolitana. Mexico, 1834.

Reglamento provicional para el gobierno interior de la Ecma. Diputación territorial de la Alta California. Monterey, 1834.

Newspapers

El Atleta, Mexico City, 1830.

El Correo de la Federación Mexicana, Mexico City, 1827 and 1828.

La Estrella de Occidente, Ures, 1860.

Gaceta del Gobierno Imperial de México, Mexico City, 1822.

Gaceta Diaria de México, Mexico City, 1825.

El Indicador de la Federación Mexicana, Mexico City, 1833.

El Noticioso General, Mexico City, 1822.

El Registro Oficial, Mexico City, 1830.

San Francisco Daily Herald, 1855.

El Sol, Mexico City, 1829 and 1830.

El Telégrafo, Mexico City, 1833 and 1834.

SECONDARY SOURCES

Books

Almada, Francisco R. *Diccionario de historia, geografía y biografía sonorenses*. Chihuahua, Mexico, 1952.

Bancroft, Hubert Howe. *History of California;* 7 vols. San Francisco, 1884–90.

———. *History of Mexico;* 6 vols. San Francisco, 1883–88.

———. *History of the North Mexican States and Texas;* 2 vols. San Francisco, 1884–89.

Benson, Nettie Lee. *La Diputación provincial y el federalismo mexicano*. Mexico, 1955.

Bentham, Jeremy. *Works,* ed. J. Bowring; 11 vols. Edinburgh, 1843.

Bolton, Herbert E. *Guide to Materials for the History of the United States in the Principal Archives of Mexico*. Washington, D.C., 1913 [1965].

Chapman, Charles Edward. *A History of California: The Spanish Period*. New York, 1930.

Cleland, Robert Glass. *The Cattle on a Thou-*

sand Hills: Southern California, 1850–1870. San Marino, Calif., 1941.

Cowan, Robert Ernest. *A Bibliography of the History of California and the Pacific West, 1510–1906*. San Francisco, 1914.

Diccionario Porrúa de historia, biografía, y geografía de México, 2nd ed. Mexico, 1965.

Eberstadt, Edward. *The Annotated Eberstadt Catalogs of Americana*, Nos. 103–138. Introduction by Archibald Hanna. New York, 1935–1965.

Eldredge, Zoeth Skinner, ed. *History of California*; 5 vols. New York, 1915.

Engelhardt, Zephyrin. *The Missions and Missionaries of California*; 4 vols. San Francisco, 1908–15; 2nd ed., vols. 1 and 2, Santa Barbara, 1929–30.

Greenwood, Robert, ed. *California Imprints, 1833–1862*. Los Gatos, Calif., 1961.

Hittell, Theodore H. *History of California*; 4 vols. San Francisco, 1885–97.

Hutchinson, C. Alan. *Frontier Settlement in Mexican California*. New Haven, Conn., 1969.

O'Gorman, Edmundo. *Historia de las divisiones territoriales de México*. Mexico, 1966.

Pitt, Leonard. *The Decline of the Californios*. Berkeley and Los Angeles, 1966.

Richman, Irving Berdine. *California Under Spain and Mexico*. Boston, 1911.

Riva Palacio, Vicente, ed. *México a través de los siglos*; 5 vols. Mexico and Barcelona, Spain, 1888–89.

Robertson, William Spence. *Iturbide of Mexico*. Durham, N.C., 1952.

Spicer, Edward H. *Cycles of Conquest*. Tucson, Ariz., 1962.

Timmons, Wilbert H. *Morelos: Priest, Soldier, Statesman of Mexico*. El Paso, Texas, 1970.

Tuthill, Franklin. *History of California*. San Francisco, 1866.

Voltaire, François Arouet de. *A Philosophical Dictionary*; 6 vols. London, 1824.

Articles

Baur, John E. "José de la Rosa, Early Ventura's Centenarian Printer." *Ventura County Historical Society Quarterly*, 18 (Summer, 1973): 14–25.

Coulter, Edith Margaret. "California Copyrights, 1851–1856." *California Historical Society Quarterly*, 22 (March 1943): 27–40.

Cowan, Robert Ernest. "Alexander S. Taylor, 1817–1876, First Bibliographer of California." *California Historical Society Quarterly*, 12 (June 1933): 18–24.

Harding, George. "A Census of California Spanish Imprints, 1833–45." *California Historical Society Quarterly*, 12 (June 1933): 125–136.

Hutchinson, C. Alan. "The Asiatic Cholera Epidemic of 1833 in Mexico." *Bulletin of the History of Medicine*, 32 (January–February 1958): 1–23, and (March–April 1958): 152–163.

————. "The Mexican Government and the Mission Indians of Upper California, 1821–1835." *The Americas*, 21 (April 1965): 335–362.

————. "General José Figueroa's Career in Mexico, 1792–1832." *New Mexico Historical Review*, 48 (October 1973): 277–298.

————. "An Official List of the Members of the Híjar–Padrés Colony for Mexican California, 1834." *Pacific Historical Review*, 42 (August 1973): 407–418.

Reynolds, Keld J. "Principal Actions of the California Junta de Fomento, 1825–1827." *California Historical Society Quarterly*, 24 (Dec. 1945): 289–320; and 25 (March 1946): 57–78; (June 1946): 149–168; (September 1946): 267–278; and (December 1946): 347–367.

————. "The Reglamento for the Híjar and Padrés Colony of 1834." *Historical Society of Southern California Quarterly*, 28 (December 1946): 142–175.

Index

Neophytes. *See* Mission Indians

Occidente (Mexican state), 4
Old California. *See* Lower California
Ortega, José Joaquín, 33

Padrés, José María: and Figueroa, 1, 2, 9, 14, 23, 34, 60, 66, 68, 90; and Gómez Farías, 9, 61, 90; and the colony, 9, 11, 21, 60, 66, 72, 74, 87, 88, 90; career of, 9, 20, 49; and Spaniards, 9; and Indians, 19; ordered to Mexico, 20, 87; conspirator, 67; and revolt at Los Angeles, 80, 84, 85, 93
Mayo Indians, 4
Mazatlán Cavalry Company, 76n*140*
Mexican California. *See* California
Mexico, Army Corps of Engineers, Military College of, 9
Mexico, Constitution of 1824. *See* Constitution of 1824 (Mexico)
Mexico, laws, decrees, orders, and regulations: regulation of 1781, 40–41; law of 6 May 1822, 29, 80; law of 18 August 1824, 44, 52; regulations of 21 November 1828, 52; law of 6 April 1830, 27, 42, 44; bill of 16 April 1833, 3, 36–37n*54*, 53n*98*; order of 16 July 1833, 31n*39*; law of 17 August 1833, 9, 21, 44, 45, 47; law of 21 November 1833, 42, 44; law of 26 November 1833, 7, 10, 14, 30n*35*, 38, 39n*60*, 42, 43, 44, 53n*98*; regulation of 4 February 1834, 34n*45*, 37, 44, 52; order of 23 April 1834, 32; order of 25 July 1834, 32; law of 9 August 1834, 27n*31*
Mier y Terán, Manuel de, 41n*65*
Military, in California, 3, 23
Mission Indians: and mission property, 2, 5, 8, 12, 30, 32, 40–41, 42, 46, 53, 57, 85, 92; and bill of 16 April 1833, 3; treated as equals of whites, 3–4, 92; as culturally deprived, 4; and secularization, 5–6, 31; and Californians, 6; forced labor of, 8; Híjar and, 15; Figueroa's views of, 15, 47, 48, 49, 50; and personal service, 46; education of, 48; as colonists, 25, 38n*58*, 50. *See also* Indians, non-Christian.
Mission temporalities. *See* Missions: property of
Missionaries. *See* Franciscan missionaries

Palacios, Miguel, 33n*42*
Parres, Joaquín, 58
Pico, Andrés, 33n*41*
Pico, Pío, 33, 33n*41*, 34
Pious Fund of the Californias, 30, 31, 38, 39, 40, 44, 58, 81
Portilla, Pablo de la, 76, 80, 85
Provincial Deputation: and mission cattle, 7; and mission lands, 7, 71n*134*; and Figueroa, 10, 27, 30, 63, 96–97; explanation of the term, 24n*23*; house rules for, 27n*29*; and Híjar, 29,

30, 31, 36n*53*, 43, 63; committee report to, 29–33; and mission Indians, 31; colonization regulations of, 35–36; and mission secularization, 39n*61*, 45, 47

Rodríguez Puebla, Juan, 4, 8
Rosa, frigate, 12, 90
Rosa, José de la, 15n*1*
Ross, California, 2, 5, 9
Russia, 5, 9, 64

San Antonio de Padua, mission, 67
San Bernardino, California, 65
San Blas, Nayarit, 9, 12, 90
San Diego, California, 5, 10, 23, 24, 29, 65, 66, 76n*140*
San Francisco, port of, 10
San Francisco Bay, 72
San Francisco de Asís, mission, 11, 70
San Francisco Solano, mission, 11, 22n*16*, 65, 68, 69, 70, 86, 93
San Gabriel Arcángel, mission, 65
San Gregorio College, Mexico City, 4
San Juan Bautista, mission, 75
San Luis Rey de Francia, mission, 65
San Pedro, California, 12
Santa Anna, Antonio López de, 5, 11, 12, 14, 29, 43
Santa Anna and Farías, California, 22n*16*
Santa Barbara, California, 12, 98
Santa Clara de Asís, mission, 75
Santa Rosa, California, 22n*16*
Sea Otter, 69
Secularization of missions. *See* Missions: secularization of
Sinaloa, Mexico, 4, 61
Sonora, Mexico, 4, 61, 75, 77, 84, 92
Sonorans: revolt at Los Angeles, 75, 89, 93
Spain, Constitution of 1812. *See* Constitution of 1812 (Spain)
Spain, laws: law of 13 March 1811, 46; law of 4 January 1813, 46; law of 23 June 1813, 36n*52* 45–46, 47, 49, 78, 79; law of 13 September 1813, 6, 7, 20, 20n*4*, 46; laws of the Indies, 46
Spaniards, 3, 9
Spanish invasion of Mexico (1829), 3
Spence, David, 76n*139*

Tampico, Tamaulipas, 4
Taylor, Alexander, S., 16n*3*
Teachers, in California 62n*116*
Tepic, Nayarit, 9
Territorial Deputation. *See* Provincial Deputation
Territorial Legislature. *See* Provincial Deputation
Torres, Francisco, 67, 70, 75, 79, 80, 87, 92; and revolt at Los Angeles, 11, 13–14, 76–77, 78, 81, 83, 84; returns to Mexico, 12, 69; and Figueroa, 89; and Híjar, 93